USGA®

GOLF RULES ILLUSTRATED

COMPILED BY
THE UNITED STATES GOLF ASSOCIATION

RULES INCIDENTS BY
DR. LEWIS BLAKEY

ILLUSTRATIONS BY
SUDDEN IMPACT MEDIA

hamlyn

CONTENTS

FOREWORD

The USGA is dedicated to clarifying and teaching the Rules that define the game we all love. The role we share with our partner, The R&A, to write a single set of Rules for the global game comes with great responsibility – not only to honor golf's traditions, but also to offer educational opportunities and resources that modernize the delivery of those Rules.

In this spirit, we are proud to present the 2016 edition of *Golf Rules Illustrated*. Updated since its last printing in 2012, this book provides an easy-to-understand, pictorial version of golf's 34 Rules – while still using the exact language found in the official 2016 Rules of Golf, our mobile app and at usga.org.

These illustrated Rules emphasize common situations that occur in playing the game, describe interesting real-world incidents, and include frequently asked questions and recent photography. These simple tools provide valuable context that will help golfers confidently apply the Rules wherever they may play.

We hope that this publication will serve as a quick reference for both seasoned players and those new to golf. More important, it should teach the underlying and fundamental ethos and spirit behind the Rules, which promote fairness and a reliance on skill as factors for success.

We firmly believe that the application of the Rules of Golf to every player worldwide – regardless of age, gender or skill level – is one of golf's greatest strengths. We are thankful that so many golfers, like you, help us preserve the game's integrity by taking time to understand them, and teach them to others.

Happy reading!

Mark Newell
Chairman, Rules of Golf Committee
United States Golf Association

PRINCIPAL CHANGES

Rules of Golf

Rule 3-3. Doubt as to Procedure

The Rule has been amended to provide further guidance on:

1. The procedure for a competitor who is uncertain of how to proceed and decides to play two balls; and
2. How the Committee should determine which ball is to count in such situations.

In addition, the Rule has been expanded to provide guidance on which ball counts when the Rules do not permit the procedure used for either ball.

Exception to Rule 6-6d. Wrong Score for Hole

This new Exception provides that a competitor is not disqualified for returning a score for any hole lower than actually taken when this is due to failure to include one or more penalty strokes that, before returning his score card, the competitor did not know he had incurred. Instead, the competitor incurs the penalty prescribed by the applicable Rule and an additional penalty of two strokes for each hole at which the competitor has committed a breach of Rule 6-6d.

Rule 14-1b. Anchoring the Club

A new Rule is introduced to prohibit anchoring the club, either "directly" or by use of an "anchor point", during the making of a stroke.

Rule 14-3. Artificial Devices and Unusual Equipment; Abnormal Use of Equipment

Several amendments have been made to Rule 14-3, including:

1. A statement of principle has been introduced to confirm what guides the governing bodies in determining whether use of any item is a breach of Rule 14-3;
2. For clarity, the previous reference to "unusual use of equipment" has been changed to "abnormal use of equipment"; and
3. The penalty for a player's first breach of Rule 14-3 during a stipulated round has been modified from disqualification to loss of hole in match play or two strokes in stroke play, with disqualification applied as the penalty for a subsequent breach of the Rule.

Rule 18-2. Ball at Rest Moved By Player, Partner, Caddie or Equipment

Rule 18-2b (Ball Moving After Address) has been withdrawn. This means that when a ball moves after a player has addressed it, the application of a penalty under Rule 18-2 will be based purely on whether the player caused the ball to move.

Rule 25-2. Embedded Ball

Notes have been introduced to:

1. clarify when a ball is embedded; and
2. confirm that a Committee may introduce a Local Rule allowing relief without penalty for a ball embedded anywhere through the green.

Rule 26-2. Ball Played Within Water Hazard

The Rule has been reformatted solely for clarity. There has been no substantive change.

Appendix I. Local Rules; Conditions of the Competition

Former Parts A and B of Appendix I relating to Local Rules are consolidated to provide all of the pertinent information on specific Local Rules in a single location.

Appendix IV. Devices and Other Equipment

Part 5 relating to distance-measuring devices is amended so that, when a Local Rule permitting the use of distance-measuring devices is in effect, there is a breach of Rule 14-3 only if a player uses the device for some other purpose that is prohibited by that Rule. Previously, when the Local Rule was in force, a player was in breach of Rule 14-3 if he used a distance-measuring device that also contained other features whose use would breach Rule 14-3, regardless of whether such other features were actually used by the player.

Appendices II, III, IV

Statements on equipment conformance and product submission processes were removed from Rules 4, 5 and 14-3 to eliminate redundancy with Appendices II, III and IV. The revision to consolidate these statements in the Appendices is non-substantive and done solely for efficiency.

HOW TO USE THE RULES BOOK

UNDERSTAND THE WORDS

The Rule book is written in a very precise and deliberate fashion. You should be aware of and understand the following differences in word use:

may	= optional
should	= recommendation
must	= instruction (and penalty if not carried out)
a ball	= you may substitute another ball (e.g., Rules 26, 27 and 28)
the ball	= you must not substitute another ball (e.g., Rules 24-2 and 25-1)

KNOW THE DEFINITIONS

There are over fifty defined terms (e.g., abnormal ground condition, through the green, etc.), and these form the foundation around which the Rules of Play are written. A good knowledge of the defined terms (which are italicized throughout the book) is very important to the correct application of the Rules.

THE FACTS OF THE CASE

To answer any question on the Rules you must consider the facts of the case in some detail. You should identify:

o The form of play (e.g., match play or stroke play, single, foursome or four-ball)
o Who is involved (e.g., the player, his partner or caddie, an outside agency)
o Where the incident occurred (e.g., on the teeing ground, in a bunker or water hazard, on the putting green)
o What actually happened
o The player's intentions (e.g., what was he doing and what does he want to do)
o The timing of the incident (e.g., has the player now returned his score card, has the competition closed)

REFER TO THE BOOK

As stated above, reference to the Rule book Index and the relevant Rule should provide the answer to the majority of questions that can arise on the course. If in doubt, play the course as you find it and play the ball as it lies. On returning to the Clubhouse, refer the matter to the Committee and it may be that reference to the "Decisions on the Rules of Golf" will assist in resolving any queries that are not entirely clear from the Rule book itself.

The USGA publication entitled *A Modification of the Rules of Golf for Golfers with Disabilities* that contains permissible modifications to The Rules of Golf to accommodate disabled golfers is available through the USGA.

*For up-to-date information regarding Appendix II, Design of Clubs, please contact the USGA or refer to www.usga.org.

Section 1
ETIQUETTE; BEHAVIOR ON THE COURSE

Introduction

This Section provides guidelines on the manner in which the game of golf should be played. If they are followed, all players will gain maximum enjoyment from the game. The overriding principle is that consideration should be shown to others on the course at all times.

The Spirit of the Game

Golf is played, for the most part, without the supervision of a referee or umpire. The game relies on the integrity of the individual to show consideration for other players and to abide by the Rules. All players should conduct themselves in a disciplined manner, demonstrating courtesy and sportsmanship at all times, irrespective of how competitive they may be. This is the spirit of the game of golf.

Safety

Players should ensure that no one is standing close by or in a position to be hit by the club, the ball or any stones, pebbles, twigs or the like when they make a stroke or practice swing.

Players should not play until the players in front are out of range.

Players should always alert greenstaff nearby or ahead when they are about to make a stroke that might endanger them.

If a player plays a ball in a direction where there is a danger of hitting someone, he should immediately shout a warning. The traditional word of warning in such situations is "fore."

Consideration for Other Players

No Disturbance or Distraction

Players should always show consideration for other players on the course and should not disturb their play by moving, talking or making unnecessary noise.

Players should ensure that any electronic device taken onto the course does not distract other players.

On the teeing ground, a player should not tee his ball until it is his turn to play.

Players should not stand close to or directly behind the ball, or directly behind the hole, when a player is about to play.

On the Putting Green

On the putting green, players should not stand on another player's line of putt or, when he is making a stroke, cast a shadow over his line of putt.

Players should remain on or close to the putting green until all other players in the group have holed out.

Scoring

In stroke play, a player who is acting as a marker should, if necessary, on the way to the next tee, check the score with the player concerned and record it.

Pace of Play

Play at Good Pace and Keep Up

Players should play at a good pace. The Committee may establish pace of play guidelines that all players should follow.

It is a group's responsibility to keep up with the group in front. If it loses a clear hole and it is delaying the group behind, it should invite the group behind to play through, irrespective of the number of players in that group. Where a group has not lost a clear hole, but it is apparent that the group behind can play faster, it should invite the faster moving group to play through.

Be Ready to Play

Players should be ready to play as soon as it is their turn to play. When playing on or near the putting green, they should leave their bags or carts in such a position as will enable quick movement off the green and towards the next tee. When the play of a hole has been completed, players should immediately leave the putting green.

Lost Ball

If a player believes his ball may be lost outside a water hazard or is out of bounds, to save time, he should play a provisional ball.

Players searching for a ball should signal the players in the group behind them to play through as soon as it becomes apparent that the ball will not easily be found. They should not search for five minutes before doing so. Having allowed the group behind to play through, they should not continue play until that group has passed and is out of range.

Priority on the Course

Unless otherwise determined by the Committee, priority on the course is determined by a group's pace of play. Any group playing a whole round is entitled to pass a group playing a shorter round. The term "group" includes a single player.

Care of the Course
Bunkers

Before leaving a bunker, players should carefully fill up and smooth over all holes and footprints made by them and any nearby made by others. If a rake is within reasonable proximity of the bunker, the rake should be used for this purpose.

Repair of Divots, Ball-Marks and Damage by Shoes

Players should carefully repair any divot holes made by them and any damage to the putting green made by the impact of a ball (whether or not made by the player himself). On completion of the hole by all players in the group, damage to the putting green caused by golf shoes should be repaired.

CARE OF THE COURSE

Always repair divot holes (1), carefully repair pitch marks on the putting green (2) and smooth over footprints and other marks when leaving a bunker (3). Do not lean on your putter when removing the ball from the hole (4).

Preventing Unnecessary Damage

Players should avoid causing damage to the course by removing divots when taking practice swings or by hitting the head of a club into the ground, whether in anger or for any other reason.

Players should ensure that no damage is done to the putting green when putting down bags or the flagstick.

In order to avoid damaging the hole, players and caddies should not stand too close to the hole and should take care during the handling of the flagstick and the removal of a ball from the hole. The head of a club should not be used to remove a ball from the hole.

Players should not lean on their clubs when on the putting green, particularly when removing the ball from the hole.

The flagstick should be properly replaced in the hole before the players leave the putting green.

Local notices regulating the movement of golf carts should be strictly observed.

Conclusion; Penalties for Breach

If players follow the guidelines in this Section, it will make the game more enjoyable for everyone.

If a player consistently disregards these guidelines during a round or over a period of time to the detriment of others, it is recommended that the Committee consider taking appropriate disciplinary action against the offending player. Such action may, for example, include prohibiting play for a limited time on the course or in a certain number of competitions. This is considered to be justifiable in terms of protecting the interest of the majority of golfers who wish to play in accordance with these guidelines.

In the case of a serious breach of etiquette, the Committee may disqualify a player under Rule 33-7.

Frequently asked question

Does a single player have any standing on the golf course?

The Etiquette section of the Rules of Golf suggests that, unless otherwise determined by the Committee, priority on the course is determined by a group's pace of play, and the term "group" includes a single player. The Pace of Play part of the Etiquette section also states, "It is a group's responsibility to keep up with the group in front. If a group loses a clear hole and this is delaying the group behind, it should invite the group behind to play through, irrespective of the number of players in that group. Where a group has not lost a clear hole, but it is apparent that the group behind can play faster, it should invite the faster moving group to play through." Therefore, a slow group should give way, where possible, to a faster group, and single golfers should have the same rights as all other players.

Fixing your own ball mark, as well as other ball marks on the putting green, will help to keep the golf course in good condition.

Section 2
DEFINITIONS

The Definitions are listed alphabetically and, in the *Rules* themselves, defined terms are in *italics*.

Abnormal Ground Conditions An "*abnormal ground condition*" is any *casual water*, *ground under repair* or hole, cast or runway on the *course* made by a *burrowing animal*, a reptile or a bird.

Addressing the Ball A player has "*addressed the ball*" when he has grounded his club immediately in front of or immediately behind the ball, whether or not he has taken his *stance*.

Advice "*Advice*" is any counsel or suggestion that could influence a player in determining his play, the choice of a club or the method of making a *stroke*.

Information on the *Rules*, distance or matters of public information, such as the position of *hazards* or the *flagstick* on the *putting green*, is not *advice*.

Ball Deemed to Move See "*Move* or *Moved*."

Ball Holed See "*Holed*."

Ball Lost See "*Lost Ball*."

Ball in Play A ball is "*in play*" as soon as the player has made a *stroke* on the *teeing ground*. It remains *in play* until it is *holed*, except when it is *lost*, *out of bounds* or lifted, or another ball has been *substituted*, whether or not the substitution is permitted; a ball so *substituted* becomes the *ball in play*.

ADDRESSING THE BALL

A player has "addressed the ball" when he grounds his club immediately in front of or immediately behind the ball, whether or not he has taken his stance.

BUNKER

A bunker face consisting of stacked turf (whether grass covered or earthen) is not part of the bunker.

A *ball in play* that has been marked but not lifted remains *in play*. A ball that has been marked, lifted and replaced is back *in play* whether or not the ball-marker has been removed.

If a ball is played from outside the *teeing ground* when the player is starting play of a hole, or when attempting to correct this mistake, the ball is not *in play* and Rule 11-4 or 11-5 applies. Otherwise, *ball in play* includes a ball played from outside the *teeing ground* when the player elects or is required to play his next *stroke* from the *teeing ground*.

Exception in match play: *Ball in play* includes a ball played by the player from outside the *teeing ground* when starting play of a hole if the *opponent* does not require the *stroke* to be canceled in accordance with Rule 11-4a.

Best-Ball See "*Forms of Match Play.*"

Bunker A "*bunker*" is a *hazard* consisting of a prepared area of ground, often a hollow, from which turf or soil has been removed and replaced with sand or the like.

Grass-covered ground bordering or within a *bunker*, including a stacked turf face (whether grass-covered or earthen), is not part of the *bunker*. A wall or lip of the *bunker* not covered with grass is part of the *bunker*. The margin of a *bunker* extends vertically downwards, but not upwards.

A ball is in a *bunker* when it lies in or any part of it touches the *bunker*.

Burrowing Animal A "*burrowing animal*" is an animal (other than a worm, insect or the like) that makes a hole for habitation or shelter, such as a rabbit, mole, groundhog, gopher or salamander.

NOTE: A hole made by a non-burrowing animal, such as a dog, is not an *abnormal ground condition* unless marked or declared as *ground under repair*.

A bunker contains sand or some other similar material.

BURROWING ANIMAL HOLE

A burrowing animal hole, such as this one, is an abnormal ground condition.

Caddie A "*caddie*" is one who assists the player in accordance with the *Rules*, which may include carrying or handling the player's clubs during play.

When one *caddie* is employed by more than one player, he is always deemed to be the *caddie* of the player sharing the *caddie* whose ball (or whose *partner's* ball) is involved, and *equipment* carried by him is deemed to be that player's *equipment*, except when the *caddie* acts upon specific directions of another player (or the *partner* of another player) sharing the *caddie*, in which case he is considered to be that other player's *caddie*.

Casual Water "*Casual water*" is any temporary accumulation of water on the *course* that is not in a *water hazard* and is visible before or after the player takes his *stance*. Snow and natural ice, other than frost, are either *casual water* or *loose impediments*, at the option of the player. Manufactured ice is an *obstruction*. Dew and frost are not *casual water*.

A ball is in *casual water* when it lies in or any part of it touches the *casual water*.

CADDIE

While typically true, an individual can serve as a caddie without carrying a player's clubs.

CASUAL WATER

Casual water is an "abnormal ground condition" and a player may take relief from such a condition under Rule 25-1.

Committee The "*Committee*" is the committee in charge of the competition or, if the matter does not arise in a competition, the committee in charge of the *course*.

Competitor A "*competitor*" is a player in a stroke-play competition. A "*fellow-competitor*" is any person with whom the *competitor* plays. Neither is *partner* of the other. In stroke-play *foursome* and *four-ball* competitions, where the context so admits, the word "*competitor*" or "*fellow-competitor*" includes his *partner*.

Course The "*course*" is the whole area within any boundaries established by the *Committee* (see Rule 33-2).

Equipment "*Equipment*" is anything used, worn, held or carried by the player or the player's *caddie*, except:
○ any ball that the player has played at the hole being played, and
○ any small object, such as a coin or a tee, when used to mark the position of the ball or the extent of an area in which a ball is to be dropped.

NOTE 1: A ball played at the hole being played is *equipment* when it has been lifted and not put back into play.

NOTE 2: *Equipment* includes objects placed on the *course* for the care of the *course*, such as rakes, while they are being held or carried.

NOTE 3: When *equipment* is shared by two or more players, the shared *equipment* is deemed to be the *equipment* of only one of the players sharing it.

If a shared golf cart is being moved by one of the players sharing it (or his *partner* or either of their *caddies*), the cart and everything in it are deemed to be that player's *equipment*. Otherwise, the cart and everything in it are deemed to be the *equipment* of the player sharing the cart whose ball (or whose *partner's* ball) is involved.

Other shared *equipment* is deemed to be the *equipment* of the player who last used, wore, held or carried it. It remains that player's *equipment* until it is used, worn, held or carried by the other player (or his *partner* or either of their *caddies*).

GROUND UNDER REPAIR

May I take a free drop from this pile of grass cuttings?

No. They have obviously been thrown under that bush to rot away. They are not piled for removal nor are they marked as ground under repair.

Fellow-Competitor See "*Competitor.*"

Flagstick The "*flagstick*" is a movable straight indicator, with or without bunting or other material attached, centered in the *hole* to show its position. It must be circular in cross-section. Padding or shock absorbent material that might unduly influence the movement of the ball is prohibited.

Forecaddie A "*forecaddie*" is one who is employed by the *Committee* to indicate to players the position of balls during play. He is an *outside agency*.

Forms of Match Play

Single: A match in which one player plays against another player.

Threesome: A match in which one player plays against two other players, and each *side* plays one ball.

Foursome: A match in which two players play against two other players, and each *side* plays one ball.

Three-Ball: Three players play a match against one another, each playing his own ball. Each player is playing two distinct matches.

Best-Ball: A match in which one player plays against the better ball of two other players or the best-ball of three other players.

Four-Ball: A match in which two players play their better ball against the better ball of two other players.

Forms of Stroke Play

Individual: A competition in which each *competitor* plays as an individual.

Foursome: A competition in which two *competitors* play as *partners* and play one ball.

Four-Ball: A competition in which two *competitors* play as *partners*, each playing his own ball. The lower score of the *partners* is the score for the hole. If one *partner* fails to complete the play of the hole, there is no penalty.

NOTE: For bogey, par and Stableford competitions, see Rule 32-1.

Four-Ball See "*Forms of Match Play*" and "*Forms of Stroke Play.*"

Foursome See "*Forms of Match Play*" and "*Forms of Stroke Play.*"

Ground Under Repair "*Ground under repair*" is any part of the *course* so marked by order of the *Committee* or so declared by its authorized representative. All ground and any grass, bush, tree or other growing thing within the *ground under repair* are part of the *ground under repair*. *Ground under repair* includes material piled for removal and a hole made by a greenkeeper, even if not so marked. Grass cuttings and other material left on the *course* that have been abandoned and are not intended to be removed are not *ground under repair* unless so marked.

When the margin of *ground under repair* is defined by stakes, the stakes are inside the *ground under repair*, and the margin of the *ground under repair* is defined by the nearest outside points of the stakes at ground level. When both stakes and lines are used to indicate *ground under repair*, the stakes identify the *ground under repair* and the lines define the margin of the *ground under repair*. When the margin of *ground under repair* is defined by a line on the ground, the line itself is in the *ground under repair*. The margin of *ground under repair* extends vertically downwards but not upwards.

A ball is in *ground under repair* when it lies in or any part of it touches the *ground under repair*.

Stakes used to define the margin of or identify *ground under repair* are *obstructions*.

NOTE: The *Committee* may make a Local Rule prohibiting play from *ground under repair* or an environmentally sensitive area defined as *ground under repair*.

HOLED

This ball is holed because it is completely below the lip of the hole.

Hazards A "*hazard*" is any *bunker* or *water hazard*.

Hole The "*hole*" must be 4¼ inches (108 mm) in diameter and at least 4 inches (101.6 mm) deep. If a lining is used, it must be sunk at least 1 inch (25.4 mm) below the *putting green* surface, unless the nature of the soil makes it impracticable to do so; its outer diameter must not exceed 4¼ inches (108 mm).

Holed A ball is "*holed*" when it is at rest within the circumference of the *hole* and all of it is below the level of the lip of the *hole*.

Honor The player who is to play first from the *teeing ground* is said to have the "*honor*."

LOOSE IMPEDIMENTS
Dirt or grass adhering to the ball is not a loose impediment.

Lateral Water Hazard A "*lateral water hazard*" is a *water hazard* or that part of a *water hazard* so situated that it is not possible, or is deemed by the *Committee* to be impracticable, to drop a ball behind the *water hazard* in accordance with Rule 26-1b. All ground and water within the margin of a *lateral water hazard* are part of the *lateral water hazard*.

When the margin of a *lateral water hazard* is defined by stakes, the stakes are inside the *lateral water hazard*, and the margin of the *hazard* is defined by the nearest outside points of the stakes at ground level. When both stakes and lines are used to indicate a *lateral water hazard*, the stakes identify the *hazard* and the lines define the *hazard* margin. When the margin of a *lateral water hazard* is defined by a line on the ground, the line itself is in the *lateral water hazard*. The margin of a *lateral water hazard* extends vertically upwards and downwards.

A ball is in a *lateral water hazard* when it lies in or any part of it touches the *lateral water hazard*.

Stakes used to define the margin of or identify a *lateral water hazard* are *obstructions*.

NOTE 1: That part of a *water hazard* to be played as a lateral water hazard must be distinctively marked. Stakes or lines used to define the margin of or identify a *lateral water hazard* must be red.

NOTE 2: The *Committee* may make a Local Rule prohibiting play from an environmentally sensitive area defined as a *lateral water hazard*.

NOTE 3: The *Committee* may define a *lateral water hazard* as a *water hazard*.

Line of Play The "*line of play*" is the direction that the player wishes his ball to take after a *stroke*, plus a reasonable distance on either side of the intended direction. The *line of play* extends vertically upwards from the ground, but does not extend beyond the *hole*.

Line of Putt The "*line of putt*" is the line that the player wishes his ball to take after a *stroke* on the *putting green*. Except with respect to Rule 16-1e, the *line of putt* includes a reasonable distance on either side of the intended line. The *line of putt* does not extend beyond the *hole*.

Loose impediments are natural objects such as:

branches

pine cones

dead animal

stones

insects

worm casts

leaves

Loose Impediments *"Loose impediments"* are natural objects including:

○ stones, leaves, twigs, branches and the like,

○ dung, and

○ worms, insects and the like, and the casts and heaps made by them,

provided they are not:

○ fixed or growing,

○ solidly embedded, or

○ adhering to the ball.

Sand and loose soil are *loose impediments* on the *putting green*, but not elsewhere.

Snow and natural ice, other than frost, are either *casual water* or *loose impediments*, at the option of the player.

Dew and frost are not *loose impediments*.

Lost Ball A ball is deemed *"lost"* if:

a. It is not found or identified as his by the player within five minutes after the player's *side* or his or their *caddies* have begun to search for it; or

b. The player has made a *stroke* at a *provisional ball* from the place where the original ball is likely to be or from a point nearer the *hole* than that place (see Rule 27-2b); or

c. The player has put another *ball into play* under penalty of stroke and distance under Rule 26-1a, 27-1 or 28a; or

d. The player has put another *ball into play* because it is known or virtually certain that the ball, which has not been found, has been moved by an *outside agency* (see Rule 18-1), is in an *obstruction* (see Rule 24-3), is in an *abnormal ground condition* (see Rule 25-1c) or is in a *water hazard* (see Rule 26-1b or c); or

e. The player has made a *stroke* at a *substituted* ball.

Time spent in playing a *wrong ball* is not counted in the five-minute period allowed for search.

Marker A *"marker"* is one who is appointed by the *Committee* to record a *competitor's* score in stroke play. He may be a *fellow-competitor*. He is not a *referee*.

Move or Moved A ball is deemed to have "*moved*" if it leaves its position and comes to rest in any other place.

Nearest Point of Relief The "*nearest point of relief*" is the reference point for taking relief without penalty from interference by an immovable *obstruction* (Rule 24-2), an *abnormal ground condition* (Rule 25-1) or a *wrong putting green* (Rule 25-3).

It is the point on the *course* nearest to where the ball lies:
(i)   that is not nearer the *hole*, and
(ii) where, if the ball were so positioned, no interference by the condition from which relief is sought would exist for the *stroke* the player would have made from the original position if the condition were not there.

NOTE: In order to determine the *nearest point of relief* accurately, the player should use the club with which he would have made his next *stroke* if the condition were not

there to simulate the *address* position, direction of play and swing for such a *stroke*.

Observer An "*observer*" is one who is appointed by the *Committee* to assist a *referee* to decide questions of fact and to report to him any breach of a *Rule*. An *observer* should not attend the *flagstick*, stand at or mark the position of the *hole*, or lift the ball or mark its position.

Obstructions An "*obstruction*" is anything artificial, including the artificial surfaces and sides of roads and paths and manufactured ice, except:
a.   Objects defining *out of bounds*, such as walls, fences, stakes and railings;
b.   Any part of an immovable artificial object that is *out of bounds*; and

BALL DEEMED TO MOVE

This ball is deemed not to have "moved" because, having left its original position, it rolled back into it again.

This ball is deemed to have "moved" because it has left its original position and come to rest in another place; the fact that it has moved vertically, rather than laterally, is irrelevant.

c. Any construction declared by the *Committee* to be an integral part of the *course*.

An *obstruction* is a movable *obstruction* if it may be moved without unreasonable effort, without unduly delaying play and without causing damage. Otherwise, it is an immovable *obstruction*.

NOTE: The *Committee* may make a Local Rule declaring a movable *obstruction* to be an immovable *obstruction*.

Opponent An "*opponent*" is a member of a *side* against whom the player's *side* is competing in match play.

Out of Bounds "*Out of bounds*" is beyond the boundaries of the *course* or any part of the *course* so marked by the *Committee*.

When *out of bounds* is defined by reference to stakes or a fence or as being beyond stakes or a fence, the *out of bounds* line is determined by the nearest inside points at ground level of the stakes or fence posts (excluding angled supports). When both stakes and lines are used to indicate *out of bounds*, the stakes identify *out of bounds* and the lines define *out of bounds*. When *out of bounds* is defined by a line on the ground, the line itself is *out of bounds*. The *out of bounds* line extends vertically upwards and downwards.

A ball is *out of bounds* when all of it lies *out of bounds*. A player may stand *out of bounds* to play a ball lying within bounds.

Objects defining *out of bounds* such as walls, fences, stakes and railings are not *obstructions* and are deemed to be fixed. Stakes identifying *out of bounds* are not *obstructions* and are deemed to be fixed.

NOTE 1: Stakes or lines used to define *out of bounds* should be white.

NOTE 2: A *Committee* may make a Local Rule declaring stakes identifying but not *defining out of bounds* to be *obstructions*.

NEAREST POINT OF RELIEF

The nearest point of relief (indicated by the white arrow) is determined by using the club that would have been used if the condition was not present.

MOVABLE OBSTRUCTIONS
Artificial/manufactured objects such as:

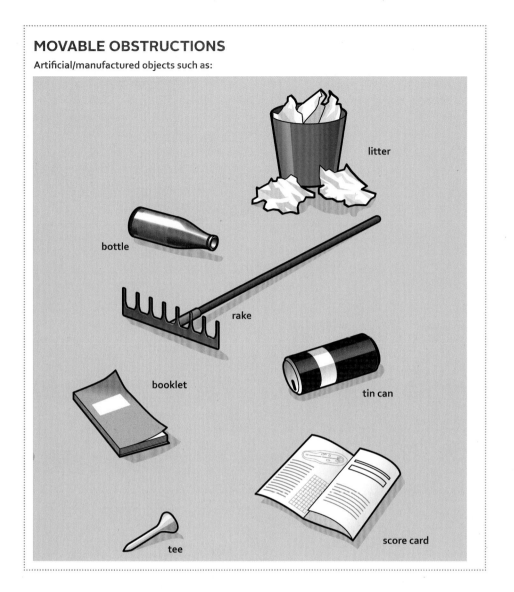

litter

bottle

rake

booklet

tin can

score card

tee

Outside Agency In match play, an "*outside agency*" is any agency other than either the player's or *opponent*'s *side*, any *caddie* of either *side*, any ball played by either *side* at the hole being played or any *equipment* of either *side*.

In stroke play, an *outside agency* is any agency other than the *competitor's side*, any *caddie* of the *side*, any ball played by the *side* at the hole being played or any *equipment* of the *side*.

An *outside agency* includes a *referee*, a *marker*, an *observer* and a *forecaddie*. Neither wind nor water is an *outside agency*.

Partner A "*partner*" is a player associated with another player on the same *side*.

In *threesome*, *foursome*, *best-ball* or *four-ball* play, where the context so admits, the word "player" includes his *partner* or *partners*.

Penalty Stroke A "*penalty stroke*" is one added to the score of a player or *side* under certain *Rules*. In a *threesome* or *foursome*, *penalty strokes* do not affect the order of play.

Provisional Ball A "*provisional ball*" is a ball played under Rule 27-2 for a ball that may be *lost* outside a *water hazard* or may be *out of bounds*.

Putting Green The "*putting green*" is all ground of the hole being played that is specially prepared for putting or otherwise defined as such by the *Committee*. A ball is on the *putting green* when any part of it touches the *putting green*.

PARTNER

A partner is a player associated with another player on the same side.

Referee A "*referee*" is one who is appointed by the *Committee* to decide questions of fact and apply the *Rules*. He must act on any breach of a *Rule* that he observes or is reported to him.

A *referee* should not attend the *flagstick*, stand at or mark the position of the *hole,* or lift the ball or mark its position.

Exception in match play: Unless a *referee* is assigned to accompany the players throughout a match, he has no authority to intervene in a match other than in relation to Rule 1-3, 6-7 or 33-7.

Rub of the Green A "*rub of the green*" occurs when a ball in motion is accidentally deflected or stopped by any *outside agency* (see Rule 19-1).

Rule or Rules The term "*Rule*" includes:
a   The Rules of Golf and their interpretations as contained in "Decisions on the Rules of Golf";
b   Any Conditions of Competition established by the *Committee* under Rule 33-1 and Appendix I;
c   Any Local Rules established by the *Committee* under Rule 33-8a and Appendix I; and
d   The specifications on:
   (i) clubs and the ball in Appendices II and III and their interpretations as contained in "A Guide to the Rules on Clubs and Balls"; and
   (ii) devices and other *equipment* in Appendix IV.

Side A "*side*" is a player, or two or more players who are *partners*. In match play, each member of the opposing *side* is an *opponent*. In stroke play, members of all *sides* are *competitors* and members of different *sides* playing together are *fellow-competitors*.

Single See "*Forms of Match Play*" and "*Forms of Stroke Play*."

Stance Taking the "*stance*" consists in a player placing his feet in position for and preparatory to making a *stroke*.

DEFINITION OF A STROKE

At this point, as the player has not started her downswing, she has not begun her stroke. It is once the player begins her downswing that she is considered to have made a stroke, unless she checks her downswing voluntarily.

Stipulated Round The "*stipulated round*" consists of playing the holes of the *course* in their correct sequence, unless otherwise authorized by the *Committee*. The number of holes in a *stipulated round* is 18 unless a smaller number is authorized by the *Committee*. As to extension of *stipulated round* in match play, see Rule 2-3.

Stroke A "*stroke*" is the forward movement of the club made with the intention of striking at and moving the ball, but if a player checks his downswing voluntarily before the clubhead reaches the ball, he has not made a *stroke*.

Substituted Ball A "*substituted ball*" is a ball put into play for the original ball that was either in *play*, *lost*, *out* of *bounds* or *lifted*, whether or not the substitution was permitted. A *substituted ball* becomes the *ball in play* when it has been dropped or placed (see Rule 20-4).

Teeing Ground The "*teeing ground*" is the starting place for the hole to be played. It is a rectangular area two club-lengths in depth, the front and the sides of which are defined by the outside limits of two tee-markers. A ball is outside the *teeing ground* when all of it lies outside the *teeing ground*.

Three-Ball See "*Forms of Match Play*."

Threesome See "*Forms of Match Play*."

Through the Green "*Through the green*" is the whole area of the *course* except:

a The *teeing ground* and *putting green* of the hole being played; and

b All *hazards* on the *course*.

Water Hazard A "*water hazard*" is any sea, lake, pond, river, ditch, surface drainage ditch or other open water course (whether or not containing water) and anything of a similar nature on the *course*. All ground and water within the margin of a *water hazard* are part of the *water hazard*.

When the margin of a *water hazard* is defined by stakes, the stakes are inside the *water hazard*, and the margin of the *hazard* is defined by the nearest outside points of the stakes at ground level. When both stakes and lines are used to indicate a *water hazard*, the stakes identify the *hazard* and the lines define the *hazard* margin. When the margin of a *water hazard* is defined by a line on the ground, the line itself is in the *water hazard*. The margin of a *water hazard* extends vertically upwards and downwards.

A ball is in a *water hazard* when it lies in or any part of it touches the *water hazard*.

Stakes used to define the margin of or identify a *water hazard* are *obstructions*.

NOTE 1: Stakes or lines used to define the margin of or identify a *water hazard* must be yellow.

NOTE 2: The *Committee* may make a Local Rule prohibiting play from an environmentally sensitive area defined as a *water hazard*.

Wrong Ball A "*wrong ball*" is any ball other than the player's:

o *ball in play*;

o *provisional ball*; or

o second ball played under Rule 3-3 or Rule 20-7c in stroke play.

Ball in play includes a ball *substituted* for the *ball in play*, whether or not the substitution is permitted. A *substituted ball* becomes the *ball in play* when it has been dropped or placed (see Rule 20-4).

Wrong Putting Green A "*wrong putting green*" is any *putting green* other than that of the hole being played. Unless otherwise prescribed by the *Committee*, this term includes a practice *putting green* or pitching green on the *course*.

TEEING GROUND

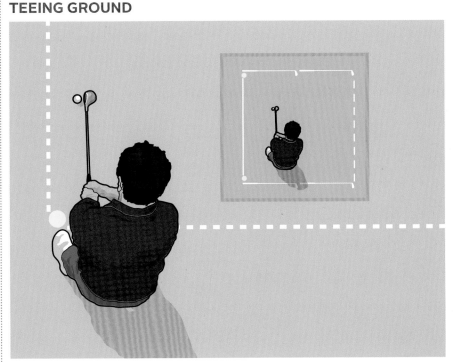

The "teeing ground" is a rectangular area two club-lengths in depth stretching back from the tee-markers. A player may, if he wishes, stand outside the teeing ground to play a ball from within it.

Rule 1

DEFINITIONS
All defined terms are
in *italics* and are listed
alphabetically in the
Definitions section –
see pages 10–23.

THE GAME
THE GAME

1-1. General

The Game of Golf consists of playing a ball with a club from the *teeing ground* into the *hole* by a *stroke* or successive *strokes* in accordance with the *Rules*.

1-2. Exerting Influence on Movement of Ball or Altering Physical Conditions

A player must not (i) take an action with the intent to influence the movement of a *ball in play* or (ii) alter physical conditions with the intent of affecting the playing of a hole.

Exceptions:

1. An action expressly permitted or expressly prohibited by another *Rule* is subject to that other *Rule*, not Rule 1-2.

2. An action taken for the sole purpose of caring for the *course* is not a breach of Rule 1-2.

---

*PENALTY FOR BREACH OF RULE 1-2:

Match play – Loss of hole; **Stroke play** – Two strokes.

*In the case of a serious breach of Rule 1-2, the *Committee* may impose a penalty of disqualification.

MATCH PLAY: AGREEMENT TO CONSIDER HOLE HALVED

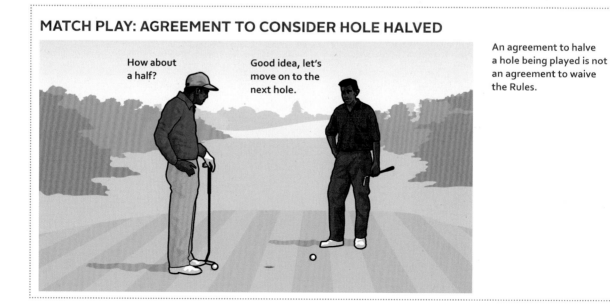

An agreement to halve a hole being played is not an agreement to waive the Rules.

NOTE 1

A player is deemed to have committed a serious breach of Rule 1-2 if the *Committee* considers that the action taken in breach of this Rule has allowed him or another player to gain a significant advantage or has placed another player, other than his *partner*, at a significant disadvantage.

NOTE 2

In stroke play, except where a serious breach resulting in disqualification is involved, a player in breach of Rule 1-2 in relation to the movement of his own ball must play the ball from where it was stopped, or, if the ball was deflected, from where it came to rest. If the movement of a player's ball has been intentionally influenced by a *fellow-competitor* or other *outside agency*, Rule 1-4 applies to the player (see Note to Rule 19-1).

1-3. Agreement to Waive Rules

Players must not agree to exclude the operation of any *Rule* or to waive any penalty incurred.

PENALTY FOR BREACH OF RULE 1-3:

Match play – Disqualification of both *sides*; **Stroke play** – Disqualification of *competitors* concerned.

(Agreeing to play out of turn in stroke play – see Rule 10-2c)

EQUITY: SOME EXAMPLES

Distractions are commonplace, but some problems less so. Wildlife needs to be protected and sometimes so does the golfer.

Ball comes to rest near bees' nest. Player is entitled to relief – Decision 1-4/10.

Bird's nest interferes with stroke. Player is entitled to relief – Decision 1-4/9.

Ball adheres to face of club after stroke. Player drops ball on spot where club was when ball stuck to it – Decision 1-4/2.

Ball comes to rest near snake. Player is entitled to relief – Decision 1-4/10.

1-4. Points Not Covered by Rules

If any point in dispute is not covered by the *Rules*, the decision should be made in accordance with equity.

RULE 1 INCIDENTS

Anticipation and forward thinking are essential for strategic effectiveness and quickly paced play. With his ball in the Road bunker at the Old Course's 17th hole during the 1990 Dunhill Cup at St. Andrews, Philip Walton walked into the sand in order to ponder his next stroke just as his fellow-competitor, Mark James, was about to play from off the road itself.

Much of what makes the Road Hole the most famous, and arguably the most difficult, par-4 in the world is that the putting surface is flanked on the right by the road and on the left by the Road bunker. Only the hard, elevated, fairly narrow piece of putting green separates the hazard from road, which is an integral part of the course and, therefore, not an obstruction. No relief is granted for a ball lying on the road.

Walton and James's predicaments were equally precarious. If misplayed, their positions might simply be exchanged. Anticipating such a possibility as he was preparing for his third shot from the road, James asked a Rules official if he could have Walton's footprints in the Road bunker raked. If his shot from the road was overplayed, James argued that he did not want to end up in one of Walton's footprints in the bunker.

The referee ruled, in equity (Rule 1-4), that James could indeed have the bunker restored to the condition it was in after James's ball came to rest on the road and before Walton walked into the sand. It is an established principle in the Decisions on the Rules of Golf that the player is entitled to the line of play he had when his ball came to rest if it is altered by another player.

During the first round of the 2010 U.S. Open at Pebble Beach, Paul Casey, playing the very difficult 14th par-5 hole, was faced with a delicate pitch shot to a tight hole location on the elevated green. While his ball appeared to be headed for a favorable outcome, it didn't clear the top of the slope before it took a turn to the right and began moving back down the hill toward where he was standing.

Long before the ball returned to the spot from where it had been struck, Casey had casually tapped down the raised grass created by his stroke. This action raised the possibility that his actions were a violation of Rule 1-2.

Although Rule 1-2 has been rewritten for 2012, the new words are only intended for clarity and the basic application of the Rule has not been changed. The provision of the Rule relating to Casey was the prohibition of taking an action with the intent to influence the movement of a ball in play. For Casey, the key word was "intent."

Fortunately for Casey, his situation at the 14th came to the attention of the Rules Committee for the championship prior to his signing of his score card. The Committee took the testimony of those present, as well as Casey and decided that the action he took may well have influenced the movement of the ball but that his action was not with such specific intent, rather with the purpose of caring for the course. He was not penalized under Rule 1-2 nor was he subject to penalty under Rule 23 as there was no loose impediment involved.

Frequently asked question

What constitutes an agreement to waive the Rules?

In match play and stroke play, if players are aware they are excluding the operation of a Rule and agree to do so, they are disqualified for a breach of Rule 1-3.

Rule 2 MATCH PLAY

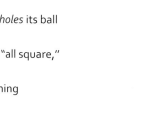

DEFINITIONS
All defined terms are in *italics* and are listed alphabetically in the Definitions section – see pages 10–23.

2-1. General

A match consists of one *side* playing against another over a *stipulated round* unless otherwise decreed by the *Committee*.

In match play the game is played by holes.

Except as otherwise provided in the *Rules*, a hole is won by the *side* that *holes* its ball in the fewer *strokes*. In a handicap match the lower net score wins the hole.

The state of the match is expressed by the terms: so many "holes up" or "all square," and so many "to play."

A *side* is "dormie" when it is as many holes up as there are holes remaining to be played.

2-2. Halved Hole

A hole is halved if each *side holes* out in the same number of *strokes*.

When a player has *holed* out and his *opponent* has been left with a *stroke* for the half, if the player subsequently incurs a penalty, the hole is halved.

2-3. Winner of Match

A match is won when one *side* leads by a number of holes greater than the number remaining to be played.

If there is a tie, the *Committee* may extend the *stipulated round* by as many holes as are required for a match to be won.

WINNER OF THE MATCH: HOLE-BY-HOLE PLAY-OFF

Good putt. That squares the match. We'll have to go back to the 1st for a hole-by-hole play-off.

No. We started this match at the 10th hole, so that is our first extra hole. As before you'll get your handicap stroke.

2-4. Concession of Match, Hole or Next Stroke

A player may concede a match at any time prior to the start or conclusion of that match.

A player may concede a hole at any time prior to the start or conclusion of that hole.

A player may concede his *opponent*'s next *stroke* at any time, provided the *opponent*'s ball is at rest. The *opponent* is considered to have *holed* out with his next *stroke,* and the ball may be removed by either *side*.

A concession may not be declined or withdrawn.

(Ball overhanging hole – see Rule 16-2)

2-5. Doubt as to Procedure; Disputes and Claims

In match play, if a doubt or dispute arises between the players, a player may make a claim. If no duly authorized representative of the *Committee* is available within a reasonable time, the players must continue the match without delay. The *Committee* may consider a claim only if it has been made in a timely manner and if the player making the claim has notified his *opponent* at the time (i) that he is making a claim or wants a ruling and (ii) of the facts upon which the claim or ruling is to be based.

A claim is considered to have been made in a timely manner if, upon discovery of circumstances giving rise to a claim, the player makes his claim (i) before any player in the match plays from the next *teeing ground*, or (ii) in the case of the last hole of the match, before all players in the match leave the *putting green*, or (iii) when the circumstances giving rise to the claim are discovered after all the players in the match have left the *putting green* of the final hole, before the result of the match has been officially announced.

STATUS OF LATE CLAIM

I've just realized that my opponent should have lost the 4th when he grounded his club in the bunker.

I'm afraid such a claim had to be made before you or your opponent played from the 5th tee. The Committee can only consider a later claim if the facts were previously unknown to you.

A claim relating to a prior hole in the match may only be considered by the *Committee* if it is based on facts previously unknown to the player making the claim and he had been given wrong information (Rules 6-2a or 9) by an *opponent*. Such a claim must be made in a timely manner.

Once the result of the match has been officially announced, a claim may not be considered by the *Committee*, unless it is satisfied that (i) the claim is based on facts which were previously unknown to the player making the claim at the time the result was officially announced, (ii) the player making the claim had been given wrong information by an *opponent* and (iii) the *opponent* knew he was giving wrong information. There is no time limit on considering such a claim.

NOTE 1

A player may disregard a breach of the *Rules* by his *opponent* provided there is no agreement by the *sides* to waive a *Rule* (Rule 1-3).

NOTE 2

In match play, if a player is doubtful of his rights or the correct procedure, he may not complete the play of the hole with two balls.

2-6. General Penalty

The penalty for a breach of a *Rule* in match play is loss of hole except when otherwise provided.

Frequently asked question

Is there a penalty for putting out on the putting green after the opponent has conceded the next stroke?

There is no penalty for putting out in this case. Once a concession is made, it may not be withdrawn. The concession stands and it is irrelevant whether the player makes the putt or misses. However, in a four-ball or best-ball match, if the act would assist a partner, the partner is, in equity, disqualified for the hole.

RULE 2 INCIDENTS

Jack Nicklaus's concession of Tony Jacklin's putt on the final hole during the final match of the 1969 Ryder Cup resulted in this match-play event's first tie, and is hailed as one of golf's finest acts of sportsmanship.

In 1969, going into the final day's competition at the Royal Birkdale Golf Club in Southport, England, the United States and Great Britain were tied at eight points each. That morning's singles matches resulted in a two-point lead by the British, which was reciprocated by the U.S. in the afternoon. This left the matches tied

at 15½ with only the final match of Nicklaus and Jacklin still on the course. Eighteen of the 32 Ryder Cup matches went to the final hole that year, and it was there that the three-day competition would be ultimately decided.

Nicklaus had the upper hand, as Jacklin had fallen behind on the back nine. As the reigning British Open Champion, Jacklin would not relent. Indeed, he eagled the 17th to go all square.

As the defending champions after their victory in 1967 at Champions Golf Club in Houston, the U.S.

Team needed only a tie at Birkdale's last hole to tie the overall 1969 competition. Under the conditions of the competition, a tie in the Ryder Cup results in the previously victorious team retaining the cup.

At the par-5 18th, Jacklin missed his putt for birdie. Nicklaus holed his four-footer for par. Jacklin was left with a short putt to tie. If he holed the putt, it would be the first time the Ryder Cup ended in a tie. A miss by Jacklin would result in an outright win by the Americans.

Before Jacklin could putt, Nicklaus picked up Jacklin's marker, conceding the Englishman's putt and ensuring the tie. "I don't think you would have missed that, Tony," Nicklaus reportedly said, "but under these circumstances I'd never give you the opportunity."

"The length of the putt has varied after 30 some years," Jacklin has said. "It's been as long as four feet. But my recollection is 20 inches. Of course, I could have missed it; there are no guarantees in golf, especially in the crucible of the Ryder Cup, but I believe I would have made it. But Jack saw the big picture."

"Two months before I had become the first British player in 18 years to win the British Open, so there was very much a pro-British fervor at the Ryder Cup in England that year. Jack saw that the putt on the last hole in 1969 meant a heck of a lot more to the Ryder Cup than who won or lost that particular match. It was a great moment."

In the 1969 Ryder Cup, Jack Nicklaus conceded a putt to Tony Jacklin on the 18th hole of the final match, resulting in a tie for the competition and the U.S. retaining the title.

Rule 3   STROKE PLAY

DEFINITIONS
All defined terms are in *italics* and are listed alphabetically in the Definitions section – see pages 10–23.

3-1. General; Winner

A stroke-play competition consists of *competitors* completing each hole of a *stipulated round* or *rounds* and, for each round, returning a score card on which there is a gross score for each hole. Each *competitor* is playing against every other *competitor* in the competition.

The *competitor* who plays the *stipulated round* or *rounds* in the fewest *strokes* is the winner.

In a handicap competition, the *competitor* with the lowest net score for the *stipulated round* or *rounds* is the winner.

3-2. Failure to Hole Out

If a *competitor* fails to *hole* out at any hole and does not correct his mistake before he makes a *stroke* on the next *teeing ground* or, in the case of the last hole of the round, before he leaves the *putting green*, **he is disqualified.**

3-3. Doubt as to Procedure
a. Procedure for Competitor

In stroke play only, if a *competitor* is doubtful of his rights or the correct procedure during the play of a hole, he may, without penalty, complete the hole with two balls. To proceed under this Rule, he must decide to play two balls after the doubtful situation has arisen and before taking further action (e.g., making a *stroke* at the original ball).

The *competitor* should announce to his *marker* or a *fellow-competitor*:

o   that he intends to play two balls; and

o   which ball he wishes to count if the *Rules* permit the procedure used for that ball.

Before returning his score card, the *competitor* must report the facts of the situation to the *Committee*. If he fails to do so, **he is disqualified.**

If the *competitor* has taken further action before deciding to play two balls, he has not proceeded under Rule 3-3 and the score with the original ball counts. The competitor incurs no penalty for playing the second ball.

b. Committee Determination of Score for Hole

When the *competitor* has proceeded under this Rule, the *Committee* will determine his score as follows:

(i)   If, before taking further action, the *competitor* has announced which ball he wishes to count and provided the *Rules* permit the procedure used for the selected ball, the score with that ball counts. If the *Rules* do not permit the procedure used for the selected ball, the score with the other ball counts provided the *Rules* permit the procedure used for that ball.

(ii) If, before taking further action, the *competitor* has failed to announce which ball he wishes to count, the score with the original ball counts provided the *Rules* permit the procedure used for that ball. Otherwise, the score with the other ball counts provided the *Rules* permit the procedure used for that ball.

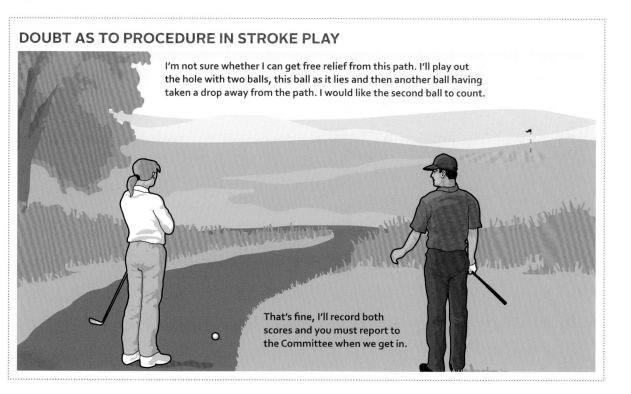

DOUBT AS TO PROCEDURE IN STROKE PLAY

I'm not sure whether I can get free relief from this path. I'll play out the hole with two balls, this ball as it lies and then another ball having taken a drop away from the path. I would like the second ball to count.

That's fine, I'll record both scores and you must report to the Committee when we get in.

(iii) If the *Rules* do not permit the procedures used for both balls, the score with the original ball counts unless the *competitor* has committed a serious breach with that ball by playing from a wrong place. If the *competitor* commits a serious breach in the play of one ball, the score with the other ball counts despite the fact that the *Rules* do not permit the procedure used for that ball. If the *competitor* commits a serious breach with both balls, **he is disqualified**.

NOTE 1

"Rules permit the procedure used for a ball" means that, after Rule 3-3 is invoked, either: (a) the original ball is played from where it had come to rest and play is permitted from that location, or (b) the *Rules* permit the procedure adopted for the ball and the ball is put into play in the proper manner and in the correct place as provided in the *Rules*.

NOTE 2

If the score with the original ball is to count, but the original ball is not one of the balls being played, the first ball put into play is deemed to be the original ball.

NOTE 3

After this Rule has been invoked, strokes made with the ball ruled not to count, and *penalty strokes* incurred solely by playing that ball, are disregarded. A second ball played under Rule 3-3 is not a *provisional* ball under Rule 27-2.

(Ball played from a wrong place – see Rule 20-7c)

3-4. Refusal to Comply with a Rule

If a *competitor* refuses to comply with a *Rule* affecting the rights of another *competitor*, **he is disqualified**.

3-5. General Penalty

The penalty for a breach of a *Rule* in stroke play is two strokes except when otherwise provided.

Frequently asked question

Can a player play two balls in match play?

No. A second ball played in match play is a wrong ball. In match play, if a player believes he is entitled to proceed under a Rule and his opponent disagrees, the opponent may make a claim under Rule 2-5.

RULE 3 INCIDENTS

Rule 3-3 is a golfer-friendly Rule in that it provides a procedure for a player who is doubtful of his rights or the correct procedure to follow. However, it only applies to stroke play.

To proceed under this Rule, he must decide to play two balls after the doubtful situation has arisen and before taking further action (e.g., making a *stroke* at the original ball). Also, he should announce to his *marker* or a *fellow-competitor* that he intends to play two balls and which ball he wishes to count if the *Rules* permit the procedure used for that ball.

To illustrate how these key provisions work in practice, consider these two situations; the first in a high-school championship and the second in a college tournament. These two situations will also illustrate that sometimes the unexpected happens with younger players who may have a somewhat limited depth of experience with the Rules or with competitive situations.

In 1998 at the Virginia Northern Region High School Championship, a stroke-play event, a considerable amount of rain fell the night before the final round. This led the Committee to post a notice informing players that ground under repair would include areas of unusual damage, including areas where maintenance vehicles had combined with wet conditions and had materially affected the ground surface. However, this was only to be the case when declared by a Committee member.

After the round had begun, an official was roving the course when he noticed a group of spectators near a player at the edge of the fairway, who motioned him over. The official asked the player if he needed assistance from a Rules official. The player pointed to a ball lying just off the fairway in a deeply rutted area apparently caused by vehicular traffic and said, "Do I get relief for that?" The official responded that indeed he would be entitled to relief according to the ground under repair Rule. The official went on to point out the nearest point of relief and instructed him to drop the ball within one club-length of that point not nearer the hole. The player responded, "I already did," to which the official said, "Tell me what happened."

The player then related the following. His coach, who was authorized to give advice according to the Note to Rule 8, had told him of Rule 3-3 and described its provisions. Then, the player had announced to his marker that he wished to play a second ball under the ground under repair Rule, to play the original ball as it lies, and to score with the second ball. He had properly determined the nearest point of relief, dropped and played the second ball onto the putting green and was about to play the original ball when he saw the roving official.

The official advised the player that the rutted area would now be marked as ground under repair, that he had proceeded correctly and that he would score with the second ball. There was no necessity to play the original ball as it lies.

The second situation occurred at the 2001 Duke University Invitational in Durham, North Carolina. There was an area of flowers that was listed on the notice to competitors as ground under repair from which relief was mandatory. Despite this listing, a player, whose ball lay in the flowerbed, preferred to play his ball as it lay. He invoked Rule 3-3 by announcing to his marker that he would play a second ball according to the ground under repair procedures and he wished to score with his original ball that he would play as it lay.

He played the original ball as it lay and played a second ball properly put into play according to the procedures of the ground under repair Rule.

Since the original ball was played from the flowerbed, an action not permitted by the notice to competitors, Rule 3-3 requires that the score with the other ball count. The player did not incur a penalty for playing the original ball as it lay since the score with that ball did not count.

Both players proceeded correctly according to the requirements of Rule 3-3a and each player scored according to the provisions of Rule 3-3b(i). The first player scored with the ball that he wished to count but the second player scored with the ball that he did not select. Neither player incurred a penalty.

Rule 4

DEFINITIONS
All defined terms are
in *italics* and are listed
alphabetically in the
Definitions section –
see pages 10–23.

CLUBS AND THE BALL
CLUBS

For detailed specifications and interpretations on the conformity of clubs under Rule 4 and
the process for consultation and submission regarding clubs, see Appendix II

4-1. Form and Make of Clubs
a. General

The player's clubs must conform with this Rule and the provisions, specifications and
interpretations set forth in Appendix II.

NOTE

The *Committee* may require, in the conditions of a competition (Rule 33-1), that
any driver the player carries must have a clubhead, identified by model and loft,
that is named on the current List of Conforming Driver Heads issued by the USGA.

b. Wear and Alteration

A club that conforms with the *Rules* when new is deemed to conform after wear through
normal use. Any part of a club that has been purposely altered is regarded as new and
must, in its altered state, conform with the *Rules*.

4-2. Playing Characteristics Changed and Foreign Material
a. Playing Characteristics Changed

During a *stipulated round*, the playing characteristics of a club must not be purposely
changed by adjustment or by any other means.

b. Foreign Material

Foreign material must not be applied to the club face for the purpose of influencing the
movement of the ball.

***PENALTY FOR CARRYING, BUT NOT MAKING STROKE WITH, CLUB OR
CLUBS IN BREACH OF RULE 4-1 OR 4-2:**

Match play – At the conclusion of the hole at which the breach is discovered,

---

NON-CONFORMING CLUB CARRIED BUT NOT USED

The penalty for carrying, but not making a stroke with, a non-conforming club is detailed in
Rule 4-1 and 4-2. The player is disqualified if he makes a stroke with a non-conforming club.
The club on the top is conforming, but the club on the bottom is not, because it has a bulge
in the grip.

the state of the match is adjusted by deducting one hole for each hole at which a breach occurred; maximum deduction per round – Two holes.

Stroke play – Two strokes for each hole at which any breach occurred; maximum penalty per round – Four strokes (two strokes at each of the first two holes at which any breach occurred).

Match play or stroke play – If a breach is discovered between the play of two holes, it is deemed to have been discovered during play of the next hole, and the penalty must be applied accordingly.

Bogey and par competitions – See Note 1 to Rule 32-1a.

Stableford competitions – See Note 1 to Rule 32-1b.

*Any club or clubs carried in breach of Rule 4-1 or 4-2 must be declared out of play by the player to his *opponent* in match play or his *marker* or a *fellow-competitor* in stroke play immediately upon discovery that a breach has occurred. If the player fails to do so, he is disqualified.

PENALTY FOR MAKING STROKE WITH CLUB IN BREACH OF RULE 4-1 OR 4-2:
Disqualification.

4-3. Damaged Clubs: Repair and Replacement
a. Damage in Normal Course of Play

If, during a *stipulated round*, a player's club is damaged in the normal course of play, he may:

(i)   use the club in its damaged state for the remainder of the *stipulated round*; or

(ii) without unduly delaying play, repair it or have it repaired; or

(iii) as an additional option available only if the club is unfit for play, replace the damaged club with any club. The replacement of a club must not unduly delay play (Rule 6-7) and must not be made by borrowing any club selected for play by any other person playing on the *course* or by assembling components carried by or for the player during the *stipulated round*.

PENALTY FOR BREACH OF RULE 4-3A:
See Penalty Statements for Rule 4-4a or b and Rule 4-4c.

NOTE
A club is unfit for play if it is substantially damaged, e.g., the shaft is dented, significantly bent or broken into pieces; the clubhead becomes loose, detached or significantly deformed; or the grip becomes loose. A club is not unfit for play solely because the club's lie or loft has been altered, or the clubhead is scratched.

b. Damage Other Than in Normal Course of Play

If, during a *stipulated round*, a player's club is damaged other than in the normal course of play rendering it non-conforming or changing its playing characteristics, the club must not subsequently be used or replaced during the round.

PENALTY FOR BREACH OF RULE 4-3B:
Disqualification.

---

c. Damage Prior to Round

A player may use a club damaged prior to a round, provided the club, in its damaged state, conforms with the *Rules.*

Damage to a club that occurred prior to a round may be repaired during the round, provided the playing characteristics are not changed and play is not unduly delayed.

PENALTY FOR BREACH OF RULE 4-3C:
See Penalty Statement for Rule 4-1 or 4-2.
(Undue delay – see Rule 6-7)

4-4. Maximum of 14 Clubs
a. Selection and Addition of Clubs

The player must not start a *stipulated round* with more than fourteen clubs. He is limited to the clubs thus selected for that round, except that if he started with fewer than fourteen clubs, he may add any number, provided his total number does not exceed fourteen.

The addition of a club or clubs must not unduly delay play (Rule 6-7) and the player must not add or borrow any club selected for play by any other person playing on the *course* or by assembling components carried by or for the player during the *stipulated round*.

b. Partners May Share Clubs

Partners may share clubs, provided that the total number of clubs carried by the *partners* so sharing does not exceed fourteen.

PENALTY FOR BREACH OF RULE 4-4A OR B, REGARDLESS OF NUMBER OF EXCESS CLUBS CARRIED

Match play – At the conclusion of the hole at which the breach is discovered, the state of the match is adjusted by deducting one hole for each hole at which a breach occurred; maximum deduction per round – Two holes.

Stroke play – Two strokes for each hole at which any breach occurred; maximum penalty per round: Four strokes (two strokes at each of the first two holes at which any breach occurred).

Match play or stroke play – If a breach is discovered between the play of two

BREACH OF 14-CLUB RULE IN MATCH PLAY

I've just realized I have 15 clubs in my bag. I'll declare my 2-iron out of play, but what is the score in our match?

As we are on the 4th tee and I was already 2 up, the two-hole penalty applies to the match score, and I am now 4 up.

holes, it is deemed to have been discovered during play of the hole just completed, and the penalty for a breach of Rule 4-4a or b does not apply to the next hole.

Bogey and par competitions – See Note 1 to Rule 32-1a.

Stableford competitions – See Note 1 to Rule 32-1b.

c. Excess Club Declared Out of Play

Any club or clubs carried or used in breach of Rule 4-3a(iii) or Rule 4-4 must be declared out of play by the player to his *opponent* in match play or his *marker* or a *fellow-competitor* in stroke play immediately upon discovery that a breach has occurred. The player must not use the club or clubs for the remainder of the *stipulated round*.

PENALTY FOR BREACH OF RULE 4-4C:

Disqualification.

RULE 4 INCIDENTS

A player must not start a round with more than 14 clubs. If he starts with 14 clubs, then he is limited to those selected clubs except when a club has been damaged in the normal course of play and if it becomes unfit for play, it may be replaced. A lost club is not one that has become unfit for play in the normal course of play and may not be replaced. A club damaged prior to the round may be used if it conforms to the Rules.

Losing a club is not the equivalent of damaging a club and must be endured as simply bad luck. A lost club cannot be replaced as Tiger Woods and his caddie, Steve Williams, learned during the 2006 Ryder Cup. At the K Club's seventh green, Williams went to a greenside lake to soak a towel. He was also holding Woods's 9-iron at the time, and lost his grip on the club. The club disappeared into the depths of the lake, where it was not retrievable. Woods was required to continue his singles match against Robert Karlsson with 13 clubs.

Just as Williams could not believe he had dropped his boss's 9-iron in a water hazard, neither could Ian Woosnam's caddie believe he had left an extra driver in his boss's bag during the final round of the 2001 British Open at Royal Lytham & St. Annes.

On the practice tee before the final round began, Woosnam was trying to decide which of two drivers to use that day. His testing apparently went a little longer than expected. His caddie hurried to the practice chipping and putting greens before moving to the first tee for their 2:15 starting time.

A championship anomaly, Royal Lytham begins with a par-3. Woosnam struck a glorious 6-iron to within inches of the hole. However, in their haste to get underway and with their focus toward the job at hand, both Woosnam and his caddie failed to count their clubs before starting. Both drivers that had been tested on the practice ground were in the bag, 15 clubs in all, when Woosnam struck his first shot from the 1st tee. The fact that the 1st hole is a par-3 may have added

Steve Williams was not able to retrieve Tiger's 9-iron, which had slipped into the water. As a result, Tiger continued his round with only thirteen clubs.

Graeme McDowell started with 13 clubs, so he was able to add his preferred driver after the round began.

as his name was being announced as the next to play. In response to his question, a Rules official advised him that, prior to teeing off, he could give the driver to a friend who was standing just beyond the ropes and who could then leave to fetch the driver that he wanted from his locker. Since he would be starting play with thirteen clubs, he would be permitted by Rule 4-4a to add a club during his round. After making his first stoke of the championship but before reaching his ball in play, the friend returned with the preferred driver, which his caddie properly added to McDowell's bag.

When a club becomes damaged is important because, under the Rules, a club damaged prior to the round must be conforming when the player begins his round. Kevin Stadler suffered under this provision of the Rules during the 2005 Michelin Championship in Las Vegas.

During the 1st hole of the fourth round, Stadler discovered that the shaft of one of his clubs was bent. He had not yet used that club during the fourth round. Additionally, nothing extraneous had taken place to damage the club during the round. Therefore, it was determined that Stadler had begun the round with the club in its bent condition.

The Rules (Appendix II, 2a) state that "the shaft must be straight from the top of the grip to a point not more than 5 inches (127 mm) above the sole ..." Because the club in question did not meet this requirement, it was non-conforming. In 2005, the penalty for beginning a round with a non-conforming club was disqualification whether or not a stroke was ever played with the club. Therefore, Stadler was disqualified.

In 2008, the rule was changed: The penalty for carrying a non-conforming club with which a stroke has not been made is the same as carrying more than 14 clubs. In stroke play, two penalty strokes are added for each hole at which any breach occurred; maximum penalty per round is four strokes. In match play, at the conclusion of the hole at which the breach is discovered, the state of the match is adjusted by deducting one hole for each hole at which a breach occurred. Maximum deduction per round is two holes.

to the distraction. Had a driver been required at the 1st, the extra driver may have been discovered before the round started. Woosnam's caddie discovered the violation on the 1st green and revealed it to his boss on the 2nd tee.

Instead of being tied for the lead in the British Open, Woosnam, following the ensuing two-stroke penalty (Rule 4-4), was reeling in disbelief. He threw his hat to the ground and the extra club into the rough. "You've only got one job to think about and that's taking care of the bloody clubs," Woosnam was overheard to say to his caddie.

Although bogeying two of the next three holes, the Welshman's tenacity in the face of adversity was admirable. He eagled the 6th and played the last 13 in three under par, finishing tied for third place, four shots behind David Duval.

In the press tent following the round, Woosnam was more forgiving of his caddie's mistake. "It is the biggest he will make in his life. He won't do it again. He's a good caddie ..." When asked if he has a system for counting his clubs, Woosnam replied, "Yeah. You start counting at one and stop when you get to 14."

Prior to the first round at the 2014 U.S. Open at Pinehurst Resort and Country Club while standing on the teeing ground of the first hole, the 2010 winner, Graeme McDowell, noticed that the driver in his bag at the tee was not the one that he intended to play with that day. Although the first hole called for a stroke with less than a driver, a bit of panic set in about what he should do

During the 2009 U.S. Open at Bethpage State Park Black Course, D. J. Trahan ran afoul of Rule 4 when he accidentally bent the shaft of his putter.

In the second round, he started on the back nine, missing a couple of short birdie putts. He three-putted the 1st hole (his 10th) from about 15 feet. Leaving the green he hit the putter against his golf bag. At the 2nd green, he called a Rules official over to examine the putter, as it was apparent that the shaft was bent. It was determined that the shaft was bent when the putter struck his golf bag at the 1st hole. This damage would not be considered as occurring in the normal course of play.

Because Trahan's putter was now non-conforming (a bent shaft), he was required to comply with Rule 4-3b governing damage that occurs other than in the normal course of play rendering the club non-conforming. This Rule requires that the club must not be used or replaced during the round. Trahan continued his round putting with his driver.

A little later in the round, while the group was on the 4th green, play was suspended because of weather conditions. When play resumed the next day, Trahan was not permitted to use or replace the putter as the next day's play was simply a continuation of the stipulated round. He finished the remaining holes on Saturday morning with the driver, missing the cut.

At the 2010 Qatar Masters, Lee Westwood discovered that the driver he was using appeared to have a cracked face and he wanted to replace it. To determine if he was entitled to replace it, he called an official for a ruling. Chief Referee Andy McFee responded with the following analysis.

If, during a stipulated round, a player's club is damaged in the normal course of play, he may replace the damaged club with any club but only if the club is unfit for play. The replacement of a club must not unduly delay play (Rule 6-7) and must not be made by borrowing any club selected for play by any other person playing on the course or by assembling components carried by or for the player during the stipulated round. A club is unfit for play if it is substantially damaged, for example, the shaft is dented, significantly bent or broken into pieces; the clubhead becomes loose, detached or significantly deformed; or the grip becomes loose.

After a careful examination, McFee determined that the face of the driver was cracked, which rendered it substantially damaged, and therefore unfit for play. In addition, in the absence of evidence that the club was damaged other than in the normal course of play, it was considered to have been damaged in the normal course of play. Westwood replaced the driver with one from his locker.

Frequently asked questions

As long as a player selects no more than 14 clubs, may he carry multiple drivers or multiple putters or carry both right and left handed clubs?
Yes, as long as the clubs are conforming, he may select any combination of clubs, including more than one of a certain type of club or left and right-handed clubs.

Is it permissible to add tape or gauze to any part of the club?
During the round, the playing characteristics of the club may not be changed – see Rule 4-2a. Prior to the player's stipulated round, tape or gauze may be applied to the grip of the club provided the application of such materials does not create a waist or bulge – see Appendix II; Part 3.
Tape applied to the club head or shaft is an external attachment, which renders the club non-conforming (see Appendix II; Part 1a). The following are exceptions to the prohibition against external attachments provided such applications are made prior to the player's stipulated round:

o   Lead tape may be applied to the head or shaft of the club for the purpose of adding weight.
o   Tape may be applied to the shaft of the club to protect it.
o   Decals may be applied to the shaft for identification purposes. These decals may also be covered by clear tape.

Rule 5

THE BALL

For detailed specifications and interpretations on the conformity of balls under Rule 5 and the process for consultation and submission regarding balls, see Appendix III

5-1. General

The ball the player plays must conform to requirements specified in Appendix III.

> **NOTE**
> The *Committee* may require, in the conditions of a competition (Rule 33-1), that the ball the player plays must be named on the current List of Conforming Golf Balls issued by the USGA.

5-2. Foreign Material

The ball the player plays must not have foreign material applied to it for the purpose of changing its playing characteristics.

PENALTY FOR BREACH OF RULE 5-1 OR 5-2: Disqualification.

5-3. Ball Unfit for Play

A ball is unfit for play if it is visibly cut, cracked or out of shape. A ball is not unfit for play solely because mud or other materials adhere to it, its surface is scratched or scraped or its paint is damaged or discolored.

If a player has reason to believe his ball has become unfit for play during play of the hole being played, he may lift the ball, without penalty, to determine whether it is unfit.

Before lifting the ball, the player must announce his intention to his *opponent* in match play or his *marker* or a *fellow-competitor* in stroke play and mark the position of the ball. He may then lift and examine it, provided that he gives his *opponent*, *marker* or *fellow-competitor* an opportunity to examine the ball and observe the lifting and replacement. The ball must not be cleaned when lifted under Rule 5-3.

If the player fails to comply with all or any part of this procedure, or if he lifts the ball without having reason to believe that it has become unfit for play during play of the hole being played, **he incurs a penalty of one stroke**.

If it is determined that the ball has become unfit for play during play of the hole being played, the player may *substitute* another ball, placing it on the spot where the original ball lay. Otherwise, the original ball must be replaced. If a player *substitutes* a ball when not permitted and he makes a *stroke* at the wrongly *substituted ball*, **he incurs the general penalty for a breach of Rule 5-3**, but there is no additional penalty under this Rule or Rule 15-2.

If a ball breaks into pieces as a result of a *stroke*, the *stroke* is canceled and the player must play a ball, without penalty, as nearly as possible at the spot from which the original ball was played (see Rule 20-5).

*PENALTY FOR BREACH OF RULE 5-3:
Match play – Loss of hole; **Stroke play** – Two strokes.
*If a player incurs the general penalty for breach of Rule 5-3, there is no additional penalty under this Rule.

THE BALL

A conforming ball stamped "practice" can still be used.

BALL UNFIT FOR PLAY

A player who has reason to believe his ball is unfit must give his opponent, marker, fellow-competitor or referee a chance to observe the lifting and replacement of the ball, as well as the ball itself.

NOTE 1

If the *opponent*, *marker* or *fellow-competitor* wishes to dispute a claim of unfitness, he must do so before the player plays another ball.

NOTE 2

If the original lie of a ball to be placed or replaced has been altered, see Rule 20-3b.

(Cleaning ball lifted from putting green or under any other Rule – see Rule 21)

RULE 5 INCIDENTS

To assist players who play in high-level events, the United States Golf Association maintains on its website (usga.org) a Conforming Golf Ball List that is updated on the first Wednesday of each month. This listing identifies golf balls that have been tested and found to conform to the Rules of Golf as established by the United States Golf Association and The R&A in St. Andrews, Scotland. This List is in operation as a Condition of Competition for professional events, as well as all USGA Championships, and only golf balls appearing on the current List may be used during those competitions.

Most players never concern themselves with the Conforming Golf Ball List or with Rule 5-1, which requires players to play a ball conforming to the requirements in Appendix III of the Rules of Golf. The reason for this is that nearly all the balls offered for sale are conforming to these requirements. On the other hand, PGA Tour players are constantly experimenting with new balls from manufacturers that might conform but are not on the List of approved balls as required for play in Tour events.

At the 1996 Cannon Greater Hartford Open in Hartford, CT, Greg Norman was playing with a ball that did not have the required markings of a ball on the List. He had been testing a ball for a manufacturer that had been submitted to the USGA and was approved but not yet published on the List. As such, it met the requirements of Rule 5-1 but not of the Conditions of the Competition that required the ball used by a player to be listed. Interestingly enough, Norman was notified by the manufacturer of the issue of which he was not aware. After being told, he informed Ben Nelson, a tour official, and he was disqualified. Nelson stated at the time that Norman had not used the ball in any other Tour events.

Later in 1996, it was discovered that Paul Azinger, Steve Elkington and Russ Cochran had played with a ball that was previously listed but inadvertently dropped from the List for the current year. At the time, tour official Jon Brendle pointed out, "The ball is obviously conforming but it's just not on the list." No penalties were assessed for these violations, as Rule 34-1b states that no penalty may be imposed after the competition has closed in a situation where the player was unaware of the violation.

Frequently asked questions

If a player runs out of golf balls during a round, may he borrow a ball from another player?
Yes. There is nothing in the Rules of Golf that prohibits a player from borrowing a golf ball from an opponent or fellow-competitor. A player who runs out of balls may get a new supply from any source, provided he does not unduly delay play (Rule 6-7) in the process. Although golf balls are part of a player's equipment, the only type of equipment that the Rules limit the borrowing of is clubs.

Must a player announce to his opponent(s) or fellow-competitor(s) that he intends to use a different ball between the play of two holes?
Although such an announcement would be courteous and is good practice, a player is not required under the Rules to inform an opponent or fellow-competitor that he intends to play a different ball between the play of two holes.

Rule 6

DEFINITIONS
All defined terms are in *italics* and are listed alphabetically in the Definitions section – see pages 10–23.

PLAYER'S RESPONSIBILITIES
THE PLAYER

6-1. Rules
The player and his *caddie* are responsible for knowing the *Rules*. During a *stipulated round*, for any breach of a *Rule* by his *caddie*, the player incurs the applicable penalty.

6-2. Handicap
a. Match Play
Before starting a match in a handicap competition, the players should determine from one another their respective handicaps. If a player begins a match having declared a handicap higher than that to which he is entitled and this affects the number of strokes given or received, **he is disqualified**; otherwise, the player must play off the declared handicap.

b. Stroke Play
In any round of a handicap competition, the *competitor* must ensure that his handicap is recorded on his score card before it is returned to the *Committee*. If no handicap is recorded on his score card before it is returned (Rule 6-6b), or if the recorded handicap is

higher than that to which he is entitled and this affects the number of strokes received, **he is disqualified** from the handicap competition; otherwise, the score stands.

NOTE

It is the player's responsibility to know the holes at which handicap strokes are to be given or received.

6-3. Time of Starting and Groups
a. Time of Starting

The player must start at the time established by the *Committee*.

PENALTY FOR BREACH OF RULE 6-3A:

If the player arrives at his starting point, ready to play, within five minutes after his starting time, the penalty for failure to start on time is loss of the first hole in match play or two strokes at the first hole in stroke play. Otherwise, the penalty for breach of this Rule is disqualification.

Bogey and par competitions – See Note 2 to Rule 32-1a.
Stableford competitions – See Note 2 to Rule 32-1b.

Exception:

Where the *Committee* determines that exceptional circumstances have prevented a player from starting on time, there is no penalty.

b. Groups

In stroke play, the *competitor* must remain throughout the round in the group arranged by the *Committee*, unless the *Committee* authorizes or ratifies a change.

PENALTY FOR BREACH OF RULE 6-3B:

Disqualification.
(Best-ball and four-ball play – see Rules 30-3a and 31-2)

6-4. Caddie

The player may be assisted by a *caddie*, but he is limited to only one *caddie* at any one time.

---

*PENALTY FOR BREACH OF RULE 6-4:

Match play – At the conclusion of the hole at which the breach is discovered, the state of the match is adjusted by deducting one hole for each hole at which a breach occurred; maximum deduction per round – Two holes.

Stroke play – Two strokes for each hole at which any breach occurred; maximum penalty per round – Four strokes (two strokes at each of the first two holes at which any breach occurred).

Match play or stroke play – If a breach is discovered between the play of two holes, it is deemed to have been discovered during play of the next hole, and the penalty must be applied accordingly.

Bogey and par competitions – See Note 1 to Rule 32-1a.
Stableford competitions – See Note 1 to Rule 32-1b.

*A player having more than one *caddie* in breach of this Rule must immediately upon the discovery that a breach has occurred ensure that he has no more than one *caddie* at any one time during the remainder of the *stipulated round*.

PLAYING THE PROPER BALL

Players are strongly encouraged to put an identifying mark on their golf ball so it is easily identified.

Otherwise, the player is disqualified.

NOTE
The *Committee* may, in the conditions of a competition (Rule 33-1), prohibit the use of *caddies* or restrict a player in his choice of *caddie*.

6-5. Ball
The responsibility for playing the proper ball rests with the player. Each player should put an identification mark on his ball.

6-6. Scoring in Stroke Play
a. Recording Scores
After each hole the *marker* should check the score with the *competitor* and record it. On completion of the round the *marker* must sign the score card and hand it to the *competitor*. If more than one *marker* records the scores, each must sign for the part for which he is responsible.

b. Signing and Returning Score Card
After completion of the round, the *competitor* should check his score for each hole and settle any doubtful points with the *Committee*. He must ensure that the *marker* or *markers* have signed the score card, sign the score card himself and return it to the *Committee* as soon as possible.

PENALTY FOR BREACH OF RULE 6-6B:
Disqualification.

c. Alteration of Score Card

No alteration may be made on a score card after the *competitor* has returned it to the *Committee*.

d. Wrong Score for Hole

The *competitor* is responsible for the correctness of the score recorded for each hole on his score card. If he returns a score for any hole lower than actually taken, **he is disqualified**. If he returns a score for any hole higher than actually taken, the score as returned stands.

Exception:

If a *competitor* returns a score for any hole lower than actually taken due to failure to include one or more *penalty strokes* that, before returning his score card, he did not know he had incurred, he is not disqualified. In such circumstances, **the competitor incurs the penalty prescribed by the applicable Rule and an additional penalty of two strokes for each hole at which the competitor committed a breach of Rule 6-6d**. This Exception does not apply when the applicable penalty is disqualification from the competition.

NOTE 1
The Committee is responsible for the addition of scores and application of the handicap recorded on the score card – see Rule 33-5.

NOTE 2
In four-ball stroke play, see also Rules 31-3 and 31-7a.

6-7. Undue Delay; Slow Play

The player must play without undue delay and in accordance with any pace of play guidelines that the *Committee* may establish. Between completion of a hole and playing from the next *teeing ground*, the player must not unduly delay play.

PENALTY FOR BREACH OF RULE 6-7:
Match play – Loss of hole; **Stroke play** – Two strokes.
Bogey and par competitions – See Note 2 to Rule 32-1a.
Stableford competitions – See Note 2 to Rule 32-1b.
For subsequent offense – Disqualification.

CORRECTNESS OF SCORE CARD

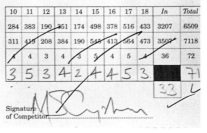

Padraig Harrington's first round score card signed by Jamie Spence as the marker and by Michael Campbell incorrectly as the competitor.

SCORING IN STROKE PLAY

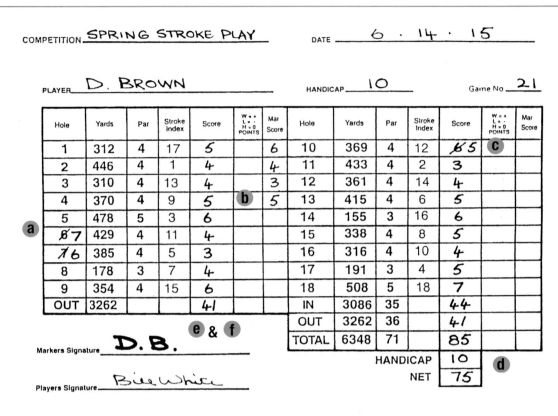

COMPETITION __SPRING STROKE PLAY__   DATE ___6 · 14 · 15___

PLAYER __D. BROWN__   HANDICAP __10__   Game No __21__

Hole	Yards	Par	Stroke Index	Score	W = + L = − H = 0 POINTS	Mar Score	Hole	Yards	Par	Stroke Index	Score	W = + L = − H = 0 POINTS	Mar Score
1	312	4	17	5		6	10	369	4	12	₆5		
2	446	4	1	4		4	11	433	4	2	3		
3	310	4	13	4		3	12	361	4	14	4		
4	370	4	9	5		5	13	415	4	6	5		
5	478	5	3	6			14	155	3	16	6		
8̶7	429	4	11	4			15	338	4	8	5		
7̶6	385	4	5	3			16	316	4	10	4		
8	178	3	7	4			17	191	3	4	5		
9	354	4	15	6			18	508	5	18	7		
OUT	3262			41			IN	3086	35		44		
							OUT	3262	36		41		
							TOTAL	6348	71		85		
							HANDICAP				10		
							NET				75		

Markers Signature __D.B.__

Players Signature __Bill White__

Competitor's Responsibilities:

1. To record the correct handicap somewhere on the score card before it is returned to the Committee.
2. To check the gross score recorded for each hole is correct.
3. To ensure that the marker has signed the card and to countersign the card himself before it is returned to the Committee.

Committee Responsibilities:

1. Issue to each competitor a score card containing the date and the competitor's name.
2. To add the scores for each hole and apply the handicap recorded on the card.

(a) Hole numbers may be altered if hole scores have been recorded in the wrong boxes.

(b) A marker need not keep a record of his own score; however, it is recommended.

(c) There is nothing in the Rules that requires an alteration to be initialed.

(d) The competitor is responsible only for the correctness of the score recorded for each hole. If the competitor records a wrong total score or net score, the Committee must correct the error, without penalty to the competitor. In this instance, the Committee have added the scores for each hole and applied the handicap.

(e) There is no penalty if a marker signs the competitor's score card in the space provided for the competitor's signature, and the competitor then signs in the space provided for the marker's signature.

(f) The initialing of the score card by the competitor is sufficient for the purpose of countersignature.

NOTE 1

If the player unduly delays play between holes, he is delaying the play of the next hole and, except for bogey, par and Stableford competitions (Rule 32), the penalty applies to that hole.

NOTE 2

For the purpose of preventing slow play, the *Committee* may, in the conditions of a competition (Rule 33-1), establish pace of play guidelines including maximum periods of time allowed to complete a *stipulated round*, a hole or a *stroke*.

In match play, the *Committee* may, in such a condition, modify the penalty for a breach of this Rule as follows:

First offense – Loss of hole;

Second offense – Loss of hole;

For subsequent offense – Disqualification.

In stroke play, the *Committee* may, in such a condition, modify the penalty for a breach of this Rule as follows:

First offense – One stroke;

Second offense – Two strokes;

For subsequent offense – Disqualification.

6-8. Discontinuance of Play; Resumption of Play
a. When Permitted

The player must not discontinue play unless:

(i) the *Committee* has suspended play;

(ii) he believes there is danger from lightning;

(iii) he is seeking a decision from the *Committee* on a doubtful or disputed point (see Rules 2-5 and 34-3); or

(iv) there is some other good reason such as sudden illness.

Bad weather is not of itself a good reason for discontinuing play.

If the player discontinues play without specific permission from the *Committee*, he must report to the *Committee* as soon as practicable. If he does so and the *Committee* considers his reason satisfactory, there is no penalty. Otherwise, **the player is disqualified**.

Exception in match play: Players discontinuing match play by agreement are not subject to disqualification, unless by so doing the competition is delayed.

NOTE

Leaving the *course* does not of itself constitute discontinuance of play.

b. Procedure When Play Suspended by Committee

When play is suspended by the *Committee*, if the players in a match or group are between the play of two holes, they must not resume play until the *Committee* has ordered a resumption of play. If they have started play of a hole, they may discontinue play immediately or continue play of the hole, provided they do so without delay. If the players choose to continue play of the hole, they are permitted to discontinue play before completing it. In any case, play must be discontinued after the hole is completed.

The players must resume play when the *Committee* has ordered a resumption of play.

UNDUE DELAY: ENTERING CLUBHOUSE

I must go into the clubhouse for a moment on our way past. I will catch up with you on the 10th tee.

OK. No doubt we will have to wait on the tee anyway, but you must not unduly delay play.

10th Tee

PENALTY FOR BREACH OF RULE 6-8B:

Disqualification.

NOTE

The *Committee* may provide, in the conditions of a competition (Rule 33-1), that in potentially dangerous situations play must be discontinued immediately following a suspension of play by the *Committee*. If a player fails to discontinue play immediately, he is disqualified, unless circumstances warrant waiving the penalty as provided in Rule 33-7.

c. Lifting Ball When Play Discontinued

When a player discontinues play of a hole under Rule 6-8a, he may lift his ball, without penalty, only if the *Committee* has suspended play or there is a good reason to lift it. Before lifting the ball the player must mark its position. If the player discontinues play and lifts his ball without specific permission from the *Committee*, he must, when reporting to the *Committee* (Rule 6-8a), report the lifting of the ball.

If the player lifts the ball without a good reason to do so, fails to mark the position of the ball before lifting it or fails to report the lifting of the ball, **he incurs a penalty of one stroke**.

d. Procedure When Play Resumed

Play must be resumed from where it was discontinued, even if resumption occurs on

DISCONTINUANCE OF PLAY

Stroke play

Let's take shelter for 10 minutes or so.

No, as this is stroke play and the Committee has not suspended play we must keep going. We'll be disqualified if we take shelter just because we're getting soaked.

Match play

We are all square with two to play, but I think it is too dark to go on. Why don't we replay tomorrow?

I agree it's too dark to finish tonight. As it is match play, we can complete the round tomorrow, but we must continue from where we left off, not start another match.

a subsequent day. The player must, either before or when play is resumed, proceed as follows:

(i) if the player has lifted the ball, he must, provided he was entitled to lift it under Rule 6-8c, place the original ball or a *substituted ball* on the spot from which the original ball was lifted. Otherwise, the original ball must be replaced;

(ii) if the player has not lifted his ball, he may, provided he was entitled to lift it under Rule 6-8c, lift, clean and replace the ball, or *substitute* a ball, on the spot from which the original ball was lifted. Before lifting the ball he must mark its position; or

(iii) if the player's ball or ball-marker is moved (including by wind or water) while play is discontinued, a ball or ball-marker must be placed on the spot from which the original ball or ball-marker was moved.

NOTE

If the spot where the ball is to be placed is impossible to determine, it must be estimated and the ball placed on the estimated spot. The provisions of Rule 20-3c do not apply.

*PENALTY FOR BREACH OF RULE 6-8D:

Match play – Loss of hole; **Stroke play** – Two strokes.

*If a player incurs the general penalty for a breach of Rule 6-8d, there is no additional penalty under Rule 6-8c.

RULE 6 INCIDENTS

Although the score card has no status in match play, in stroke play it is the ultimate testament to a player's performance. The score card must not contain a score lower than actually taken, it must be signed by the competitor, attested by the competitor's marker and returned as soon as possible to the Committee. Failure to meet any of these criteria generally results in disqualification.

However, there is a major exception to the first of these three criteria that appears in the 2016 Rules of Golf for the first time: if a competitor returns a score for any hole lower than actually taken due to failure to include one or more penalty strokes that, before returning his score card, he did not know he had incurred, he is not disqualified. In such circumstances, the competitor incurs the penalty prescribed by the applicable Rule and an additional penalty of two strokes for every hole at which the competitor committed a breach of Rule 6-6d. This exception does not apply when the applicable penalty is disqualification from the competition.

Two incidents exhibit the change to Rule 6-6d. In the first, Carl Pettersson returned his score card with an incorrect score merely because one hole was incorrectly recorded. In the second, P. H. Horgan III incurred a penalty, but did not know it at the time. In 2016, Pettersson would still be disqualified, while Horgan would be able to continue playing, although with additional penalty strokes.

In 2000, Carl Pettersson, now a PGA Tour player, competed for North Carolina State University. After his final round at the NCAA East Region, his team had apparently qualified for the NCAA Championships and Pettersson was the overall low scorer. Before the results were announced, it was discovered he had inadvertently signed an incorrect score card with the score for one hole lower than he had actually taken. He was disqualified from the competition and his final round score of 70 would not count toward NC State's team total. As a result, his team did not qualify for the NCAA Championship. Pettersson's error was in not checking the scores properly before returning the score card, therefore, the Exception to Rule 6-6d would not apply and he would still be disqualified in 2016.

A befuddled Padraig Harrington following his final day disqualification from the 2000 Benson & Hedges International for failing to sign his first round score card.

At the 1996 Nike Shreveport Open, while the final round was concluding with two groups yet to finish, it appeared that P. H. Horgan III, the leading money winner on the Nike Tour, would be in a play-off with Tim Loustalot for the championship, as they had tied with a four-round score of 277. While waiting for the final groups to finish, Horgan was in a conversation with the tournament director and casually mentioned an incident that occurred the day before where he had dropped his ball and moved his ball-marker on the 8th green. Both he and his fellow-competitor, Steve Gotsche, had agreed that there was no penalty, whereas the player who moves his ball-marker in such a situation will incur a one-stroke penalty since Rule 20-1 stipulates that the ball-marker will remain in position until the ball is replaced. Horgan was disqualified for signing an incorrect score card and Loustalot received the trophy. Since the reason for Horgan's incorrect score was a penalty he did not know he had incurred, he would no longer be disqualified in 2016. Instead, his score for the third round would be adjusted by adding the one penalty stroke for the violation of Rule 20-1 and an additional two penalty strokes under the Exception to Rule 6-6d.

Failure to sign his first round score card arguably cost Padraig Harrington the 2000 Benson & Hedges International Open at the Belfry. As he prepared to begin the final round with a five-shot lead, officials informed the 28-year-old Irishman that there was a problem.

Anticipating the ultimate victory, members of the Club had begun to collect Harrington's three previous score cards for souvenir purposes when it was noticed that he had not signed his first round card. Jamie Spence, Harrington's first round marker, had signed the card as required, but Michael Campbell, the third player in the group, had mistakenly signed Harrington's card instead of Harrington signing it. The resulting penalty under Rule 6-6b was disqualification.

Robert De Vicenzo signed for a score higher than he actually made in the final round of the 1968 Masters Tournament. The higher score did not disqualify him but it did keep the Argentinean from forcing a play-off with Bob Goalby.

Playing in front of Goalby on Sunday, De Vicenzo, the reigning British Open Champion, sank a five-foot birdie putt on the 17th hole for a 3. He followed that with a bogey at the 18th, giving him 66 for the day and 277 for the tournament. Goalby managed a five-footer for par at the 18th that also gave him 66 for the day and a total of 277.

However, De Vicenzo's fellow-competitor and marker, Tommy Aaron, had mistakenly recorded a 4 for De Vicenzo at the 17th rather than the 3. De Vicenzo did not notice the mistake, signed and returned the score card and was rushed away from the scorer's table to talk to the press. A little later, Aaron noticed the mistake and brought it to the attention of tournament officials.

Augusta National founder, Bob Jones, searched for a way around the ensuing ruling but none could be found. Once the score card was signed and returned, the decision under the Rules was unavoidable: The higher score must stand (Rule 6-6d). Goalby was the Masters Champion.

An hour later De Vicenzo told the media, "It's my fault. Tommy feels like I feel, very bad. I think the Rule is hard." The day's drama was compounded by the fact that it was De Vicenzo's 45th birthday.

Frequently asked questions

It is recommended for the player to place an identification mark on his golf ball. May a line or an arrow that will also help in aligning the club face be used?
Rules 6-5 and 12-2 state that each player should put an identification mark on his ball. Thus, the Rules do not limit the type of markings a player may put on the ball (i.e., arrows, lines, words, etc.). Additionally, there is no penalty for using such lines to "line up" prior to a stroke on the putting green or any other place on the course.

If my score card is lost or becomes wet during the round and is unreadable, am I disqualified?
No. A different score card may be returned, provided it contains the correct score for each hole and is signed by both you and your marker.

Rule 7

DEFINITIONS
All defined terms are in *italics* and are listed alphabetically in the Definitions section – see pages 10–23.

PRACTICE

7-1. Before or Between Rounds
a. Match Play
On any day of a match-play competition, a player may practice on the competition *course* before a round.

b. Stroke Play
Before a round or play-off on any day of a stroke-play competition, a *competitor* must not practice on the competition *course* or test the surface of any *putting green* on the *course* by rolling a ball or roughening or scraping the surface.

When two or more rounds of a stroke-play competition are to be played over consecutive days, a *competitor* must not practice between those rounds on any competition *course* remaining to be played, or test the surface of any *putting green* on such *course* by rolling a ball or roughening or scraping the surface.

Exception:
Practice putting or chipping on or near the first *teeing ground* or any practice area before starting a round or play-off is permitted.

PENALTY FOR BREACH OF RULE 7-1B:
Disqualification.

NOTE
The *Committee* may, in the conditions of a competition (Rule 33-1), prohibit practice on the competition course on any day of a match-play competition or permit practice on the competition *course* or part of the course (Rule 33-2c) on any day of or between rounds of a stroke-play competition.

7-2. During Round
A player must not make a practice *stroke* during play of a hole.

Between the play of two holes, a player must not make a practice *stroke*, except that he may practice putting or chipping on or near:
a. the *putting green* of the hole last played,
b. any practice *putting green*, or
c. the *teeing ground* of the next hole to be played in the round,
provided a practice *stroke* is not made from a *hazard* and does not unduly delay play (Rule 6-7).

Strokes made in continuing the play of a hole, the result of which has been decided, are not practice *strokes*.

Exception:
When play has been suspended by the *Committee*, a player may, prior to resumption of play, practice (a) as provided in this Rule, (b) anywhere other than on the competition *course* and (c) as otherwise permitted by the *Committee*.

PRACTICE DURING A ROUND

Practice putting and chipping on or near the teeing ground of the next hole to be played is permitted as long as play is not delayed.

PENALTY FOR BREACH OF RULE 7-2:

Match play – Loss of hole; **Stroke play** – Two strokes.

In the event of a breach between the play of two holes, the penalty applies to the next hole.

NOTE 1

A practice swing is not a practice *stroke* and may be taken at any place, provided the player does not breach the *Rules*.

NOTE 2

The *Committee* may, in the conditions of a competition (Rule 33-1), prohibit:

(a) practice on or near the *putting green* of the hole last played, and
(b) rolling a ball on the *putting green* of the hole last played.

RULE 7 INCIDENTS

After a suspension of play during the final round of the 2001 Players Championship at Sawgrass, both the penultimate group and the final group were required to resume play from the 10th tee. Tiger Woods, playing in the final group, was aware that the group in front would resume play first, and his group would have an additional wait on the tee before their resumption.

Concerned that Woods might continue to hit practice shots on the practice range after the signal for resumption of play had been sounded, officials advised Woods and his fellow-competitor that such action would be in breach of Rule 7-2, which prohibits practice during the round. Play was resumed without incident, and Woods went on to win The Players Championship by one stroke over Vijay Singh.

Also under Rule 7-2, players may practice, with certain restrictions, on the course while play is suspended and prior to resumption. During the first round of the 2000 U.S. Open at Pebble Beach, thick fog forced a suspension of play and the players were advised to remain in position on the course in hope that the fog would lift and play could be resumed.

Therefore those players who were between holes were permitted to practice under the provisions of Rule 7-2. Walking officials confirmed this point with the players in their group.

When it became evident that the fog would not clear quickly, the players were evacuated from the course and returned to the clubhouse. The following morning, when play was resumed, practice under Rule 7-2 was again applicable before the siren signaled the resumption of play.

Frequently asked questions

May a player practice on the competition course before the stipulated round?
Before a match-play competition, a player may practice on the competition course unless prohibited by the Committee – see the Note to Rule 7-1. However, in stroke play, a competitor is not permitted to practice on the competition course before the competition or test the surface of any putting green unless specifically permitted by the Committee.

Is practice putting permitted between the play of two holes?
In both match play and stroke play, a player may practice putting or chipping on or near the putting green of the hole last played, any practice putting green or the teeing ground of the next hole to be played, provided such a practice stroke is not played from a hazard and does not unduly delay play. However, the Committee can limit certain practice – see Note 2 to Rule 7-2.

In match play, if one player hits his second shot from the fairway out of bounds and concedes the hole to his opponent, can they finish the hole?
Yes, each player can play the remainder of the hole with one ball as these strokes are not considered practice strokes.

Rule 8

DEFINITIONS
All defined terms are in *italics* and are listed alphabetically in the Definitions section – see pages 10–23.

ADVICE; INDICATING LINE OF PLAY

8-1. Advice

During a *stipulated round*, a player must not:

a. give *advice* to anyone in the competition playing on the *course* other than his *partner*, or

b. ask for *advice* from anyone other than his *partner* or either of their *caddies*.

8-2. Indicating Line of Play
a. Other Than on Putting Green

Except on the *putting green*, a player may have the *line of play* indicated to him by anyone, but no one may be positioned by the player for that purpose on or close to the line or an extension of the line beyond the *hole* while the *stroke* is being made. Any mark placed by the player or with his knowledge, for the purpose of indicating the *line of play*, must be removed before the *stroke* is made.

Exception:
Flagstick attended or held up – see Rule 17-1.

b. On the Putting Green

When the player's ball is on the *putting green*, the *line of putt* may be indicated before, but not during, the *stroke* by the player, his *partner* or either of their *caddies*; in doing so the *putting green* must not be touched. A mark must not be placed anywhere for the purpose of indicating a *line of putt*.
(Touching line of putt – see Rule 16-1a)

ADVICE

My yardage book shows that I have 150 yards to the green from this bunker, but I'm still not sure what club to use.

Don't ask me or you'll be penalized for seeking advice.

INDICATING LINE OF PLAY

PENALTY FOR BREACH OF RULE:

Match play – Loss of hole; **Stroke play** – Two strokes.

NOTE

The *Committee* may, in the conditions of a team competition (Rule 33-1), permit each team to appoint one person who may give *advice* (including pointing out a *line of putt*) to members of that team. The *Committee* may establish conditions relating to the appointment and permitted conduct of that person, who must be identified to the *Committee* before giving *advice*.

RULE 8 INCIDENTS

It may be that no good deed goes unpunished, but that does not mean it goes unrewarded. Mark Wilson was contending for the 2007 Honda Classic at PGA National when it became incumbent upon him to penalize himself.

Wilson was playing the 217-yard, par-3 5th hole when his caddie, Chris Jones, reflexively offered advice to Camilo Villegas, who was playing with Wilson. Following Wilson's tee shot with an 18-degree hybrid club, Villegas took his place on the tee and contemplated his club selection. Villegas asked his own caddie what club he thought Wilson had hit. Villegas's caddie speculated that a 2- or 3-iron had been used.

"Oh, it's an 18-degree," Jones injected reflexively.

Wilson was fully aware of the violation under Rule 8-1 that prohibits a player or his caddie from giving advice to a fellow-competitor in stroke play or an opponent in match play.

"I played out that hole," Wilson said later, "and immediately called an official over to see what he thought. He wasn't sure at first if that was necessarily advice, but within 60 seconds, he made the decision."

Jones said he was shaken when his boss pointed out the violation. "I heard Camilo and his caddie talking, and I just blurted it out. I was getting too comfortable and too friendly." Wilson forgave his caddie and told him to shake it off.

"I've called penalties on myself before," Wilson said following a tournament-winning play-off three days later that included Villegas and Boo Weekly (see incident for Rule 17), "and I've never won. It didn't work out those times ... It was the right thing to do. I don't think I'd be here [in the winner's circle] if I hadn't called it on myself. And, if I would be sitting here and hadn't called it on myself, every time I looked at that trophy, it would be tarnished." When the giving of advice is penalized in golf, it is usually due to a light-hearted friendly moment. Tom Watson and Lee Trevino were playing together in the 1980 Tournament of Champions when Watson casually told Trevino about a little flaw he noticed in his fellow-competitor's swing. Overheard by the television audience, Watson was asked about it following the round. Watson agreed that he had indeed given Trevino a swing tip. Fortunately, the penalty was assessed before Watson returned his score card. Equally fortunate was that he had a three-stroke lead at the time and still won the tournament. As he had not asked for advice, Trevino incurred no penalty.

Also addressed under Rule 8 are the regulations regarding indicating the line of play. At the 2013 U.S. Amateur Public Links Championship at Laurel Hill GC in Lorton, Virginia, James Erkenbeck, first-team All-American at the University of New Mexico, was playing a first round match and putting for an eagle on the par-5 ninth hole. His caddie was attending the flagstick for Erkenbeck's 30-foot putt when he told the player to putt at his left foot.

The caddie did not initially place his foot in position for the purpose of pointing out the line of putt so there was no violation of Rule 8-2b for touching the putting green in pointing out the line of putt. However, when the caddie subsequently suggested that the player aim at his left foot, the player would be in breach of the Rule if the caddie did not move his foot to another position that did not indicate the line of putt prior to the stroke.

The referee assigned to the match heard what the caddie had said to the player and promptly told the caddie that he must move the foot prior to the stroke to avoid a penalty.

The caddie moved his foot but Erkenbeck missed the putt for eagle. The match ended on the 14th hole with Erkenbeck the winner by a margin of five up with four holes to play.

James Erkenbeck and his caddie at the 2013 U.S. Amateur Public Links.

Frequently asked questions

Can players share information attained from a distance measuring device?
Information on distance is considered public information and therefore, by definition, is not advice. If a Local Rule has been enacted permitting the use of devices which measure distance only, information obtained from such a device may be shared between or amongst players. However, there is no obligation under the Rules to share this information if asked.

Rule 9

DEFINITIONS

All defined terms are in *italics* and are listed alphabetically in the Definitions section – see pages 10–23.

INFORMATION AS TO STROKES TAKEN

9-1. General

The number of *strokes* a player has taken includes any *penalty strokes* incurred.

9-2. Match Play

a. Information as to Strokes Taken

An *opponent* is entitled to ascertain from the player, during the play of a hole, the number of *strokes* he has taken and, after play of a hole, the number of *strokes* taken on the hole just completed.

b. Wrong Information

A player must not give wrong information to his *opponent*. If a player gives wrong information, **he loses the hole**.

A player is deemed to have given wrong information if he:

(i) fails to inform his *opponent* as soon as practicable that he has incurred a penalty, unless (a) he was obviously proceeding under a *Rule* involving a penalty and this was observed by his *opponent*, or (b) he corrects the mistake before his *opponent* makes his next *stroke*; or

(ii) gives incorrect information during play of a hole regarding the number of *strokes* taken and does not correct the mistake before his *opponent* makes his next *stroke*; or

(iii) gives incorrect information regarding the number of *strokes* taken to complete a hole and this affects the *opponent*'s understanding of the result of the hole, unless he corrects the mistake before any player makes a *stroke* from the next *teeing ground* or,

INFORMATION AS TO STROKES TAKEN

OK. Thanks for letting me know.

Before you play, I had to deem my ball unplayable in there, so my next stroke will be my third.

in the case of the last hole of the match, before all players leave the *putting green*.
A player has given wrong information even if it is due to the failure to include a penalty
that he did not know he had incurred. It is the player's responsibility to know the *Rules*.

9-3. Stroke Play

A *competitor* who has incurred a penalty should inform his *marker* as soon as practicable.

RULE 9 INCIDENTS

The One Ball Condition from Appendix I in the Rules of Golf is straightforward enough when adopted for individual competition. It becomes a little less obvious in foursome play, or so it seemed at the 1991 Ryder Cup Matches.

On the 7th tee of Kiawah Island's Ocean Course during the first morning's foursomes, Chip Beck and Paul Azinger were overheard by their European opponents discussing which type of ball they would select to optimize their performance on that hole.

The One Ball Condition adopted for the competition stated: "Each player must use the same brand and type of ball for the entire round." This was interpreted to mean that when it was a player's turn to drive, he was required to use the same type of ball that he used for his first tee shot.

With one player driving the odd-numbered holes and the other driving the even-numbered holes, as required in foursome competition, the Americans erred when Beck, driving from the 7th tee, selected the ball type used by his partner, rather than the ball type that he used in driving from the 1st tee. The European side of Seve Ballesteros and Jose Maria Olazabal suspected this was a breach of the Rules. Nothing was said to Beck and Azinger. Sam Torrance, a fellow European Team member who was not playing in the morning foursomes, was in the gallery following the match. He was called over by Ballesteros, told of the situation and sent to fetch the European Captain Bernard Gallacher.

While Gallacher was being located, play of the 7th, 8th and 9th holes was completed. On the way to the 10th tee, the Europeans made a claim concerning what had taken place on the 7th hole. The Chief Referee was called for a ruling.

In match play, Rule 9-2 requires a player who has incurred a penalty to notify his opponents as soon as practicable. If he does not, even when he doesn't know he has incurred a penalty, he is considered to have given wrong information. In this case, the Americans gave wrong information as a penalty was associated with their playing of the wrong type of ball from the 7th tee. However, since the European side was aware of the error and did not make a claim (Rule 2-5) before anyone played from the 8th tee, their belated claim could not be considered. It was as if the statute of limitations ran out for that particular violation.

The match continued from the 10th tee without Beck and Azinger being penalized for their infraction at the 7th.

Frequently asked questions

If a player unknowingly gives incorrect information on the Rules to a fellow-competitor or opponent, is it a penalty?

No. However, if the player knowingly gave misinformation on the Rules, he could be disqualified under Rule 33-7.

Rule 10

ORDER OF PLAY

DEFINITIONS
All defined terms are in *italics* and are listed alphabetically in the Definitions section – see pages 10–23.

10-1. Match Play
a. When Starting Play of Hole

The *side* that has the *honor* at the first *teeing ground* is determined by the order of the draw. In the absence of a draw, the *honor* should be decided by lot.

The *side* that wins a hole takes the *honor* at the next *teeing ground*. If a hole has been halved, the *side* that had the *honor* at the previous *teeing ground* retains it.

b. During Play of Hole

After both players have started play of the hole, the ball farther from the *hole* is played first. If the balls are equidistant from the *hole* or their positions relative to the *hole* are not determinable, the ball to be played first should be decided by lot.

Exception:

Rule 30-3b (*best-ball* and *four-ball* match play).

NOTE

When it becomes known that the original ball is not to be played as it lies and the player is required to play a ball as nearly as possible at the spot from which the original ball was last played (see Rule 20-5), the order of play is determined by the spot from which the previous *stroke* was made. When a ball may be played from a spot other than where the previous *stroke* was made, the order of play is determined by the position where the original ball came to rest.

c. Playing Out of Turn

If a player plays when his *opponent* should have played, there is no penalty, but the *opponent* may immediately require the player to cancel the *stroke* so made and, in correct order, play a ball as nearly as possible at the spot from which the original ball was last played (see Rule 20-5).

10-2. Stroke Play
a. When Starting Play of Hole

The *competitor* who has the *honor* at the first *teeing ground* is determined by the order of the draw. In the absence of a draw, the *honor* should be decided by lot.

The *competitor* with the lowest score at a hole takes the *honor* at the next *teeing ground*. The *competitor* with the second lowest score plays next and so on. If two or more *competitors* have the same score at a hole, they play from the next *teeing ground* in the same order as at the previous t*eeing ground*.

Exception:

Rule 32-1 (handcap bogey, par and Stableford competitions).

b. During Play of Hole

After the *competitors* have started play of the hole, the ball farthest from the *hole* is played first. If two or more balls are equidistant from the *hole* or their positions relative to the *hole* are not determinable, the ball to be played first should be decided by lot.

Exceptions:

Rules 22 (ball assisting or interfering with play) and 31-4 (*four-ball* stroke play).

NOTE

When it becomes known that the original ball is not to be played as it lies and the *competitor* is required to play a ball as nearly as possible at the spot from which the original ball was last played (see Rule 20-5), the order of play is determined by the spot from which the previous *stroke* was made. When a ball may be played from a spot other than where the previous *stroke* was made, the order of play is determined by the position where the original ball came to rest.

c. Playing Out of Turn

If a *competitor* plays out of turn, there is no penalty and the ball is played as it lies. If, however, the *Committee* determines that *competitors* have agreed to play out of turn to give one of them an advantage, **they are disqualified**.

(Making stroke while another ball in motion after stroke from putting green — see Rule 16-1f)

(Incorrect order of play in foursome stroke play — see Rule 29-3)

10-3. Provisional Ball or Another Ball from Teeing Ground

If a player plays a *provisional ball* or another ball from the *teeing ground*, he must do so after his *opponent* or *fellow-competitor* has made his first *stroke*. If more than one player elects to play a *provisional ball* or is required to play another ball from the *teeing ground*, the original order of play must be retained. If a player plays a *provisional ball* or another ball out of turn, Rule 10-1c or -2c applies.

RULE 10 INCIDENTS

While there is no penalty for playing out of turn, the strategic consequences of doing so can have impressively different weight in stroke play and match play.

There are many speculative reasons why Sam Snead came so close but never won the U.S. Open Championship. In a play-off with Lew Worsham in 1947, Snead came as close as it is possible to come without success.

Of the 1,356 entries that year, it had come down to Worsham and Snead who played the regulation 72 holes in two-under-par (282). An 18-hole play-off ensued. Coming to the last tee of the play-off round, the two men were still tied. After playing to the final green, both were left with putts for par from about the same distance.

Rule 10 is unequivocal: In stroke play, "after the competitors have started play of the hole, the ball farthest from the hole is played first." It also states that no penalty is incurred if a competitor plays out of turn,

as long as it has not been agreed upon in order to create an advantage.

Snead and Worsham were each less than three feet from the hole. Worsham voiced no objection when Snead began his procedure for putting first. This would indicate that it must have been apparent to both men that Snead was away.

Snead recalled not only addressing his putt but also actually taking the club back before Worsham objected. "In the middle of my backswing, Lew said, 'Sam, I think I'm away,'" Snead recalled later. At that point, Snead interrupted his stroke.

Isaac Grainger was the Rules official with the group. "When Ike came over," Snead remembered, "I said, 'I know I can continue putting and, besides, I am away as well.'"

Grainger, an authority on the Rules who would

serve as president of the USGA from 1954–1955, was renowned for being fastidious.

"Ike never replied," Snead said, "but he did have a ruler."

The players backed slightly away and watched intently as Grainger measured from the hole to each ball. Snead recalled that his ball was 30½ inches from the flagstick. The distance to Worsham's ball was 30 inches. It was, indeed, Snead's turn to play.

The interruption proved distracting, as Snead missed. Worsham holed and, with a score of 69, became the 1947 U.S. Open Champion.

A large number of Rules have Exceptions or Notes within them; some have both. These items should never be overlooked by those who study or apply the Rules.

But doesn't Rule 10-1b simply say in match play that during play of a hole the ball farther from the hole is played first? Yes, but suppose a player's original ball lies at a spot in a water hazard. He might either play it from there or from a spot outside the hazard with a penalty stroke under the water hazard Rule and this latter spot might be a significant distance from the hole compared to where the original ball lies. Which of these two spots is the reference point for determining whose turn it is to play? The answer is found in the Note to Rule 10-1b, which states that, "When a ball may be played from a spot other than from where the previous stroke was made, the order of play is determined by the position where the original ball came to rest."

This Note came into play at the 2013 U.S. Amateur Public Links Championship at Laurel Hill GC in Lorton, Virginia. During play of the par-5 36th hole of the final match, Michael Kim, who was one down to his opponent Jordan Niebrugge, played his second shot about 30-yards from the hole but just short of the putting green where the ball came to rest in a water hazard. Niebrugge had previously played his second shot to the left of the putting green, about 50-yards from the hole. Kim decided to take relief from the water hazard and dropped a ball in the dropping zone about 80-yards from the hole.

Before Kim could play his ball from the dropping zone, the referee, Bill Fallon, correctly reminded the players that according to the Note it was Niebrugge's turn to play since Kim's original ball had come to rest in the water hazard closer to the hole than where Niebrugge's ball had come to rest.

Niebrugge played his ball that lay 50-yards from the hole onto the putting green, followed by Kim who played his ball that lay 80-yards from the hole onto the putting green. Subsequently, the hole was halved in a score of par with Niebrugge winning the Championship by a margin of 1up.

Rule 10 played an integral part in the final match of the 2013 U.S. Amateur Public Links between Jordan Niebrugge and Michael Kim.

Frequently asked question

Player A's ball lies 15 feet from the hole, but in a bunker. Player B's ball lies 30 feet from the hole on the putting green. Who plays first?

Player B should play first, since his ball is further from the hole than A's ball, even though A's ball is not on the putting green.

Rule 11

TEEING GROUND
TEEING GROUND

DEFINITIONS
All defined terms are in *italics* and are listed alphabetically in the Definitions section – see pages 10–23.

11-1. Teeing

When a player is putting a ball into play from the *teeing ground*, it must be played from within the *teeing ground* and from the surface of the ground or from a conforming tee (see Appendix IV) in or on the surface of the ground.

For the purposes of this Rule, the surface of the ground includes an irregularity of surface (whether or not created by the player) and sand or other natural substance (whether or not placed by the player).

If a player makes a *stroke* at a ball on a non-conforming tee, or at a ball teed in a manner not permitted by this Rule, **he is disqualified**.

A player may stand outside the *teeing ground* to play a ball within it.

11-2. Tee-Markers

Before a player makes his first *stroke* with any ball on the *teeing ground* of the hole being played, the tee-markers are deemed to be fixed. In these circumstances, if the player moves or allows to be moved a tee-marker for the purpose of avoiding interference with his *stance*, the area of his intended swing or his *line of play*, **he incurs the penalty for a breach of Rule 13-2**.

11-3. Ball Falling Off Tee

If a ball, when not *in play*, falls off a tee or is knocked off a tee by the player in *addressing* it, it may be re-teed, without penalty. However, if a *stroke* is made at the ball in these circumstances, whether the ball is moving or not, the *stroke* counts, but there is no penalty.

11-4. Playing from Outside Teeing Ground
a. Match Play

If a player, when starting a hole, plays a ball from outside the *teeing ground* there is no penalty, but the *opponent* may immediately require the player to cancel the *stroke* and play a ball from within the *teeing ground*.

b. Stroke Play

If a *competitor*, when starting a hole, plays a ball from outside the *teeing ground*, **he incurs a penalty of two strokes** and must then play a ball from within the *teeing ground*.

    If the *competitor* makes a *stroke* from the next *teeing ground* without first correcting his mistake or, in the case of the last hole of the round, leaves the *putting green* without first declaring his intention to correct his mistake, **he is disqualified**.

    The *stroke* from outside the *teeing ground* and any subsequent *strokes* by the *competitor* on the hole prior to his correction of the mistake do not count in his score.

11-5. Playing from Wrong Teeing Ground

The provisions of Rule 11-4 apply.

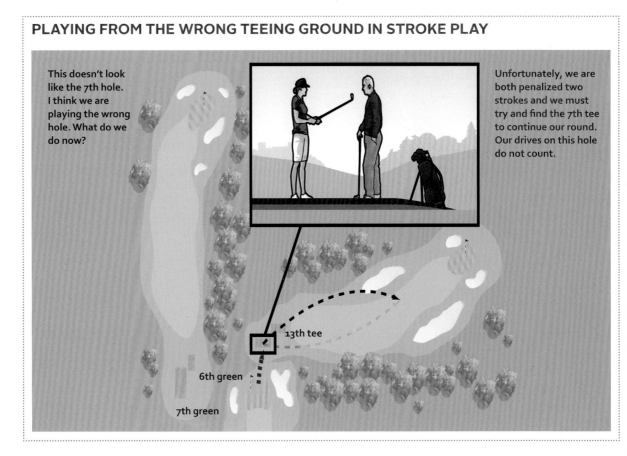

PLAYING FROM THE WRONG TEEING GROUND IN STROKE PLAY

This doesn't look like the 7th hole. I think we are playing the wrong hole. What do we do now?

Unfortunately, we are both penalized two strokes and we must try and find the 7th tee to continue our round. Our drives on this hole do not count.

13th tee

6th green

7th green

Rule 11 Incidents

"Most of the time nothing happens," reflects C. Grant Spaeth, then president of the USGA and a former chairman of the Rules of Golf Committee, recalling the 1990 U.S. Open Championship play-off, "but when it does, you better be ready."

The final result of the championship lent substantiation to the USGA's 18-hole play-off policy. At eight-under-par, 280, Mike Donald and Hale Irwin were tied after 72 holes of regulation play at Medinah C.C.

The competitive tension had been intense all week, as is usually the case at the Open. Irwin summoned a surge of talent reflective of his 33 professional victories that included two previous U.S. Open victories (1974 and 1979). Indeed, he holed a 45-foot birdie putt on the 72nd hole to force an 18-hole play-off the following day with Donald, whose sole PGA Tour victory had come the previous year in Williamsburg, Virginia.

A momentary lapse of concentration regarding the Rules might have determined the winner had it not been for Spaeth's diligence as the attending referee.

"After a long week, I was tired," Spaeth recalled. "Walking off the 17th green (of the play-off round), I was tempted not to go down a hill to the 18th tee, which sits out on a peninsula that stretches into the lake. I thought I might cut over to the 18th fairway, contrary to the strictures in the book [that suggest walking officials be present at each teeing ground]. Thank God I resisted and trudged back to the tee."

After days of athletic and psychological competition, the players walked off the 17th green with Donald leading by a stroke and with the honor. On the 18th tee, Donald mistakenly teed his ball in front of the tee markers. Spaeth noticed the error and, as a dutiful referee, brought it to the attention of Donald, who re-teed appropriately within the teeing ground.

Rule 11, as it applies to stroke play, is exact. If a competitor plays from outside the teeing ground, he incurs a penalty of two strokes and must then play a ball from within the teeing ground. Had Donald's mistake been observed a few moments after his ball was played, the resulting two-stroke penalty would have reversed the state of the play-off and given Irwin a one-stroke lead.

Spaeth's intervention prevented the breach. Donald's bogey and Irwin's par at the 90th hole resulted in both men scoring 74 in the play-off round. By the conditions outlined in the entry form, and for the first time in U.S. Open history, the championship then moved to hole-by-hole play-off to determine the champion.

On the first hole-by-hole play-off hole, the 91st of the championship, Irwin holed an eight-foot birdie putt to become the U.S. Open's oldest winner.

Frequently asked question

May a player use a tee that he has found or is this a breach sharing equipment?
A player may use a conforming tee (see Appendix IV) that he has found (including a broken tee). There is no general Rule that prohibits the sharing of equipment other than clubs.

If I knock my ball off the tee while addressing it, is it a penalty?
No, since the ball was not in play, there is no penalty. You may re-tee the ball and play your first stroke.

Rule 12

DEFINITIONS
All defined terms are in *italics* and are listed alphabetically in the Definitions section – see pages 10–23.

PLAYING THE BALL
SEARCHING FOR AND IDENTIFYING BALL

12-1. Seeing Ball; Searching for Ball

A player is not necessarily entitled to see his ball when making a *stroke*.

In searching for his ball anywhere on the *course*, the player may touch or bend long grass, rushes, bushes, whins, heather or the like, but only to the extent necessary to find or identify the ball, provided that this does not improve the lie of the ball, the area of his intended *stance* or swing or his *line of play*; if the ball is *moved*, Rule 18-2 applies except as provided in clauses a–d of this Rule.

In addition to the methods of searching for and identifying a ball that are otherwise permitted by the *Rules*, the player may also search for and identify a ball under Rule 12-1 as follows:

a. Searching for or Identifying Ball Covered by Sand

If the player's ball lying anywhere on the course is believed to be covered by sand, to the extent that he cannot find or identify it, he may, without penalty, touch or move the sand in order to find or identify the ball. If the ball is found, and identified as his, the player must re-create the lie as nearly as possible by replacing the sand. If the ball is moved during the touching or moving of sand while searching for or identifying the ball or during the re-creation of the lie, there is no penalty; the ball must be replaced and the lie re-created.

In re-creating a lie under this Rule, the player is permitted to leave a small part of the ball visible.

b. Searching for or Identifying Ball Covered by Loose Impediments in Hazard

In a *hazard*, if the player's ball is believed to be covered by *loose impediments* to the extent that he cannot find or identify it, he may, without penalty, touch or move *loose impediments* in order to find or identify the ball. If the ball is found or identified as his, the player must replace the *loose impediments*. If the ball is *moved* during the touching or moving of *loose impediments* while searching for or identifying the ball, Rule 18-2 applies; if the ball is *moved* during the replacement of the *loose impediments*, there is no penalty and the ball must be replaced.

If the ball was entirely covered by *loose impediments*, the player must re-cover the ball but is permitted to leave a small part of the ball visible.

c. Searching for Ball in Water in Water Hazard

If a ball is believed to be lying in water in a *water hazard*, the player may, without penalty, probe for it with a club or otherwise. If the ball in water is accidentally *moved* while probing, there is no penalty; the ball must be replaced, unless the player elects to proceed under Rule 26-1. If the *moved* ball was not lying in water or the ball was accidentally *moved* by the player other than while probing, Rule 18-2 applies.

d. Searching for Ball Within Obstruction or Abnormal Ground Condition

If a ball lying in or on an *obstruction* or in an *abnormal ground condition* is accidentally

SEARCHING FOR A BALL IN SAND

If a player believes his ball is buried in sand, he may touch or move the sand in order to find or identify it. If the ball moves, there is no penalty but the ball must be replaced and the lie re-created.

moved during search, there is no penalty; the ball must be replaced unless the player elects to proceed under Rule 24-1b, 24-2b or 25-1b as applicable. If the player replaces the ball, he may still proceed under one of those Rules, if applicable.

PENALTY FOR BREACH OF RULE 12-1:
Match play – Loss of hole; **Stroke play** – Two strokes.
(Improving lie, area of intended stance or swing, or line of play – see Rule 13-2)

12-2. Lifting Ball for Indentification

The responsibility for playing the proper ball rests with the player. Each player should put an identification mark on his ball.

If a player believes that a ball at rest might be his, but he cannot identify it, the player may lift the ball for identification, without penalty. The right to lift a ball for identification is in addition to the actions permitted under Rule 12-1.

Before lifting the ball, the player must announce his intention to his *opponent* in match play or his *marker* or a *fellow-competitor* in stroke play and mark the position of the ball. He may then lift the ball and identify it, provided that he gives his *opponent*, *marker* or *fellow-competitor* an opportunity to observe the lifting and replacement. The ball must not be cleaned beyond the extent necessary for identification when lifted under Rule 12-2.

If the ball is the player's ball and he fails to comply with all or any part of this procedure, or he lifts his ball in order to identify it without having good reason to do so, **he incurs a penalty of one stroke**. If the lifted ball is the player's ball, he must replace it. If he fails to do so, **he incurs the general penalty for a breach of Rule 12-2**, but there is no additional penalty under this Rule.

NOTE
If the original lie of a ball to be replaced has been altered, see Rule 20-3b.

*PENALTY FOR BREACH OF RULE 12-2:
Match play – Loss of hole; **Stroke play** – Two strokes.
*If a player incurs the general penalty for a breach of Rule 12-2, there is no additional penalty under this Rule.

LIFTING BALL FOR IDENTIFICATION

A player may lift a ball in order to identify it, but the ball must be marked first and the player must give his opponent or fellow-competitor a chance to watch the lifting and replacement. The ball cannot be cleaned beyond what is needed to identify the ball.

RULE 12 INCIDENTS

Nick Faldo discovered that within the Rules of Golf there are protective nuances that can come in handy even while you are up a tree at the U.S. Open.

In the second round of the 1992 championship at Pebble Beach, Faldo's second shot at the par-5 14th finished dangerously close to the out-of-bounds that runs along the right rough. For his third, the Englishman chose a short iron in order to play over the singular tree that protects the green. As the ball climbed in elevation, it struck the trunk of the tree and no one saw it fall to the ground.

Faldo asked the walking Rules official if a provisional ball could be played under the circumstances. Because the official did not see the ball come down from the tree, he replied that Faldo was entitled to play a provisional ball, as the original might be lost.

After playing the provisional ball and as the group walked toward the tree to look for the original ball, the two-time British Open and two-time Masters Champion (at the time) asked the Rules official if it was permissible to climb the tree in order to search for his ball. The official affirmed that it was, but cautioned

Faldo that if the ball moved as a result of his being in the tree, there would be a penalty stroke assessed and the ball would have to be replaced.

That provision not withstanding, the Rules official further advised Faldo that if, before climbing or shaking the tree, he stated his intention to deem his ball unplayable should he find it, there would be no penalty for moving the ball during search. With such prior notification, one penalty stroke would be assessed for a ball unplayable (Rule 28) but no additional penalty would be incurred for moving a ball at rest (Rule 18).

Faldo took the official's advice. Before climbing the tree, he declared that should he find the ball he intended to proceed under Rule 28. He then climbed to search. Having no luck, he shook the tree in hope of dislodging the ball.

"Where's Jane?" he quipped while standing on a high limb.

Unable to find his original ball, Faldo's provisional ball became the ball in play under penalty of stroke and distance (Rule 27).

The second part of Rule 12-2 spells out to the player a procedure to follow for lifting a ball for identification if he believes a ball at rest is his but he cannot identify it.

The procedure is precise but straightforward and includes a requirement before lifting the ball of announcing his intention to his opponent in or his marker or a fellow-competitor. This announcement can also be made to his referee if his group is assigned one, or a member of the Committee. If the lifted ball is the player's ball and he fails to comply with the procedure of announcing, the penalty incurred is one stroke.

During the third round of the 2013 British Open at Muirfield, Martin Laird had just scored a nine at the par-4 third hole and possibly was not focused as well as he needed to be at the tenth hole when he struck his tee shot into the deep Muirfield rough. His second shot failed to get the ball out of the rough into which it disappeared. A spotter located a ball but told Laird that he was unsure of whose ball it might be. Before lifting the ball, Laird told the spotter that he would lift it for identification but he failed to tell either his fellow-competitor, Dustin Johnson, or his referee.

Laird marked the position of the ball and rotated it slightly in order to see his mark on the ball. The ball was his but he incurred a penalty of one stroke for not following the procedure regarding the requirement for announcing.

Golf balls can come to rest in some odd places. At the 1992 U.S. Open Nick Faldo scaled a tree in search of his ball that had apparently come to rest there.

Frequently asked question

Can I lift a ball in a hazard so I can identify it as mine?

Yes, you are allowed to lift a ball you believe may be yours anywhere on the course, including in a hazard, provided the correct procedure in Rule 12-2 is followed.

Rule 13 BALL PLAYED AS IT LIES

DEFINITIONS
All defined terms are in *italics* and are listed alphabetically in the Definitions section – see pages 10–23.

13-1. General

The ball must be played as it lies, except as otherwise provided in the *Rules*.
(Ball at rest moved – see Rule 18)

13-2. Improving Lie, Area of Intended Stance or Swing, or Line of Play

A player must not improve or allow to be improved:
o   the position or lie of his ball,
o   the area of his intended *stance* or swing,
o   his *line of play* or a reasonable extension of that line beyond the *hole*, or
o   the area in which he is to drop or place a ball,
by any of the following actions:
o   pressing a club on the ground,
o   moving, bending or breaking anything growing or fixed (including immovable *obstructions* and objects defining *out of bounds*),
o   creating or eliminating irregularities of surface,
o   removing or pressing down sand, loose soil, replaced divots or other cut turf placed in position, or
o   removing dew, frost or water.
However, the player incurs no penalty if the action occurs:
o   in grounding the club lightly when *addressing the ball*,
o   in fairly taking his *stance*,
o   in making a *stroke* or the backward movement of his club for a *stroke* and the *stroke* is made,
o   in creating or eliminating irregularities of surface within the *teeing ground* or in removing dew, frost or water from the *teeing ground*, or
o   on the *putting green* in removing sand and loose soil or in repairing damage (Rule 16-1).

Exception:
Ball in *hazard* – see Rule 13-4.

STATUS OF SAND AND LOOSE SOIL

Sand and loose soil are only loose impediments when they lie on the putting green (left). They are not loose impediments on other parts of the course (far left).

IMPROVING AREA OF INTENDED SWING OR LINE OF PLAY

A player must not break an interfering branch or remove sand or loose soil which is off the putting green but on the line of play.

CREATING OR ELIMINATING IRREGULARITIES OF SURFACE

May I replace this divot in its hole which is on my line of play?

I am afraid you can't do that as you would be improving your line of play by eliminating an irregularity of surface.

13

IMPROVING AREA OF INTENDED STANCE

This out of bounds stake interferes with my stance when I try to address my ball. Can I remove it?

No. You must not improve your stance by moving a boundary stake as such a stake is deemed to be fixed

BALL IN BUNKER: PROHIBITED ACTIONS

Before making a stroke at a ball which is in a bunker the player must not:

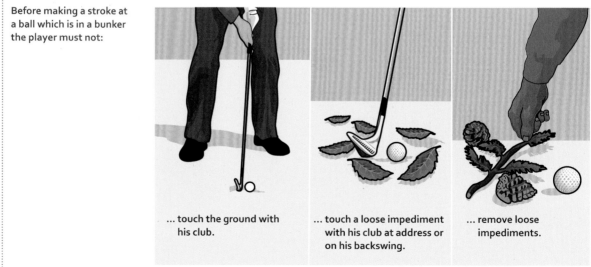

... touch the ground with his club.

... touch a loose impediment with his club at address or on his backswing.

... remove loose impediments.

13-3. Building Stance

A player is entitled to place his feet firmly in taking his *stance*, but he must not build a *stance*.

13-4. Ball in Hazard; Prohibited Actions

Except as provided in the *Rules*, before making a *stroke* at a ball that is in a *hazard* (whether a *bunker* or a *water hazard*) or that, having been lifted from a *hazard*, may be dropped or placed in the *hazard*, the player must not:

a. Test the condition of the *hazard* or any similar *hazard*;

b. Touch the ground in the *hazard* or water in the *water hazard* with his hand or a club; or

c. Touch or move a *loose impediment* lying in or touching the *hazard*.

Exceptions:

1. Provided nothing is done that constitutes testing the condition of the *hazard* or improves the lie of the ball, there is no penalty if the player (a) touches the ground or *loose impediments* in any *hazard* or water in a *water hazard* as a result of or to prevent falling, in removing an *obstruction*, in measuring or in marking the position of, retrieving, lifting, placing or replacing a ball under any *Rule* or (b) places his clubs in a *hazard*.

2. At any time, the player may smooth sand or soil in a *hazard* provided this is for the sole purpose of caring for the *course* and nothing is done to breach Rule 13-2 with respect to his next *stroke*. If a ball played from a *hazard* is outside the *hazard* after the *stroke*, the player may smooth sand or soil in the *hazard* without restriction.

3. If the player makes a *stroke* from a *hazard* and the ball comes to rest in another *hazard*, Rule 13-4a does not apply to any subsequent actions taken in the *hazard* from which the *stroke* was made.

NOTE

At any time, including at *address* or in the backward movement for the *stroke*, the player may touch, with a club or otherwise, any *obstruction*, any construction declared by the *Committee* to be an integral part of the *course* or any grass, bush, tree or other growing thing.

PENALTY FOR BREACH OF RULE:

Match play – Loss of hole; **Stroke play** – Two strokes.

(Searching for ball – see Rule 12-1)

(Relief for ball in water hazard – see Rule 26)

RULE 13 INCIDENTS

The tenet of playing the ball as it lies is protected under Rule 13 in the most obvious instances, as well as seemingly minor ones. Principles embedded in the Rules are the same regardless of the magnitude of circumstances under which they are brought to bear.

Richie Ramsay became the first Scotsman to win the U.S. Amateur since 1898 but not before encountering a penalty for grounding his club in a hazard during the semifinals. Rule 13-4b is explicit in prohibiting the player from touching the ground in a hazard with his hand or a club. In match play, the penalty is loss of hole. In stroke play, the penalty is two strokes.

Hazeltine National G.C.'s 16th hole is a beautiful par-4 that runs beside Lake Hazeltine from tee to green. Although Ramsay was unaware of having grounded his club in a hazard at the 16th, two officials who were walking with the match, as well as a television commentator and an official assisting the commentator in the broadcast booth witnessed the violation. All confirmed that Ramsay had grounded his club while addressing his ball in the hazard.

Ramsay, 1-up after the Rule 13 loss-of-hole infraction, remained stoic for the last two holes and won 1-up over Webb Simpson.

At the 2010 PGA Championship, Dustin Johnson grounded his club in a bunker on the 72nd hole,

incurring a two-stroke penalty to miss a play-off by one stroke.

The venue was Whistling Straits, a links-style course set along two miles of Lake Michigan shoreline in Wisconsin with over 1,000 bunkers. These bunkers were the subject of a notice to competitors containing the words, "All areas of the course that were designed and built as sand bunkers will be played as bunkers (hazards), whether or not they have been raked. This will mean that many bunkers positioned outside the ropes, as well as some areas of bunkers inside the ropes, close to the rope line, will likely include numerous footprints, heel prints and tire tracks during play of the Championship. Such irregularities of surface are a part of the game and no free relief will be available from these conditions."

Johnson acknowledged that he had grounded his club in the area of concern but said after the event, "Walking up there, it never once crossed my mind that I was in a sand trap." It was also reported that Johnson said he had not read the notice to competitors.

The Rules have always treated sand bunkers differently from other parts of the course. And the definition of a bunker gives that difference, "A 'bunker' is a hazard consisting of a prepared area of ground, often a hollow, from which turf or soil has been removed and replaced with sand or the like."

Richie Ramsay is informed of his Rule 13 infraction during the semifinals of the 2006 U.S. Amateur. He unknowingly grounded his club in a hazard. Although he lost the hole, Ramsay ultimately prevailed in this match and the championship.

At the 2010 Kia Classic tournament at La Costa, CA, Michelle Wie was penalized for grounding her club in a lateral water hazard. Although the Rule itself is concise and straightforward, the incident was anything but.

At the 11th hole, Wie's shot to the green found the water hazard but in a playable position in shallow water. To make a stroke at the ball, she placed her right foot in the water and the left foot on the bank with nearly all of her weight on the right foot. She made the stroke, the water splashed, the ball arced several feet in the air but only advanced forward about two feet, making land, but still within the hazard. After finishing her stroke, she rested her club, still in her left hand, on the ground within the hazard line.

Informed by TV commentators of the potential problem, LPGA Tour official Doug Brecht, who had witnessed the incident from across the fairway, reviewed TV footage of the incident and went to the course to interview Wie about what had happened.

Wie claimed that she was allowed to ground her club to prevent falling and that was the reason she had done so. As an exception, the Rule does permit grounding to prevent falling, but review of the incident by other officials saw insufficient evidence to support the player's claim and she was assessed a two-stroke penalty for the violation.

Although it is an infraction for a player to touch the ground in a hazard or water in a water hazard with his hand or a club, or to touch or move loose impediments in a hazard while his ball is in that hazard, the Rules do permit touching obstructions, integral parts of the golf course, and growing plants or trees. Lee Westwood caused some unnecessary concern among television commentators when he played from a bridge in a water hazard during the final of the 2004 HSBC World Match Play Championship.

John Paramor, the referee with the match, in which Westwood was playing Ernie Els, was aware that Westwood's ball had come to rest on the bridge at the 7th hole of Wentworth's West Course. Walking to the ball, Paramor and Westwood discussed what was permitted and what was not.

With Paramor standing a few yards away, the television commentators were taken aback when Westwood took a practice swing and hit the bridge with his club, just as they were when he grounded his club on the bridge at address prior to making his stroke. The Note under Rule 13-4 permits such actions, at any time.

However, the authority to touch the bridge did not remove the prohibition against Westwood removing loose impediments on the bridge, and Paramor was careful to be certain that Westwood understood that distinction.

Frequently asked questions

Is it permissible to place the rake or clubs in a bunker or water hazard while I play my stroke from the same hazard?
Yes, provided the lie of the ball is not improved, or the player does not test the condition of the hazard.

After making a stroke in a bunker from point A to point B (the ball is still in the bunker), may a player smooth the area from which the last stroke was made?
Yes, as long as she is doing so with the sole intention of caring for the course and nothing is done to improve the areas covered by Rule 13-2 for her stroke from point B.

Rule 14 STRIKING THE BALL

DEFINITIONS
All defined terms are in *italics* and are listed alphabetically in the Definitions section – see pages 10–23.

14-1. Ball to Be Fairly Struck At
a. Fairly Striking the Ball
The ball must be fairly struck at with the head of the club and must not be pushed, scraped or spooned.

b. Anchoring the Club
In making a stroke, the player must not anchor the club, either "directly" or by use of an "anchor point."

NOTE 1:
The club is anchored "directly" when the player intentionally holds the club or a gripping hand in contact with any part of his body, except that the player may hold the club or a gripping hand against a hand or forearm.

NOTE 2:
An "anchor point" exists when the player intentionally holds a forearm in contact with any part of his body to establish a gripping hand as a stable point around which the other hand may swing the club.

14-2. Assistance
a. Physical Assistance and Protection from Elements
A player must not make a *stroke* while accepting physical assistance or protection from the elements.

b. Positioning of Caddie or Partner Behind Ball
A player must not make a *stroke* with his *caddie*, his *partner* or his *partner's caddie* positioned on or close to an extension of the *line of play* or *line of putt* behind the ball.

Exception:
There is no penalty if the player's *caddie*, his *partner* or his *partner's caddie* is inadvertently located on or close to an extension of the *line of play* or *line of putt* behind the ball.

PENALTY FOR BREACH OF RULE 14-1 OR 14-2:
Match play – Loss of hole; Stroke play – Two strokes.

14-3. Artificial Devices and Unusual Equipment; Abnormal Use of Equipment
Rule 14-3 governs the use of equipment and devices (including electronic devices) that might assist a player in making a specific stroke or generally in his play.

Golf is a challenging game in which success should depend on the judgment, skills and abilities of the player. This principle guides the USGA in determining whether the use of any item is in breach of Rule 14-3.

For detailed specifications and interpretations on the conformity of *equipment* and devices under Rule 14-3 and the process for consultation and submission regarding equipment and devices, see Appendix IV.

PROHIBITED STROKES

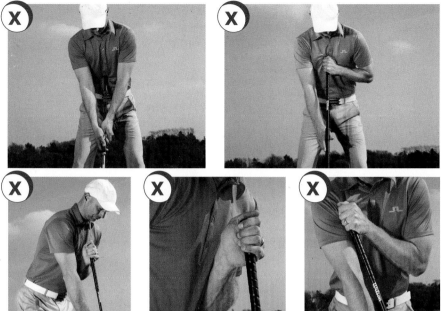

In making a stroke, the player must not anchor the club, either directly or by use of an anchor point.

PERMITTED STROKES

Rule 14-1b only applies to strokes made with the club anchored, either directly or through the use of a forearm to establish an anchor point. Longer than standard putters can still be used provided there is no such anchoring.

Except as provided in the *Rules*, during a *stipulated round* the player must not use any artificial device or unusual *equipment*, or use any equipment in an abnormal manner:

a. That might assist him in making a *stroke* or in his play; or

b. For the purpose of gauging or measuring distance or conditions that might affect his play; or

c. That might assist him in gripping the club, except that:

    (i) gloves may be worn provided that they are plain gloves;

ASSISTANCE

If this player makes a stroke while her caddie holds the umbrella to shield her from the sun, she would be penalized two strokes in stroke play or lose the hole in match play.

DISTANCE MEASURING DEVICE

If the Committee allows, a player may use a device which measures or gauges distance only.

(ii) resin, powder and drying or moisturizing agents may be used; and

(iii) a towel or handkerchief may be wrapped around the grip.

Exceptions:

1. A player is not in breach of this Rule if (a) the *equipment* or device is designed for or has the effect of alleviating a medical condition, (b) the player has a legitimate medical reason to use the *equipment* or device, and (c) the *Committee* is satisfied that its use does not give the player any undue advantage over other players.

2. A player is not in breach of this Rule if he uses *equipment* in a traditionally accepted manner.

PENALTY FOR BREACH OF RULE 14-3:

Match play – Loss of hole; **Stroke play** – Two strokes.

For subsequent offense – Disqualification.

NOTE

The *Committee* may make a Local Rule allowing players to use a distance-measuring device.

14-4. Striking the Ball More than Once

If a player's club strikes the ball more than once in the course of a *stroke*, the player must count the *stroke* and **add a *penalty stroke***, making two *strokes* in all.

BALL TO BE FAIRLY STRUCK AT WITH CLUBHEAD

A player may strike the ball with the back or toe of the clubhead.

14-5. Playing Moving Ball

A player must not make a *stroke* at his ball while it is moving.

Exceptions:

o   Ball falling off tee – Rule 11-3.

o   Striking the ball more than once – Rule 14-4.

o   Ball moving in water – Rule 14-6.

When the ball begins to move only after the player has begun the *stroke* or the backward movement of his club for the *stroke*, he incurs no penalty under this Rule for playing a moving ball, but he is not exempt from any penalty under Rule 18-2 (Ball at rest moved by player).

(Ball purposely deflected or stopped by player, partner or caddie – see Rule 1-2)

14-6. Ball Moving in Water

When a ball is moving in water in a *water hazard*, the player may, without penalty, make a *stroke*, but he must not delay making his *stroke* in order to allow the wind or current to improve the position of the ball. A ball moving in water in a *water hazard* may be lifted if the player elects to invoke Rule 26.

PENALTY FOR BREACH OF RULE 14-5 OR 14-6:

Match play – Loss of hole; **Stroke play** – Two strokes.

RULE 14 INCIDENTS

Rule 14 is clear in stating that there is a one-stroke penalty for striking a ball more than once in the course of a stroke. In nearly all cases, a player is completely aware when such misfortune finds him.

From the thick rough, short and right of Oakland Hills' 5th green during the 1985 U.S. Open, T. C. Chen encountered that unfortunate fluke in golf when one swing of the club strikes the ball more than once.

Chen's third shot left his ball about 10 feet off the right front of the green with an additional 10 feet of putting green to the hole. He was faced with a delicate pitch that needed enough clubhead speed to get the lofted club through the grass but not so much that the force imparted to the ball would cause it to run past the hole.

Practice swings left the necessary feeling in Chen's hands for gauging the grabbing effect of the grass. He addressed the ball and swung slowly but firmly. On the downswing, as the club approached the ball, the tall grass slowed the club. Chen firmly but

gently pulled the club into the ball. It rebounded slowly off the decelerating clubface rising ahead of the clubface and into the air. As the club finished its path through the grass, the resistance it was encountering became less and the club was released.

However, the firm pulling action still left in Chen's swing gave the club added momentum as it left the grass. In a spurt of speed, the clubhead caught up with the slow-moving ball and collided with it a second time. As the ball ricocheted off the clubface, a spectator rose from his kneeling position, directly behind Chen, raising two fingers as an indication of what he had just witnessed.

As the lofted clubface was going up at the moment of the second impact, the ball was pushed a little higher in the air and slightly to Chen's left. It came to rest on the apron of the putting green about 10 feet from the hole.

Prior to the infraction, Chen led the championship by four strokes with 14 holes to play. Visibly shaken, he took three more to finish the par-4 hole with an eight. His hopes of winning the U.S. Open were dashed. He tied for second with Denis Watson and Dave Barr, just one shot behind Andy North.

Rule 14-3 prohibits the use of artificial devices, unusual equipment and equipment in an unusual manner during a stipulated round. Prior to 2016, the penalty for a breach of this Rule was disqualification. With publication of the 2016 Rules of Golf, the penalty for the first offense is loss of hole in match play and two strokes in stroke play; for a subsequent offense during the same round the penalty is disqualification. There are two exceptions where there is no penalty: one pertaining to use of equipment designed for a medical reason and the other where a player uses equipment in a traditionally accepted manner.

This latter exception includes the use of a booklet containing illustrations of the holes on a course with yardage between various points or the use of a club as a plumb-line to assist the player in determining the slope on a putting green.

The key to applying this Rule is to note that it prohibits the use of devices, not simply carrying them during a round.

Distance-measuring devices are not permitted by Rule 14-3, but the Rule gives Committees the authority to establish a Local Rule allowing players to use a

One of golf's most infamous Rules situations involved T.C. Chen at the 1985 U.S. Open. This incident, which had a dramatic effect on the final results of the championship, is retold below.

distance-measuring device, which in effect overrides the provisions of Rule 14-3. Even when the Local Rule is in effect, the device must not be used for any purposes that are prohibited by Rule 14-3.

There are many items of equipment that are acceptable under this Rule when used for their designed purpose, such as plain eyeglasses or binoculars, hand warmers and stretching devices that are not used in a golf swing.

Various training aids designed to be used in a golf swing may not be used to make a practice swing or stroke during a round. Examples are use of a weighted headcover, or a "donut" attached to a club for a practice swing or a rod to check a player's alignment or swing plane.

During the 2010 LPGA Safeway Classic on the Ghost Creek Course at Pumpkin Ridge Golf Club in Oregon, Julie Inkster faced a 10-minute delay at the 10th hole of her third and final round. While waiting, she placed a donut on her 9-iron and took a few swings with the club and donut. As a result, she was disqualified under the Rules in effect at that time. Afterward it was reported that she issued a statement, "I had a 30-minute wait and I needed to loosen up," she said. "It had no effect on my game whatsoever, but it is what it is. I'm very disappointed."

While use of the donut in a swing during a round, as in the Inkster case, was a violation of the Rule, it would have been permissible to use a weighted training club provided the club was conforming and it was one of the 14 clubs selected for the round. A player could also swing two or three clubs at once in a practice swing.

A similar situation arose at the 2013 Crowne Plaza Invitational where Jeff Overton faced a delay during his third round. Coming off the ninth putting green, he noticed several groups waiting to tee off at the tenth hole. Like Inkster, he wanted to use the time to his advantage. Unlike Inkster, who was using an artificial device during a practice swing, Overton wanted to practice his putting stroke on an adjacent practice putting green. An official told him that such practice was permitted by Rule 7-2 in a case like his where he would not be delaying play.

However, Overton did not ask and he was not told that he could not use the alignment sticks that he carried in his bag while making a practice stroke. Although there was no penalty for carrying the sticks, which are artificial devices, Rule 14-3 prohibits the use of such a device during his round in either a practice swing or stroke. As with Inkster, Overton was disqualified under the Rules in effect at that time, but would only receive a two-stroke penalty starting in 2016.

The key to applying this Rule is to note that it prohibits the use of artificial devices not simply carrying them during a round.

Frequently asked question

If I make a stroke with my club and my hand touches my clothing, am I in breach of Rule 14-1b?

If you merely touch an article of clothing with the club or gripping hand in making the stroke, generally there is no penalty. This might occur if you are wearing loose-fitting clothes or rain gear and are holding the club close to your body, and the club inadvertently touches the clothing in making the stroke.

The answer would be different if you intentionally used the club or a gripping hand to press an article of clothing against any part of the body, other than a forearm or gripping hand. Intentionally using a gripping hand to hold an article of clothing is a breach of Rule 14-3.

Rule 15 SUBSTITUTED BALL; WRONG BALL

DEFINITIONS
All defined terms are in *italics* and are listed alphabetically in the Definitions section – see pages 10–23.

15-1. General

A player must *hole* out with the ball played from the *teeing ground,* unless the ball is *lost* or *out of bounds* or the player *substitutes* another ball, whether or not substitution is permitted (see Rule 15-2). If a player plays a *wrong ball*, see Rule 15-3.

15-2. Substituted Ball

A player may *substitute* a ball when proceeding under a *Rule* that permits the player to play, drop or place another ball in completing the play of a hole. The *substituted ball* becomes the *ball in play*.

If a player *substitutes* a ball when not permitted to do so under the *Rules* (including an unintentional *substitution* when a *wrong ball* is dropped or placed by the player), that *substituted ball* is not a *wrong* ball; it becomes the *ball in play*. If the mistake is not corrected as provided in Rule 20-6 and the player makes a *stroke* at an incorrectly *substituted ball*, **he loses the hole in match play or incurs a penalty of two strokes in stroke play under the applicable Rule** and, in stroke play, must play out the hole with the *substituted* ball.

Exception:

If a player incurs a penalty for making a *stroke* from a wrong place, there is no additional penalty for substituting a ball when not permitted.
(Playing from wrong place – see Rule 20-7)

15-3. Wrong Ball
a. Match Play

If a player makes a *stroke* at a *wrong ball*, **he loses the hole**.

If the *wrong ball* belongs to another player, its owner must place a ball on the spot from which the *wrong ball* was first played.

If the player and *opponent* exchange balls during the play of a hole, the first to make a *stroke* at a *wrong ball*, **loses the hole**; when this cannot be determined, the hole must be played out with the balls exchanged.

PLAYING A SUBSTITUTED BALL

I lifted my ball from the putting green to clean it, but I have just noticed that I have played the other ball I had in my pocket.

Unfortunately, you have substituted a ball when not permitted to do so. It is now the ball in play and you incur a two-stroke penalty. If we had been playing a match, you would have lost the hole.

PLAYING WRONG BALL IN STROKE PLAY

This is not my ball. I must have played the wrong one from under that bush. What do I do now?

I am afraid you are penalized two strokes for playing a wrong ball and we must try and find your ball. If we don't find it in what remains of the five-minute search period, you will have to proceed under the lost ball Rule.

Exception:

There is no penalty if a player makes a *stroke* at a *wrong ball* that is moving in water in a *water hazard*. Any *strokes* made at a *wrong ball* moving in water in a *water hazard* do not count in the player's score. The player must correct his mistake by playing the correct ball or by proceeding under the *Rules*.

(Placing and Replacing – see Rule 20-3)

b. Stroke Play

If a *competitor* makes a *stroke* or *strokes* at a *wrong ball*, **he incurs a penalty of two strokes**.

The *competitor* must correct his mistake by playing the correct ball or by proceeding under the *Rules*. If he fails to correct his mistake before making a *stroke* on the next *teeing ground* or, in the case of the last hole of the round, fails to declare his intention to correct his mistake before leaving the *putting green*, **he is disqualified**.

Strokes made by a *competitor* with a *wrong ball* do not count in his score. If the *wrong ball* belongs to another *competitor*, its owner must place a ball on the spot from which the *wrong ball* was first played.

Exception:

There is no penalty if a *competitor* makes a *stroke* at a *wrong ball* that is moving in water in a *water hazard*. Any *strokes* made at a *wrong ball* moving in water in a *water hazard* do not count in the *competitor's* score.

(Placing and Replacing – see Rule 20-3)

RULE 15 INCIDENTS

It's not often that anyone makes a stroke at a wrong ball from the middle of the fairway. It's virtually unknown that two experienced tour professionals would do so while playing in a national championship.

During the second round at the 2014 U.S. Open at Pinehurst Resort and Country Club, while playing the 18th hole, Hunter Mahan and Jamie Donaldson hit their tee shots down the left of center of the fairway. Neither player's ball at rest was visible from the tee as there was a slight rise to the fairway leading to the putting green. Mahan's caddie was the first one to arrive where he thought his player's ball would lie and indeed there was a ball there. Without identifying the ball, he checked the yardage to the hole. When Mahan arrived a few moments later, he also did not identify the ball, which he then played to the putting green. Donaldson played the other ball nearby onto the putting where it was then learned that the two players had make strokes at each other's ball, that is, they had both played a wrong ball.

Both players returned to where their original balls lay and played from there with a two stroke penalty to be added to their score for the hole. The strokes made at the wrong ball did not count in either player's score for the hole.

If this incident had occurred in match play between two players, the first player to make a stroke at a wrong ball would lose the hole. When this cannot be determined, the hole would be played out with the balls exchanged.

Ian Poulter learned the hard way that once you have marked the position of and lifted your ball in play, it is necessary to keep a firm grip on it.

At the 4th green during the final round of The Players Championship in 2004, Poulter lifted his ball, lost his grip on it and then watched as it sank to the

Hunter Mahan and Jamie Donaldson returning to the 18th fairway to correct their mistake.

bottom of the adjacent lake. Facing a two-stroke penalty for having to substitute a ball when not permitted to do so under the Rules (Rule 15-2 and Rule 16-1b), Poulter looked for a way to retrieve his ball. Kam Bhambra, Poulter's fitness coach, was following the group and saw what had taken place. Bhambra stripped down to his boxer shorts, jumped into the water and retrieved the ball.

"It was the first ball I found," Bhambra said. "I was a bit worried about alligators, but duty called." Poulter replaced the ball and completed the hole with a par. The two-stroke penalty that he did not incur would have dropped him 20 places on the leader board and cost him $20,000 in prize money.

Frequently asked question

May a player change golf balls during the play of a hole or a stipulated round? When the player is permitted to substitute another golf ball, may he change to a ball of a different brand or type?

Rules 15-1 and 15-2 explain that the player must complete play of the hole with the ball with which he began the hole unless he is proceeding under a Rule that permits him to substitute a ball. The player may change balls between the play of two holes as well.

Rules 26-1 (Water Hazard Rule), 27-1 (Ball Lost or Out of Bounds) and 28 (Ball Unplayable) are examples of Rules that permit the player to substitute another ball. Rule 5-3 permits a player to substitute another ball during the play of a hole when his original ball has become unfit for play during the play of that hole. Other Rules (e.g., Rule 18, Rule 24 and Rule 25-1) permit the player to substitute another ball only if the original ball is not immediately recoverable.

Note that Rule 16-1b, the Rule that allows the player to lift his ball from the putting green, does not permit the player to substitute another ball; this precludes the player from substituting a "putting ball."

When changing balls, the player is permitted to substitute a ball of another brand or type unless the Committee has adopted the One Ball Condition (see Appendix I; Part B; Section 1c). This optional condition (usually referred to as "The One Ball Rule") is generally adopted only in events that are limited to professional golfers or highly skilled amateur golfers. Generally, this condition of competition is not adopted in club-level competitions.

Rule 16

THE PUTTING GREEN

16-1. General
a. Touching Line of Putt

The *line of putt* must not be touched except:

(i) the player may remove *loose impediments*, provided he does not press anything down;

(ii) the player may place the club in front of the ball when *addressing* it, provided he does not press anything down;

(iii) in measuring – Rule 18-6;

(iv) in lifting or replacing the ball – Rule 16-1b;

(v) in pressing down a ball-marker;

(vi) in repairing old *hole* plugs or ball marks on the *putting green* – Rule 16-1c; and

(vii) in removing movable *obstructions* – Rule 24-1.

(Indicating line for putt on putting green – see Rule 8-2b)

b. Lifting and Cleaning Ball

A ball on the *putting green* may be lifted and, if desired, cleaned. The position of the ball must be marked before it is lifted, and the ball must be replaced (see Rule 20-1). When another ball is in motion, a ball that might influence the movement of the ball in motion must not be lifted.

c. Repair of Hole Plugs, Ball Marks and Other Damage

The player may repair an old *hole* plug or damage to the *putting green* caused by the impact of a ball, whether or not the player's ball lies on the *putting green*. If a ball or ball-marker is accidentally *moved* in the process of the repair, the ball or ball-marker must be replaced. There is no penalty, provided the movement of the ball or ball-marker is directly

TOUCHING LINE OF PUTT: EXAMPLES OF WHEN PERMITTED

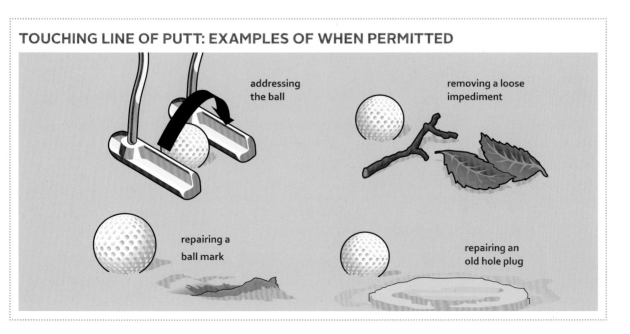

addressing the ball

removing a loose impediment

repairing a ball mark

repairing an old hole plug

REMOVING LOOSE IMPEDIMENTS FROM LINE OF PUTT

Can I remove these leaves using my cap rather than my hand?

Yes, loose impediments can be removed from your line of putt by any means, provided you do not press anything down.

attributable to the specific act of repairing an old *hole* plug or damage to the *putting green* caused by the impact of a ball. Otherwise, Rule 18 applies.

Any other damage to the *putting green* must not be repaired if it might assist the player in his subsequent play of the hole.

d. Testing Surface

During the *stipulated round*, a player must not test the surface of any *putting green* by rolling a ball or roughening or scraping the surface.

Exception:

Between the play of two holes, a player may test the surface of any practice *putting green* and the *putting green* of the hole last played, unless the *Committee* has prohibited such action (see Note 2 to Rule 7-2).

e. Standing Astride or on Line of Putt

The player must not make a *stroke* on the *putting green* from a *stance* astride, or with either foot touching, the *line of putt* or an extension of that line behind the ball.

Exception:

There is no penalty if the *stance* is taken inadvertently on or astride the *line of putt* (or an extension of that line behind the ball) or is taken to avoid standing on another player's *line of putt* or prospective *line of putt*.

f. Making Stroke While Another Ball in Motion

The player must not make a *stroke* while another ball is in motion after a *stroke* from the *putting green*, except that if a player does so, there is no penalty if it was his turn to play. (Lifting ball assisting or interfering with play while another ball in motion – see Rule 22)

STANDING ON EXTENSION OF THE LINE OF PUTT

There is no penalty in this case since the line of putt does not extend beyond the hole.

CLEANING BALL AND REPAIRING DAMAGE

A player may not repair spike marks or other damage if it might assist his play.

BALL OVERHANGING HOLE

PENALTY FOR BREACH OF RULE 16-1:
Match play – Loss of hole; **Stroke play** – Two strokes.
(Position of *caddie* or *partner* – see Rule 14-2)
(Wrong *putting green* – see Rule 25-3)

16-2. Ball Overhanging Hole

When any part of the ball overhangs the lip of the *hole*, the player is allowed enough time to reach the *hole* without unreasonable delay and an additional ten seconds to determine whether the ball is at rest. If by then the ball has not fallen into the *hole*, it is deemed to be at rest. If the ball subsequently falls into the *hole*, the player is deemed to have *holed* out with his last *stroke*, and **must add a *penalty stroke*** to his score for the hole; otherwise, there is no penalty under this Rule.
(Undue delay – see Rule 6-7)

RULE 16 INCIDENTS

Television giveth, and television taketh away.

When a ball overhangs a hole, the player is permitted enough time to reach the hole without unreasonable delay and an additional 10 seconds to determine whether the ball is at rest. If the ball subsequently falls into the hole, the player is deemed to have holed out with his last stroke and must add a penalty stroke to his score for the hole. Estimating

those 10 seconds is imprecise; videotape of such an event is exact, both of which Soren Hansen discovered at the 2000 Qatar Masters.

Hansen's 10-foot putt hung on the edge of the hole before ultimately dropping into it. Mathias Gronberg, a fellow-competitor in the same group, stated that he had been counting and 11 seconds had passed before the ball dropped. Therefore, it was reasoned, Hansen should add a penalty stroke to his score and the ball would be considered holed with his last stroke. However, Hansen was not so sure, and a Rules official was summoned to make a ruling.

After the official listened to the accounts of various witnesses, he ruled that a penalty stroke was in order under Rule 16-2. After leaving the scene and returning to the tournament office, it occurred to the official that there might be television videotape of the incident. There was and, fortunately, it showed that only eight seconds elapsed before the ball fell into the hole. Hansen was exonerated and the penalty rescinded.

Meg Mallon, on the other hand, tarried in circumstances similar to Hansen's. While leading during the second round of the 1996 Jami Farr Classic, Mallon's birdie putt on the 17th hole stopped just short of going in.

Video of the incident shows Mallon taking perhaps a bit too long to reach her putt and then waiting more than 20 seconds before watching it fall into the hole. Believing that her ball was holed without penalty, Mallon did not include the penalty stroke she had incurred and then returned a score for the hole that was lower than she had actually taken. She was subsequently disqualified under Rule 6-6d.

Frequently asked questions

Is there such a thing as an illegal hole location?

There are no Rules regarding hole locations, so there is no such thing as an "illegal" hole location. Many factors affect selection of hole locations.

There must be enough putting green surface between the hole and the front and sides of the putting green to accommodate the required shot. For example, if the hole requires a long iron or wood shot to the putting green, the hole should be located deeper in the putting green and further from its sides.

It is recommended that generally the hole be located at least four paces from any edge of the putting green. An area two to three feet in radius around the hole should be as nearly level as possible and of uniform grade. In no case should holes be located in tricky places or on sharp slopes where a ball can gather speed.

There should be a balanced selection of hole locations for the entire course with respect to left, right, central, front and back positions. For a competition played over several days, the course should be kept in balance daily as to degree of difficulty.

The person who cuts the holes should make sure that the Rules of Golf are observed, especially the requirements that the hole not exceed 4 1/4 inches in outer diameter and that the hole-liner be sunk at least one inch below the putting green surface.

More information regarding the selection of hole locations can be found in the USGA publication "How to Conduct a Competition."

Our group reaches the putting green, and we noticed the hole is damaged. What should we do?

If the damage is a ball mark, you may repair it (Rule 16-1c). However, if the damage is something other than a ball mark, the answer depends on the extent of the damage. A hole that is damaged, but the dimensions of the hole have not been materially changed, must not be touched, and you must continue play of the hole. If the hole is damaged materially, a member of the Committee should be requested to repair the damage. In this case, you may only repair the hole if a Committee member is not readily available. Repairing the hole when not permitted will result in a breach of Rule 16-1a for touching the line of putt.

Rule 17 THE FLAGSTICK

17

DEFINITIONS

All defined terms are in *italics* and are listed alphabetically in the Definitions section – see pages 10–23.

17-1. Flagstick Attended, Removed or Held Up

Before making a *stroke* from anywhere on the *course*, the player may have the *flagstick* attended, removed or held up to indicate the position of the *hole*.

If the *flagstick* is not attended, removed or held up before the player makes a *stroke*, it must not be attended, removed or held up during the *stroke* or while the player's ball is in motion if doing so might influence the movement of the ball.

NOTE 1

If the *flagstick* is in the *hole* and anyone stands near it while a *stroke* is being made, he is deemed to be attending the *flagstick*.

NOTE 2

If, prior to the *stroke*, the *flagstick* is attended, removed or held up by anyone with the player's knowledge and he makes no objection, the player is deemed to have authorized it.

NOTE 3

If anyone attends or holds up the *flagstick* while a *stroke* is being made, he is deemed to be attending the *flagstick* until the ball comes to rest.

(Moving attended, removed or held-up flagstick while ball in motion – see Rule 24-1)

ATTENDING THE FLAGSTICK

While most commonly seen for a stroke from the putting green, the flagstick can be attended before a stroke from anywhere on the course.

BALL STRIKING ATTENDED FLAGSTICK IN STROKE PLAY

I'm sorry, the flagstick was jammed in the hole and won't come out. I hope it didn't stop your ball from going in.

Unfortunately, it's even worse than that, as I'm also penalized two stokes.

BALL RESTING AGAINST FLAGSTICK

17-2. Unauthorized Attendance

If an *opponent* or his *caddie* in match play or a *fellow-competitor* or his *caddie* in stroke play, without the player's authority or prior knowledge, attends, removes or holds up the *flagstick* during the *stroke* or while the ball is in motion, and the act might influence the movement of the ball, the *opponent* or *fellow-competitor* incurs the applicable penalty.

---

*PENALTY FOR BREACH OF RULE 17-1 OR 17-2:

Match play – Loss of hole; **Stroke play** – Two strokes.

*In stroke play, if a breach of Rule 17-2 occurs and the *competitor's* ball subsequently strikes the *flagstick*, the person attending or holding it or anything carried by him, the *competitor* incurs no penalty. The ball is played as it lies, except that if the *stroke* was made on the *putting green*, the *stroke* is canceled and the ball must be replaced and replayed.

17-3. Ball Striking Flagstick or Attendant

The player's ball must not strike:

a. The *flagstick* when it is attended, removed or held up;
b. The person attending or holding up the *flagstick* or anything carried by him;
c. The *flagstick* in the *hole*, unattended, when the *stroke* has been made on the *putting green*.

Exception:

When the *flagstick* is attended, removed or held up without the player's authority – see Rule 17-2.

PENALTY FOR BREACH OF RULE 17-3:

Match play – Loss of hole; **Stroke play** – Two strokes and the ball must be played as it lies.

17-4. Ball Resting Against Flagstick

When a player's ball rests against the *flagstick* in the *hole* and the ball is not *holed*, the player or another person authorized by him may move or remove the *flagstick*, and if the ball falls into the *hole*, the player is deemed to have *holed* out with his last *stroke*; otherwise, the ball, if *moved*, must be placed on the lip of the *hole*, without penalty.

RULE 17 INCIDENTS

No good deed goes unpunished, or at least no deed intended to be good.

At the 2007 Arnold Palmer Invitational, Boo Weekly hoped to come to the aid of his fellow-competitor and it cost him a two-stroke penalty.

Weekly and Tom Johnson were playing the par-3 second hole at Bay Hill. Johnson's ball was on the right-hand side of the putting green, about 85 feet from the back, left hole location. Because of the steep slope of the green, he chose to chip his ball from the putting surface to the fringe in hope of it being slowed by the longer grass and then trickling down toward the hole.

Although playing from the putting green, he did not, however, ask that the flagstick be attended. Perhaps because he was chipping to a point off the green, he forgot that he would incur a two-stroke penalty if his ball subsequently struck the unattended flagstick in the hole after he made his stroke from the putting green.

Johnson's chip was well played and, as it made its way to the hole, Weekly came to the realization that if the ball struck the flagstick, Johnson would be penalized. Wishing to come to the aid of his fellow-competitor, Weekly raced to the hole and removed the flagstick.

In his heart, Weekly's action had been taken to prevent a possible violation by Johnson. However, Rule 17-1 cautions that if the flagstick is not attended before the player makes a stroke, it must not be removed while the player's ball is in motion if doing so might influence the movement of the ball.

Once Johnson played his ball, the resulting situation and any of its ramifications were his reward and his responsibility, and his alone. Weekly's attempt to change that situation violated that basic premise of the game.

Before Johnson played, he could have asked that the flagstick be attended; or Weekly could have asked if Johnson wanted him to attend it. But once Johnson's stroke was made, the die was cast.

The Rules official who made the ruling, Mark Russell, commented, "I've never heard of that [happening] in my 27 years in golf."

Boo Weekly said, "I learned another Rule in the game of golf."

There are 14 double putting greens at St. Andrews' Old Course that often result in situations where a player is playing a pitch shot from one side of the green to a hole location some distance away but on the same green. An awareness of Rule 17 is particularly important in such circumstances.

During the 1995 British Open, Peter Fowler of Australia found himself on the front edge of the 2nd green with the hole having been cut in the back left corner beyond the huge humps and swales that are a feature of that green. He asked the Rules official if he was permitted to make his stroke from the green with a wedge, which, of course, the Rules permit. He pitched to within three feet of the hole.

Corey Pavin, who was playing the 16th hole, which shares a putting surface with the 2nd, congratulated Fowler on his inspired pitch but warned, "Next time have the flag attended. It's a two-stroke penalty if you hit the stick."

As these incidents illustrate, golf sometimes requires imagination in formulating how best to get to the hole. At Pebble Beach's par-3 17th hole, Miguel Angel Jimenez

The shape and contours of the 17th green at Pebble Beach Golf Links resulted in an unusual sight at the 2000 U.S. Open.

found himself in such a situation during the 100th U.S. Open.

When H. Chandler Egan made design changes to the course prior to the 1929 U.S. Amateur Championship, one of those changes included redesigning the 17th green into the shape of an hourglass divided by a diagonal ridge. The effect was to create a double green. Hence when the hole is cut at the back right position, it is difficult for a ball played from the front right position to get close to the hole. This was Jimenez's dilemma in 2000.

The pinched, hourglass shape brought the rough into the line of putt necessary for him to get close to the hole. Like Tom Johnson and Peter Fowler in the incidents above, Jimenez chose to play a pitch shot from the green, over the rough and the ridge, to the hole on the other side of the same green.

Jimenez was, however, aware of the Rule regarding the flagstick and wisely sought confirmation from the Rule official walking with his group. In order to avoid an infraction that could be caused by his ball striking the flagstick, he directed his caddie to attend the flagstick.

Rule 17-3a also states that an infraction occurs if a ball strikes an attended flagstick regardless of from where the shot is played. The penalty in stroke play is two strokes. Therefore, Jimenez's caddie was further directed to remove the flagstick if it looked as though the ball might strike it or go into the hole.

Playing a delicate pitch, Jimenez took a small divot. His ball landed on the downward slope of the ridge and ran to about 10 feet from the hole. Two putts were taken for bogey.

Frequently asked questions

May the player have the flagstick attended even if his ball is not on the putting green?
Yes. Rule 17-1 states that, before making a stroke from anywhere on the course, the player may have the flagstick attended, removed or held up.

Can the flagstick be replaced after it has been removed from the hole?
Yes. If a player makes a stroke from the putting green with the flagstick removed from the hole and she putts the ball and it rolls off the green, she may have the flagstick replaced in the hole prior to her next stroke.

Rule 18

DEFINITIONS

All defined terms are in *italics* and are listed alphabetically in the Definitions section – see pages 10–23.

BALL MOVED, DEFLECTED OR STOPPED
BALL AT REST MOVED

18-1. By Outside Agency

If a ball at rest is *moved* by an *outside agency*, there is no penalty and the ball must be replaced.

> **NOTE**
>
> It is a question of fact whether a ball has been *moved* by an *outside agency*. In order to apply this Rule, it must be known or virtually certain that an *outside agency* has *moved* the ball. In the absence of such knowledge or certainty, the player must play the ball as it lies or, if the ball is not found, proceed under Rule 27-1.
>
> (Player's ball at rest moved by another ball – see Rule 18-5)

18-2. By Player, Partner, Caddie or Equipment

Except as permitted by the *Rules*, when a player's ball is *in play*, if:

(i) the player, his *partner* or either of their *caddies*:

o lifts or *moves* the ball,

o touches it purposely (except with a club in the act of *addressing* the ball), or

o causes the ball to *move*, or

(ii) the *equipment* of the player or his *partner* causes the ball to *move*, **the player incurs a penalty of one stroke**.

If the ball is *moved*, it must be replaced, unless the movement of the ball occurs after the player has begun the *stroke* or the backward movement of the club for the *stroke* and the *stroke* is made.

Under the *Rules* there is no penalty if a player accidentally causes his ball to *move* in the following circumstances:

o In searching for a ball covered by sand or in re-creating the lie of a ball that has been altered during such a process, in the replacement of *loose impediments* moved in a *hazard* while finding or identifying a ball, in probing for a ball lying in water in a *water hazard* or in searching for a ball in an *obstruction* or an *abnormal ground condition* – Rule 12-1

o In repairing a *hole* plug or ball mark – Rule 16-1c

o In measuring – Rule 18-6

o In lifting a ball under a *Rule* – Rule 20-1

o In placing or replacing a ball under a *Rule* – Rule 20-3a

o In removing a *loose impediment* on the *putting green* – Rule 23-1

o In removing movable *obstructions* – Rule 24-1.

18-3. By Opponent, Caddie or Equipment in Match Play
a. During Search

If, during search for a player's ball, an *opponent*, his *caddie* or his *equipment moves* the ball, touches it or causes it to *move*, there is no penalty. If the ball is *moved*, it must be replaced.

b. Other Than During Search

If, other than during search for a player's ball, an *opponent*, his *caddie* or his *equipment moves* the ball, touches it purposely or causes it to *move*, except as otherwise provided in the *Rules*, **the *opponent* incurs a penalty of one stroke**. If the ball is *moved*, it must be replaced.

BALL AT REST MOVED

By Outside Agency – no penalty and replace ball (Rule 18-1).

By Player, Partner, Caddie or Equipment – one stroke penalty and replace ball (Rule 18-2).

By Opponent, Caddie or Equipment Not During Search – opponent incurs one stroke penalty and replace ball (Rule 18-3b).

By Opponent, Caddie or Equipment During Search – no penalty and replace ball (Rule 18-3a).

By Another Ball – replace moved ball (Rule 18-5).

By Fellow-Competitor, Caddie or Equipment – no penalty and replace ball (Rule18-4).

In Measuring – no penalty and replace ball (Rule 18-6).

(Playing a wrong ball – see Rule 15-3)
(Ball moved in measuring – see Rule 18-6)

18-4. By Fellow-Competitor, Caddie or Equipment in Stroke Play

If a *fellow-competitor*, his *caddie* or his *equipment moves* the player's ball, touches it or causes it to *move*, there is no penalty. If the ball is *moved*, it must be replaced.
(Playing a wrong ball – see Rule 15-3)

18-5. By Another Ball

If a *ball in play* and at rest is *moved* by another ball in motion after a *stroke*, the *moved* ball must be replaced.

18-6. Ball Moved in Measuring

If a ball or ball-marker is *moved* in measuring while proceeding under or in determining the application of a *Rule*, the ball or ball-marker must be replaced. There is no penalty, provided the movement of the ball or ball-marker is directly attributable to the specific act of measuring. Otherwise, the provisions of Rules 18-2, 18-3b or 18-4 apply.

---

*PENALTY FOR BREACH OF RULE:

Match play – Loss of hole; **Stroke play** – Two strokes.

*If a player who is required to replace a ball fails to do so, or if he makes a *stroke* at a ball *substituted* under Rule 18 when such substitution is not permitted, he incurs the general penalty for breach of Rule 18, but there is no additional penalty under this Rule.

NOTE 1

If a ball to be replaced under this Rule is not immediately recoverable, another ball may be *substituted*.

NOTE 2

If the original lie of a ball to be placed or replaced has been altered, see Rule 20-3b.

NOTE 3

If it is impossible to determine the spot on which a ball is to be placed or replaced, see Rule 20-3c.

RULE 18 INCIDENTS

Widely regarded as one of the most famous examples of sportsmanship in golf, a first round Rule 18 infraction, called on himself, ultimately cost Bob Jones the 1925 U.S. Open Championship.

At Worcester C.C. in Massachusetts, Jones saw his ball move after he addressed it on a steep bank at the 11th hole. He added a penalty stroke to his score for the hole and carried on.

Later, praised for his honesty, Jones replied, "You just might as well praise me for not breaking into banks. There is only one way to play this game."

Jones began the final round in a tie for fourth place and, by the end of the day, was able to force a 36-hole play-off with Willie Macfarlane. The following day, Jones (75–73) lost to Macfarlane (75–72) by one stroke.

A ball moved by an outside agency is another matter. At the 1998 Players Championship, a seagull flew off with Brad Fabel's ball that was at rest on the putting green of the 17th hole. Fabel, who made the first hole-in-one on the 17th in 1986, had safely played his tee shot onto the island green of the par-3 hole. As Fabel's group walked to the green, a seagull landed on the green and began pushing Fabel's ball toward the water hazard with its beak. Upon reaching the edge of the water hazard, the bird was able to lift the ball with its beak and fly off over the water. The ball proved too heavy for the bird and was ultimately dropped from about 30 feet in the air into the water below.

Under Rule 18-1, Fabel was entitled, without penalty, to replace his ball on the spot from which the seagull had moved it. Because his original ball was at the bottom of the lake, Fabel was entitled to substitute another ball.

If a player's ball at rest is moved by another ball in motion after a stroke, the ball that was moved must be replaced. An approach played by Mhairi McKay during the third round of the 2003 U.S. Women's Open flew into a greenside bunker where it struck and moved the ball of her fellow-competitor, Hilary Lunke.

The tracks in the sand made by the two balls were clearly discernible and were used to determine the spot on which Lunke's ball was to be replaced. Failure to replace the ball before her stroke would have resulted in a two-stroke penalty. Under the Rule, the ball in motion, McKay's ball in this incident, must be played from where it finishes.

During the final round of the 2011 Zurich Classic of New Orleans, Webb Simpson was clinging to a one-shot lead over Bubba Watson when he struck his 30-foot putt on the 15th green to within tap-in range. As he settled over the short putt placing his feet in position for the stroke, he briefly grounded his putter several inches behind the ball. After he did so, the ball moved, presumably due the presence of strong gusting winds combined with the firm and slick putting surface.

In 2011, Rule 18-2b (withdrawn for 2016) provided that if a player's ball in play moved after he had addressed it (other than as a result of a stroke), the player was deemed to have moved the ball and incurred a penalty stroke. Simpson was the only one to notice that the ball had moved ever so slightly but immediately called for an official to determine if there was a penalty. It was confirmed that the ball had moved after it had been addressed. Simpson was assessed a one-stroke penalty and the ball was replaced. Simpson and Watson were now tied and after 72 holes wound up in a play-off in which Watson prevailed.

In 2016 and beyond, without Rule 18-2b to apply to situations where the ball moves at address, the basic question is: Did the player cause the ball to move (Rule 18-2) or is there evidence that some other agency caused the ball to move? Perhaps today's answer to the Simpson case would be that the wind caused the ball to move and there would be no penalty to be assessed.

Frequently asked questions

While making a practice swing, the ball in play is accidentally moved by the club. What is the ruling?

The player incurs a one-stroke penalty and must replace the ball to its original position. If she fails to replace the ball, she will incur a total penalty of loss of hole in match play or two strokes in stroke play. Please refer to the Penalty Statement under Rule 18 (Rule 18-2 and Decision 18-2/20).

A player replaces his ball on the putting green and then it moves due to wind or gravity. Is it replaced or played from its new position?

Since wind and gravity are not outside agencies, the ball is played from its new position. If the ball rolls into the hole, it is considered holed with the previous stroke. If the ball rolls into a water hazard, the ball must be played as it lies or Rule 26-1 can be employed.

Rule 19 BALL IN MOTION DEFLECTED OR STOPPED

DEFINITIONS
All defined terms are in *italics* and are listed alphabetically in the Definitions section – see pages 10–23.

19-1. By Outside Agency

If a player's ball in motion is accidentally deflected or stopped by any *outside agency*, it is a *rub of the green*, there is no penalty and the ball must be played as it lies, except:

a. If a player's ball in motion after a *stroke* other than on the *putting green* comes to rest in or on any moving or animate *outside agency*, the ball must *through the green* or in a *hazard* be dropped, or on the *putting green* be placed, as near as possible to the spot directly under the place where the ball came to rest in or on the *outside agency*, but not nearer the *hole*, and

b. If a player's ball in motion after a *stroke* on the *putting green* is deflected or stopped by, or comes to rest in or on, any moving or animate *outside agency*, except a worm, insect or the like, the *stroke* is canceled. The ball must be replaced and replayed.

If the ball is not immediately recoverable, another ball may be *substituted*.

Exception:

Ball striking person attending or holding up *flagstick* or anything carried by him – see Rule 17-3b.

NOTE

If a player's ball in motion has been deliberately deflected or stopped by an *outside agency*:

(a) After a stroke from anywhere other than on the *putting green*, the spot where the ball would have come to rest must be estimated. If that spot is:

(i) *through the green* or in a *hazard*, the ball must be dropped as near as possible to that spot;

(ii) *out of bounds*, the player must proceed under Rule 27-1; or

(iii) on the *putting green*, the ball must be placed on that spot.

(b) After a *stroke* on the *putting green*, the *stroke* is canceled. The ball must be replaced and replayed.

If the *outside agency* is a *fellow-competitor* or his *caddie*, Rule 1-2 applies to the *fellow-competitor*.

(Player's ball deflected or stopped by another ball — see Rule 19-5)

19-2. By Player, Partner, Caddie or Equipment

If a player's ball is accidentally deflected or stopped by himself, his *partner* or either of their *caddies* or *equipment*, **the player incurs a penalty of one stroke**. The ball must be played as it lies, except when it comes to rest in or on the player's, his *partner's* or either of their *caddies'* clothes or *equipment*, in which case the ball must *through the green* or in a *hazard* be dropped, or on the *putting green* be placed, as near as possible to the spot directly under the place where the ball came to rest in or on the article, but not nearer the *hole*.

Exceptions:

1. Ball striking person attending or holding up a *flagstick* or anything carried by him – see Rule 17-3b.

2. Dropped ball – see Rule 20-2a.

(Ball purposely deflected or stopped by player, partner or caddie – see Rule 1-2)

BALL IN MOTION DEFLECTED OR STOPPED

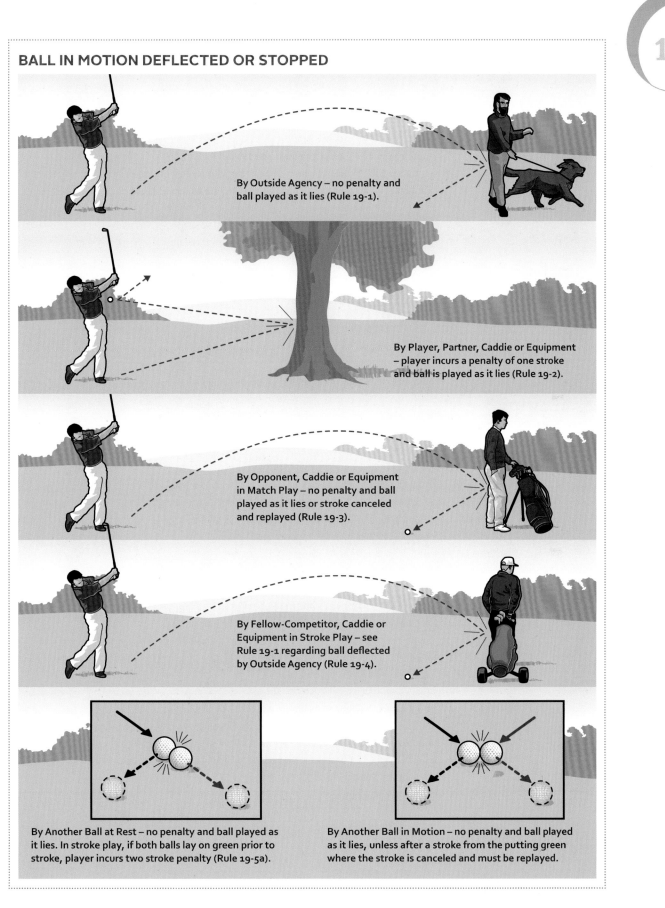

By Outside Agency – no penalty and ball played as it lies (Rule 19-1).

By Player, Partner, Caddie or Equipment – player incurs a penalty of one stroke and ball is played as it lies (Rule 19-2).

By Opponent, Caddie or Equipment in Match Play – no penalty and ball played as it lies or stroke canceled and replayed (Rule 19-3).

By Fellow-Competitor, Caddie or Equipment in Stroke Play – see Rule 19-1 regarding ball deflected by Outside Agency (Rule 19-4).

By Another Ball at Rest – no penalty and ball played as it lies. In stroke play, if both balls lay on green prior to stroke, player incurs two stroke penalty (Rule 19-5a).

By Another Ball in Motion – no penalty and ball played as it lies, unless after a stroke from the putting green where the stroke is canceled and must be replayed.

19-3. By Opponent, Caddie or Equipment in Match Play

If a player's ball is accidentally deflected or stopped by an *opponent*, his *caddie* or his *equipment*, there is no penalty. The player may, before another *stroke* is made by either *side*, cancel the *stroke* and play a ball, without penalty, as nearly as possible at the spot from which the original ball was last played (see Rule 20-5) or he may play the ball as it lies. However, if the player elects not to cancel the *stroke* and the ball has come to rest in or on the *opponent*'s or his *caddie*'s clothes or *equipment*, the ball must *through the green* or in a *hazard* be dropped, or on the *putting green* be placed, as near as possible to the spot directly under the place where the ball came to rest in or on the article, but not nearer the *hole*.

Exception:

Ball striking person attending or holding up *flagstick* or anything carried by him – see Rule 17-3b.

(Ball purposely deflected or stopped by *opponent* or caddie – see Rule 1-2)

19-4. By Fellow-Competitor, Caddie or Equipment in Stroke Play

See Rule 19-1 regarding ball deflected by *outside agency*.

Exception:

Ball striking person attending or holding up *flagstick* or anything carried by him – see Rule 17-3b.

19-5. By Another Ball
a. At Rest

If a player's ball in motion after a *stroke* is deflected or stopped by a *ball in play* and at rest, the player must play his ball as it lies. In match play, there is no penalty. In stroke play, there is no penalty, unless both balls lay on the *putting green* prior to the *stroke*, in which case **the player incurs a penalty of two strokes**.

b. In Motion

If a player's ball in motion after a *stroke* other than on the *putting green* is deflected or stopped by another ball in motion after a *stroke*, the player must play his ball as it lies, without penalty.

If a player's ball in motion after a *stroke* on the *putting green* is deflected or stopped by another ball in motion after a *stroke*, the player's *stroke* is canceled. The ball must be replaced and replayed, without penalty.

NOTE

Nothing in this Rule overrides the provisions of Rule 10-1 (Order of Play in Match Play) or Rule 16-1f (Making Stroke While Another Ball in Motion).

PENALTY FOR BREACH OF RULE 19-5:

Match play – Loss of hole; **Stroke play** – Two strokes.

RULE 19 INCIDENTS

When a ball in motion is deflected or stopped, the consequences under the Rules vary depending on who or what interfered. Sometimes it is a rub of the green, sometimes a penalty is involved and sometimes it must be estimated where the ball would have ended up, had it not been deflected or stopped, so it can be put into play at that spot.

At the 2003 Masters Tournament, Jeff Maggert accidentally deflected his own ball in an attempt to play from the fairway bunker at the 3rd hole.

Maggert was playing in the final group on the final day when his drive at the par-4 finished in one of four bunkers at the left of the landing zone. The ball was far enough behind the forward lip of the bunker so that he judged that he could play a full approach to the putting green. However, once struck, the ball smashed into the lip, ricocheted backwards and hit him. The Rules official stationed on that hole informed Maggert that a two-stroke penalty had been incurred and the ball had to be played as it lay (Rule 19-2).

In 2008, a change to Rule 19 reduced the penalty to one stroke in such an instance.

If a player's ball in motion has been deliberately deflected or stopped by an outside agency, the player must follow the Note to Rule 19-1.

Tiger Woods found himself in such a situation during second round play of the 1st hole at the 2006 PGA Championship. Wood's drive went left towards the gallery lining the fairway. It bounced near a fairway bunker, was deflected by a spectator and came to rest near the rope line restricting the gallery.

A Rules official in the area immediately asked for information from spectators and marshals who were present, including whether the ball was purposefully or accidentally deflected. No one was of the opinion that the ball had been purposefully deflected and, therefore, it was played as it lay.

At events with large numbers of spectators it is common to have a player's ball after a stroke be deflected by one of the spectators as in the incidents above. Sometimes the ball comes to rest in an odd location and the question

If a player accidentally deflects his own ball, as Jeff Maggert did at the 2003 Masters, the player incurs a one-stroke penalty.

arises as to whether the ball may be played from where it lies, placed or dropped somewhere else.

There are many examples of these situations but this one illustrates the principles involved in the application of Rule 19 to a situation where a ball comes to rest in one of these odd locations.

During the second round of the 2014 Tour Championship by Coca-Cola at East Lake Golf Club, Rory McIlroy's tee shot at the 14th hole went off to the right, struck a tree and eventually came to rest in a spectator's pocket. The spectator, an outside agency, remained where the ball had entered his pocket until McIlroy arrived. Rule 19-1a applied and McIlroy dropped the ball as near as possible to the spot directly under the place where the ball came to rest in the outside agency. This reference spot was established once the ball came to rest and had the spectator left the scene with the ball, McIlroy would have proceeded as he did with respect to the established reference spot with permission to substitute another ball since the original ball would not have been immediately recoverable.

Frequently asked questions

A ball in motion is deflected by a direction post or bounces off a sprinkler head next to a putting green. What is the ruling?

Since both objects are considered outside agencies in each case, it is in each case a rub of the green and the ball must be played as it lies.

What do I do if my ball is stopped or deflected by a rake held by my caddie?

A rake that is being carried or held by a player's caddie is considered to be the equipment of the player at that time (see Note 2 to the Definition of "Equipment"). The player incurs a penalty of one stroke and must play the ball as it lies.

Rule 20

DEFINITIONS
All defined terms are in *italics* and are listed alphabetically in the Definitions section – see pages 10–23.

RELIEF SITUATIONS AND PROCEDURE
LIFTING, DROPPING AND PLACING; PLAYING FROM WRONG PLACE

20-1. Lifting and Marking

A ball to be lifted under the *Rules* may be lifted by the player, his *partner* or another person authorized by the player. In any such case, the player is responsible for any breach of the *Rules*.

The position of the ball must be marked before it is lifted under a *Rule* that requires it to be replaced. If it is not marked, **the player incurs a penalty of one stroke** and the ball must be replaced. If it is not replaced, **the player incurs the general penalty for breach of this Rule**, but there is no additional penalty under Rule 20-1.

If a ball or ball-marker is accidentally *moved* in the process of lifting the ball under a *Rule* or marking its position, the ball or ball-marker must be replaced. There is no penalty, provided the movement of the ball or ball-marker is directly attributable to the specific act of marking the position of or lifting the ball. Otherwise, **the player incurs a penalty of one stroke under this Rule or Rule 18-2a.**

MARKING A GOLF BALL

To mark the position of the ball, a player can use items such as a tee, coin or even a ball mark repair tool.

DROPPING THE BALL

Martin Kaymer drops his ball at the 2014 U.S. Open at Pinehurst. The player must stand up straight, hold the ball at arm's length and at shoulder height and drop it.

PROCEDURE FOR LIFTING BALL

Although I want your ball lifted because it is interfering with my play, why are you marking it?

Because when a ball is lifted anywhere on the course and has to be replaced, its position must be marked.

Exception:

If a player incurs a penalty for failing to act in accordance with Rule 5-3 or 12-2, there is no additional penalty under Rule 20-1.

NOTE

The position of a ball to be lifted should be marked by placing a ball-marker, a small coin or other similar object immediately behind the ball. If the ball-marker interferes with the play, *stance* or *stroke* of another player, it should be placed one or more clubhead-lengths to one side.

WHEN TO RE-DROP BALL

Ball rolls and comes to rest in a hazard.	Ball rolls out of and comes to rest outside a hazard.	Ball rolls onto and comes to rest on a putting green.	Ball rolls and comes to rest out of bounds.
Ball rolls back into and comes to rest in condition.	Ball rolls and comes to rest nearer the hole than its original position or the nearest point of relief.	Ball rolls and comes to rest more than two club-lengths away.	Ball rolls and comes to rest nearer the hole than the appropriate reference point.

20-2. Dropping and Re-Dropping
a. By Whom and How

A ball to be dropped under the *Rules* must be dropped by the player himself. He must stand erect, hold the ball at shoulder height and arm's length and drop it. If a ball is dropped by any other person or in any other manner and the error is not corrected as provided in Rule 20-6, **the player incurs a penalty of one stroke**.

If the ball, when dropped, touches any person or the *equipment* of any player before or after it strikes a part of the *course* and before it comes to rest, the ball must be re-dropped, without penalty. There is no limit to the number of times a ball must be re-dropped in these circumstances.

(Taking action to influence position or movement of ball – see Rule 1-2)

b. Where to Drop

When a ball is to be dropped as near as possible to a specific spot, it must be dropped not nearer the *hole* than the specific spot which, if it is not precisely known to the player, must be estimated.

A ball when dropped must first strike a part of the *course* where the applicable *Rule* requires it to be dropped. If it is not so dropped, Rules 20-6 and 20-7 apply.

c. When to Re-Drop

A dropped ball must be re-dropped, without penalty, if it:

(i)   rolls into and comes to rest in a *hazard*;

(ii) rolls out of and comes to rest outside a *hazard*;

(iii) rolls onto and comes to rest on a *putting green*;

(iv) rolls and comes to rest *out of bounds*;

(v) rolls to and comes to rest in a position where there is interference by the condition from which relief was taken under Rule 24-2b (immovable obstruction), Rule 25-1 (abnormal ground conditions), Rule 25-3 (wrong putting green) or a Local Rule (Rule 33-8a) or rolls back into the pitch-mark from which it was lifted under Rule 25-2 (embedded ball);

(vi) rolls and comes to rest more than two club-lengths from where it first struck a part of the *course*; or

(vii) rolls and comes to rest nearer the *hole* than:

   (a) its original position or estimated position (see Rule 20-2b) unless otherwise permitted by the *Rules*; or

   (b) the *nearest point of relief* or maximum available relief (Rule 24-2, 25-1 or 25-3); or

   (c) the point where the original ball last crossed the margin of the *water hazard* or *lateral water hazard* (Rule 26-1).

If the ball when re-dropped rolls into any position listed above, it must be placed as near as possible to the spot where it first struck a part of the *course* when re-dropped.

NOTE 1

If a ball when dropped or re-dropped comes to rest and subsequently *moves*, the ball must be played as it lies, unless the provisions of any other *Rule* apply.

NOTE 2

If a ball to be re-dropped or placed under this Rule is not immediately recoverable, another ball may be *substituted*.

(Use of Dropping Zone – see Appendix I; Part A; Section 6)

LIE OF BALL ALTERED IN BUNKER

LIFTING, DROPPING AND PLACING; PLAYING FROM WRONG PLACE | **RULE 20**

20-3. Placing and Replacing
a. By Whom and Where

A ball to be placed under the *Rules* must be placed by the player or his *partner*.

A ball to be replaced under the *Rules* must be replaced by any one of the following: (i) the person who lifted or *moved* the ball, (ii) the player, or (iii) the player's *partner*. The ball must be placed on the spot from which it was lifted or *moved*. If the ball is placed or replaced by any other person and the error is not corrected as provided in Rule 20-6, **the player incurs a penalty of one stroke**. In any such case, the player is responsible for any other breach of the *Rules* that occurs as a result of the placing or replacing of the ball.

If a ball or ball-marker is accidentally *moved* in the process of placing or replacing the ball, the ball or ball-marker must be replaced. There is no penalty, provided the movement of the ball or ball-marker is directly attributable to the specific act of placing or replacing the ball or removing the ball-marker. Otherwise, **the player incurs a penalty of one stroke under Rule 18-2 or 20-1**.

If a ball to be replaced is placed other than on the spot from which it was lifted or *moved* and the error is not corrected as provided in Rule 20-6, **the player incurs the general penalty, loss of hole in match play or two strokes in stroke play, for a breach of the applicable Rule**.

b. Lie of Ball to Be Placed or Replaced Altered

If the original lie of a ball to be placed or replaced has been altered:

(i) except in a *hazard*, the ball must be placed in the nearest lie most similar to the original lie that is not more than one club-length from the original lie, not nearer the *hole* and not in a *hazard*;

(ii) in a *water hazard*, the ball must be placed in accordance with Clause (i) above, except that the ball must be placed in the *water hazard*;

LIE OF BALL ALTERED IN WATER HAZARD

I am going to play my ball from the water hazard and your ball is in my way. Would you mind marking and lifting it?

Not at all, but let's note just what kind of lie I have. If, as a result of your shot, my lie is altered I must place my ball in the hazard in the nearest lie most similar, not more than one club-length away and not nearer the hole.

PLAYING FROM THE WRONG PLACE

If a player moves his ball-marker a putter-head length to one side, he must remember to put it back before he putts. Otherwise, the player will be penalized for playing from a wrong place.

(iii) in a *bunker*, the original lie must be re-created as nearly as possible and the ball must be placed in that lie.

NOTE

If the original lie of a ball to be placed or replaced has been altered and it is impossible to determine the spot where the ball is to be placed or replaced, Rule 20-3b applies if the original lie is known, and Rule 20-3c applies if the original lie is not known.

Exception:

If the player is searching for or identifying a ball covered by sand – see Rule 12-1a.

c. Spot Not Determinable

If it is impossible to determine the spot where the ball is to be placed or replaced:

(i) *through the green*, the ball must be dropped as near as possible to the place where it lay but not in a *hazard* or on a *putting green*;

(ii) in a *hazard*, the ball must be dropped in the *hazard* as near as possible to the place where it lay;

(iii) on the *putting green*, the ball must be placed as near as possible to the place where it lay but not in a *hazard*.

Exception:

When resuming play (Rule 6-8d), if the spot where the ball is to be placed is impossible to determine, it must be estimated and the ball placed on the estimated spot.

d. Ball Fails to Come to Rest on Spot

If a ball when placed fails to come to rest on the spot on which it was placed, there is no penalty and the ball must be replaced. If it still fails to come to rest on that spot:

(i) except in a *hazard*, it must be placed at the nearest spot where it can be placed at rest that is not nearer the *hole* and not in a *hazard*;

(ii) in a *hazard*, it must be placed in the *hazard* at the nearest spot where it can be placed at rest that is not nearer the *hole*.

If a ball when placed comes to rest on the spot on which it is placed, and it subsequently *moves*, there is no penalty and the ball must be played as it lies, unless the provisions of any other *Rule* apply.

---

*PENALTY FOR BREACH OF RULE 20-1, 20-2 OR 20-3:

Match play – Loss of hole; **Stroke play** – Two strokes.

*If a player makes a *stroke* at a ball *substituted* under one of these Rules when such *substitution* is not permitted, he incurs the general penalty for breach of that Rule, but there is no additional penalty under that Rule. If a player drops a ball in an improper manner and plays from a wrong place or if the ball has been put into play by a person not permitted by the *Rules* and then played from a wrong place, see Note 3 to Rule 20-7c.

20-4. When Ball Dropped, Placed or Replaced is in Play

If the player's *ball in play* has been lifted, it is again in *play* when dropped or placed. A ball that has been replaced is *in play* whether or not the ball-marker has been removed.

A substituted ball becomes the *ball in play* when it has been dropped or placed.

(Ball incorrectly substituted – see Rule 15-2)

(Lifting ball incorrectly substituted, dropped or placed – see Rule 20-6)

20-5. Making Next Stroke from Where Previous Stroke Made

When a player elects or is required to make his next *stroke* from where a previous *stroke* was made, he must proceed as follows:

(a) On the Teeing Ground: The ball to be played must be played from within the *teeing ground*. It may be played from anywhere within the *teeing ground* and may be teed.

(b) Through the Green: The ball to be played must be dropped and when dropped must first strike a part of the *course through the green*.

(c) In a Hazard: The ball to be played must be dropped and when dropped must first strike a part of the *course* in the *hazard*.

(d) On the Putting Green: The ball to be played must be placed on the *putting green*.

PENALTY FOR BREACH OF RULE 20-5:

Match play – Loss of hole; **Stroke play** – Two strokes.

20-6. Lifting Ball Incorrectly Substituted, Dropped or Placed

A ball incorrectly *substituted*, dropped or placed in a wrong place or otherwise not in accordance with the *Rules* but not played may be lifted, without penalty, and the player must then proceed correctly.

20-7. Playing from Wrong Place

a. General

A player has played from a wrong place if he makes a stroke at his *ball in play*:

(i) on a part of the *course* where the *Rules* do not permit a *stroke* to be made or a ball to be dropped or placed; or

(ii) when the *Rules* require a dropped ball to be re-dropped or a *moved* ball to be replaced.

NOTE

For a ball played from outside the *teeing ground* or from a wrong *teeing ground* – see Rule 11-4.

b. Match Play

If a player makes a *stroke* from a wrong place, **he loses the hole.**

c. Stroke Play

If a *competitor* makes a *stroke* from a wrong place, **he incurs a penalty of two strokes under the applicable *Rule*.** He must play out the hole with the ball played from the wrong place, without correcting his error, provided he has not committed a serious breach (see Note 1).

If a *competitor* becomes aware that he has played from a wrong place and believes that he may have committed a serious breach, he must, before making a *stroke* on the next *teeing ground*, play out the hole with a second ball played in accordance with the *Rules*. If the hole being played is the last hole of the round, he must declare, before leaving the *putting green*, that he will play out the hole with a second ball played in accordance with the *Rules*.

If the *competitor* has played a second ball, he must report the facts to the *Committee* before returning his score card; if he fails to do so, **he is disqualified**. The *Committee* must determine whether the *competitor* has committed a serious breach of the applicable *Rule*. If he has, the score with the second ball counts and **the *competitor* must add two *penalty strokes*** to his score with that ball. If the *competitor* has committed a serious breach and has failed to correct it as outlined above, **he is disqualified**.

NOTE 1

A *competitor* is deemed to have committed a serious breach of the applicable *Rule* if the *Committee* considers he has gained a significant advantage as a result of playing from a wrong place.

NOTE 2

If a *competitor* plays a second ball under Rule 20-7c and it is ruled not to count, *strokes* made with that ball and *penalty strokes* incurred solely by playing that ball are disregarded. If the second ball is ruled to count, the *stroke* made from the wrong place and any *strokes* subsequently taken with the original ball including *penalty strokes* incurred solely by playing that ball are disregarded.

NOTE 3

If a player incurs a penalty for making a *stroke* from a wrong place, there is no additional penalty for:

(a) *substituting* a ball when not permitted;

(b) dropping a ball when the *Rules* require it to be placed, or placing a ball when the *Rules* require it to be dropped;

(c) dropping a ball in an improper manner; or

(d) a ball being put into play by a person not permitted to do so under the *Rules*.

RULE 20 INCIDENTS

Finishing tied after 72 holes, Ian Poulter and Robert Karlsson went head-to-head for the 2010 Dubai World Championship title. The pair halved the first extra hole in the play-off with birdies and both found the putting green on the second play-off hole. Poulter had left himself a 30-foot birdie putt and had marked and lifted the ball. After assessing the putt, he bent down with the intention of replacing his ball, when the ball slipped out of his hand and moved his ball-marker.

Rule 20-3a provides that if a ball-marker is accidentally moved in the process of replacing the ball, the ball or ball-marker must be replaced and there is no penalty, provided the movement of the ball-marker is directly attributable to the specific act of replacing the ball. But if the movement of the ball-marker is not in the specific act of replacing the ball, the player incurs a penalty of one stroke and must replace the ball or ball-marker.

Decision 20-1/15 provides that in order for the movement of the ball-marker to be considered directly attributable to the specific act of replacing the ball, the movement has to occur when the ball was actually placed in front of the ball-marker such that the player's hand or the placement of the ball causes the ball-marker to move. The Decision also clarifies that any accidental movement of the ball-marker that occurs before the specific act, such as dropping the ball, regardless of the height from which it was dropped, is not considered directly attributable to the specific act of replacing the ball.

Consequently, in Poulter's case as he had dropped his ball prior to the specific act of replacing it, he was penalized one stroke for the accidental movement of the ball-marker. He then replaced his ball on the original spot from which it was lifted, composed himself and attempted the putt for what was now a par, but it wasn't to be. Poulter missed out on the title, world ranking points and over €300,000 in earnings for his accidental error.

After the event, Poulter commented that he had the ball-marker (a platinum coin) specially made at the beginning of 2010. "It has my kids' names on it and it's my lucky coin," he said. "After the year I've had, I still consider it lucky."

Once the criteria for relief under the Rules have been applied, the figurative Rules clock is re-set and play continues.

On the 18th hole of the 2002 EMC World Cup at Vista Vallarta in Mexico, Thomas Levet could not have realized how quickly his water hazard penalty would repeat itself. With his partner, Rafael Jacquelin, out of the hole and the French team leading by one, Levet played his approach from the fairway into a lateral water hazard at the front and left of the putting green.

He took relief, and the resulting penalty, under Rule 26-1, dropped a ball on the steep, closely mown grass bank beside the hazard where it came to rest. The ball was in play.

Gathering his wits, Levet walked onto the green, toward the hole, in order to assess what would be needed from his pitch. On his way back to his ball, the ball began to move and rolled back into the lateral water hazard from which he had just taken relief.

Because the ball had been at rest after his taking relief from the hazard, and because Levet had not addressed the ball or done anything to cause it to move, the ball was back in the hazard and could only be removed by playing it or under penalty of an additional stroke, again taking relief under the water hazard Rule. So, he was two in the hazard the first time, three out with the first penalty, and four out with the second penalty. A new point of reference for where the ball last crossed the margin of the hazard had to be determined for the second drop. Levet played his fifth shot expeditiously.

After taking relief from a water hazard at the EMC World Cup, Thomas Levet's ball came to rest and then subsequently rolled back into the same hazard. Levet was forced to take a second drop and a second penalty stroke.

Frequently asked questions

Must a player use a small coin or similar object to mark the position of his ball before lifting it?

The Note to Rule 20-1 states in part that the position of the ball should be marked by placing a ball-marker, small coin or other small object immediately behind the ball. When the word "should" is used in the Rules of Golf it is a recommendation only and failure to comply does not result in a penalty. The intention is to emphasize that use of a ball-marker or other small object (such as a coin) is considered to be the best way to mark a ball.

Is the person who lifted the player's ball the only person who may replace it?

No. Up to a maximum of three different people may replace a ball, depending on the circumstances. The player, his partner or the person who lifted or moved it may replace the ball. For example, in a Four-Ball match, if a player were to authorize his caddie to lift his ball, the caddie, the player or the player's partner could replace it. However, if the player lifts the ball himself, only the player or his partner may replace it – see Rule 20-3a.

Is a player required to use his longest club when measuring under the Rules?

No, the player may use any club he has selected for play during that round.

Rule 21 CLEANING BALL

DEFINITIONS
All defined terms are in *italics* and are listed alphabetically in the Definitions section – see pages 10–23.

A ball on the *putting green* may be cleaned when lifted under Rule 16-1b. Elsewhere, a ball may be cleaned when lifted, except when it has been lifted:

a. To determine if it is unfit for play (Rule 5-3);

b. For identification (Rule 12-2), in which case it may be cleaned only to the extent necessary for identification; or

c. Because it is assisting or interfering with play (Rule 22).

If a player cleans his ball during play of a hole except as provided in this Rule, **he incurs a penalty of one stroke** and the ball, if lifted, must be replaced.

   If a player who is required to replace a ball fails to do so, **he incurs the general penalty under the applicable *Rule***, but there is no additional penalty under Rule 21.

Exception:
If a player incurs a penalty for failing to act in accordance with Rule 5-3, 12-2 or 22, there is no additional penalty under Rule 21.

RULE 21 INCIDENTS

Several years ago, the 1987 US Open Champion, Scott Simpson, was involved in a minor incident resulting from a request from another player asking Simpson to lift his ball under Rule 22 because his ball interfered with the play of the other player. This Rule prohibits cleaning of the ball during the process unless the ball lies on the putting green.

In responding to the other player's request, Simpson authorized his caddie to lift his ball. Having marked the position of the ball, the caddie lifted it and returned it to Simpson by throwing it to him. The referee with the Simpson group raised the issue of whether the act of throwing and catching the ball would constitute cleaning the ball in violation of Rule 21 or Rule 22.

Whether the ball was cleaned is a question of fact and the action of throwing and catching could result in a ball being cleaned. Any doubt should be resolved against the player. At the time, it was determined that the facts did not support the conclusion that Simpson had cleaned the ball with the result that no penalty was assessed.

At the 2009 U.S. Senior Open at Crooked Stick Golf Club, Simpson was involved in a similar incident during the first round at the par-3 13th hole. His tee shot at the 185-yard hole resulted in the ball coming to rest on the fringe just short of the putting green. A fellow-competitor judged that the ball interfered with his play and requested that the ball be lifted. This time Simpson himself marked the position of the ball, lifted it and put it into his pocket causing the referee with the group to ponder whether this act resulting in cleaning of the ball.

With knowledge of the prior event, the referee considered all the facts in the present situation: (i) the ball struck from the tee was in pristine condition, (ii) the ball at rest on the smooth fringe appeared to be in a similar condition with no visible foreign material adhering to the ball, (iii) the turf surrounding the ball was very tight and in an extremely dry condition, (iv) there was a lack of any wet soil or cut-grass blades present on the fringe or on the ball at rest, and (v) there was very low humidity present. Based on these facts, it was concluded that the condition of the ball at rest on the fringe was the same as the condition of the ball when struck from the tee. The referee thus determined that no cleaning had resulted from Simpson putting the ball into his pocket and no violation of Rule 21 had occurred.

Rule 22 BALL ASSISTING OR INTERFERING WITH PLAY

DEFINITIONS
All defined terms are in *italics* and are listed alphabetically in the Definitions section – see pages 10–23.

22-1. Ball Assisting Play

Except when a ball is in motion, if a player considers that a ball might assist any other player, he may:

a.   Lift the ball if it is his ball, or

b.   Have any other ball lifted.

A ball lifted under this Rule must be replaced (see Rule 20-3). The ball must not be cleaned, unless it lies on the *putting green* (see Rule 21).

In stroke play, a player required to lift his ball may play first rather than lift the ball.

In stroke play, if the *Committee* determines that *competitors* have agreed not to lift a ball that might assist any *competitor*, **they are disqualified**.

NOTE

When another ball is in motion, a ball that might influence the movement of the ball in motion must not be lifted.

22-2. Ball Interfering with Play

Except when a ball is in motion, if a player considers that another ball might interfere with his play, he may have it lifted.

A ball lifted under this Rule must be replaced (see Rule 20-3). The ball must not be cleaned, unless it lies on the *putting green* (see Rule 21).

In stroke play, a player required to lift his ball may play first rather than lift the ball.

NOTE 1

Except on the *putting green*, a player may not lift his ball solely because he considers that it might interfere with the play of another player. If a player lifts his ball without being asked to do so, he incurs a penalty of one stroke for a breach of Rule 18-2, but there is no additional penalty under Rule 22.

NOTE 2

When another ball is in motion, a ball that might influence the movement of the ball in motion must not be lifted.

PENALTY FOR BREACH OF RULE:

Match play – Loss of hole; **Stroke play** – Two strokes.

BALL INTERFERING WITH OR ASSISTING PLAY

Frequently asked questions

Is it permissible for two fellow-competitors in stroke play to agree to leave the ball of one of the players near the hole to assist the other player in playing his ball from just off the putting green?

No. If the fellow-competitors agree not to lift a ball that might assist another player, they are disqualified – Rule 22-1.

In match play, the player has requested for the opponent to leave his ball near the hole. Is this request permissible? Is there a penalty if the opponent does lift the ball?

Except while a ball is in motion, the opponent has the right under Rule 22-1 to mark the position of and lift his ball before the player plays his stroke, if he believes that his ball will assist the player in his play of the hole. Therefore, in this case, the player's opponent may mark the position of and lift his ball under Rule 22-1. There's no penalty for making this request; however, the player can not deny the opponent of his right to lift the ball.

RULE 22 INCIDENT

Golf's playing field is the largest of any sport. For this reason, it is rare when one ball comes into contact with or interferes with another. It is even more bizarre when there is such an occurrence at the major championship level.

And yet, Jesper Parnevik and Scott Hoch found themselves in just such a predicament near the 6th green at Pinehurst No. 2 during the 1999 U.S. Open.

Rule 22 allows any player to lift his ball if he believes it will assist another player, or have any ball lifted that might interfere with his play or assist any other player. Except on the putting green, a ball lifted under Rule 22 may not be cleaned.

Hoch and Parnevik both played just to the left side of the par-3, 222-yard hole. From the tee, it was difficult to discern whether the balls were on the fringe of the green or in the rough. Their fellow-competitor's ball, belonging to Steve Jones, was visible on the green. Arriving greenside, Hoch and Parnevik found that their balls lay about three inches off the fringe in the Bermuda grass rough and actually touching. Both balls were held slightly off the ground by the stiff consistency of the grass. Because Hoch's ball was closer to the hole, it was necessary that it be lifted in order for Parnevik to play his shot.

Before Hoch lifted his ball, the walking Rules official with the group closely inspected the lie of both balls firstly to be certain that Hoch, upon replacing his ball after Parnevik's stroke, would be afforded the same lie or if that were not possible, the most similar lie and secondly that

Parnevik's ball could be accurately replaced should it move when Hoch lifted his ball.

As anticipated, when Hoch lifted his ball, Parnevik's moved an inch closer to the hole. Under the official's watchful eye, Parnevik attempted to replace his ball at its original location. However, the supporting nature of the Bermuda grass could not be re-introduced and Parnevik's ball sunk a little deeper into the rough than its original position. Under the Rules, it doesn't matter if the movement is vertical or horizontal. The ball could not be replaced in its original position so that it would remain at rest.

Rule 20-3d covers such a situation by stating that if a ball, when placed or replaced, fails to come to rest on that spot, it must be replaced. If it again fails to remain at rest, it must be placed at the nearest spot where it can be placed at rest that is not nearer the hole and not in a hazard.

Parnevik found such a spot and chipped onto the green. In so doing, he altered Hoch's lie. Hoch was entitled to the lie that his tee shot had afforded him, which is one of the Rules' cardinal principles. Since his lie had been altered, Hoch found the nearest lie most similar to his original lie, within one club-length, and placed his ball on that spot. He then chipped in for a birdie two.

All of this was under the discerning eyes of both the walking Rules official and a Rules rover, who was monitoring the group's pace of play. Parnevik and Jones finished the hole, and the three players went to the 7th tee.

Rule 23 LOOSE IMPEDIMENTS

DEFINITIONS

All defined terms are in *italics* and are listed alphabetically in the Definitions section – see pages 10–23.

23-1. Relief

Except when both the *loose impediment* and the ball lie in or touch the same *hazard*, any *loose impediment* may be removed without penalty.

If the ball lies anywhere other than on the *putting green* and the removal of a *loose impediment* by the player causes the ball to *move*, Rule 18-2 applies.

On the *putting green*, if the ball or ball-marker is accidentally moved in the process of the player removing a *loose impediment*, the ball or ball-marker must be replaced. There is no penalty, provided the movement of the ball or ball-marker is directly attributable to the removal of the loose *impediment*. Otherwise, **the player incurs a penalty of one stroke under Rule 18-2**.

When a ball is in motion, a *loose impediment* that might influence the movement of the ball must not be removed.

NOTE

If the ball lies in a *hazard*, the player must not touch or move any *loose impediment* lying in or touching the same *hazard* – see Rule 13-4c.

PENALTY FOR BREACH OF RULE:

Match play – Loss of hole; **Stroke play** – Two strokes.

(Searching for ball in hazard – see Rule 12-1)

(Touching line of putt – see Rule 16-1a)

RULE 23-1. RELIEF

A player is entitled to remove any loose impediment without penalty, except when both the loose impediment and the player's ball lie in or touch the same hazard.

RULE 23 INCIDENTS

Consistency lies at the heart of the Rules of Golf even when rulings are made that superficially or visually seem inconsistent. Except when both the loose impediment and a player's ball lie in or touch the same hazard, any loose impediment may be removed without penalty.

When Tiger Woods was permitted to gain assistance from his substantial gallery in order to move a boulder lying on the desert floor, it did not look appropriate, but it was – and it was consistent within the Rules.

During the final round of 1999 Phoenix Open, Woods's drive from the 13th tee traveled 360 yards before finishing in the desert just off the left side of the fairway. The ball stopped about two feet directly behind a boulder that was roughly four feet wide, two feet high, and two feet thick. The rock was too heavy for Woods to move by himself, and his ball was too close to it to play over or around. With the rock in place, Woods's best option was to play sideways onto the fairway.

With 225 yards left to reach the putting green, Woods was not enamored with the idea of pitching out to the fairway and then playing his approach to the green. PGA Tour Rules Official Orlando Pope appeared on the scene, and Woods inquired as to his options. With a glimmer of a smile, Woods kicked the rock and asked, "It's not a pebble, but is it a loose impediment?"

The definition within the Rules states that loose impediments are natural objects that are not fixed or growing, not solidly embedded, and do not adhere to the ball. There is no restriction for size or weight. Thus, stones of any size are loose impediments and may be removed as long as they are not solidly embedded and their removal does not unduly delay play.

Pope replied to Woods, "It's readily movable if you have people who can move it real quick."

"Really?" Woods responded to the revelation quietly.

Then Pope added in an inquiring tone, "But it kind of looks embedded to me."

"It's embedded?" Woods asked as they both stepped back to look.

Pope then decided that the rock was simply lying on the desert floor and was not solidly embedded. He also knew that it was permissible for spectators, caddies, fellow-competitors, essentially anyone to assist in removing a large, loose impediment.

Several men rolled the stone out of Woods' line of play as others watched and cheered. Following the removal, Woods shook each man's hand and then played his shot on a direct line to the green.

Golf's leading players have always enjoyed and suffered the effects of their large galleries. Bob Jones had to be protected by Marines when he completed his Grand Slam at Merion in 1930. Sam Snead, Arnold Palmer and Jack Nicklaus often had errant shots stopped by those who followed them.

In addition situations in which they may have been helped, imagine the number of times those same stars have been distracted by a movement or noise from the spectators, photographers, reporters, and security officers that follow them. It has never been the function of the

Loose impediments are natural objects that come in all shapes and sizes. At the 1999 Phoenix Open, Tiger Woods learned that a player can receive assistance in removing a large loose impediment. Details of the incident can be read above.

Rules of Golf to attempt to equalize such variations.

Almost all Rules have exceptions, many of which are emphasized through placement of the exception at the end of the Rule but some exceptions are provisions within the main text of the Rule.

Rule 23 provides the player with authority for the removal of loose impediments and the opening statement of the Rule reads, "Except when both the loose impediment and the ball lie in or touch the same hazard, any loose impediment may be removed without penalty." However, an important restriction to this permission to remove loose impediments lies in the fourth paragraph of the Rule, "When a ball is in motion, a loose impediment that might influence the movement of the ball must not be removed."

Nearly all players are familiar with the provision in the Rule allowing removal of loose impediments. Some, which in 2011 included PGA Tour player Camilo Villegas, may not be acquainted with that fourth paragraph.

In the 2011 Hyundai Tournament of Champions at Kapalua, HI, Villegas was disqualified for a score card violation stemming from a breach of Rule 23 that a television viewer called in after the opening round.

During the first round of the tournament, Villegas pitched his ball up the steep slope in front of the 15th green but the ball didn't have enough speed to make it to the top and began to roll back in the direction from which he just played. As the ball was in motion, Villegas walked over and with his club casually moved the detached divot that he had just created out of the way of the moving ball. While the divot was clearly a loose impediment, the exception in the Rule prohibits its removal while the ball is in motion if this action might influence the movement of the ball. The penalty for doing so is two strokes in stroke play.

Because Villegas was unaware of the violation, he recorded a score of seven on the par-5 hole and returned his first round score card without including the penalty in his score for the hole. He was disqualified for returning an incorrect score card. Because of addition of the exception to Rule 6-6d in 2016, had this incident occurred in 2016, Villegas would not have been disqualified but rather would have been penalized two strokes for a violation of Rule 23 and an additional two strokes for a breach of Rule 6-6d. (See Rule 6 incidents for other situations where Rule 6-6d might apply).

There are some things to note with respect to this situation. The fact that Villegas was unaware of the Rule is not relevant to his being subject to penalty for the violation. Additionally, his intent in moving the loose impediment is also not relevant as Rule 23 is based on the outcome of his actions, not his intent as is the case with Rule 1-2. Finally, Rule 23 uses the words "might influence the movement of the ball," which means that a determination must be made of the probable effect of the action at the moment the action is taken, not after the movement of the ball is completed. The PGA Tour official responsible for this determination in the Villegas case was Slugger White, vice-president of Rules who said, ""Unfortunately, it was very obvious what he did."

Frequently asked questions

Can I remove sand that lies on the putting green even although my ball lies off the putting green?

Except when the ball lies in a hazard, Rule 23-1 allows the player to remove loose impediments without penalty regardless of where the ball lies. However, as sand and loose soil are loose impediments only when they lie on the putting green, it is the position of the sand and loose soil that is key. Provided the sand or loose soil lie on the putting green, it may be removed.

Can stones in bunkers be removed if they interfere with my play?

Stones are loose impediments and normally cannot be removed if they lie in the same hazard as the ball. However, the Committee may introduce a Local Rule stating that stones in bunkers are movable obstructions. If the Local Rule is introduced, Rule 24-1 applies and players can remove stones in bunkers.

Rule 24 OBSTRUCTIONS

DEFINITIONS

All defined terms are in *italics* and are listed alphabetically in the Definitions section – see pages 10–23.

24-1. Movable Obstruction

A player may take relief, without penalty, from a movable *obstruction* as follows:

a. If the ball does not lie in or on the *obstruction*, the *obstruction* may be removed. If the ball *moves*, it must be replaced, and there is no penalty, provided that the movement of the ball is directly attributable to the removal of the *obstruction*. Otherwise, Rule 18-2 applies.

b. If the ball lies in or on the *obstruction*, the ball may be lifted and the *obstruction* removed. The ball must *through the green* or in a *hazard* be dropped, or on the *putting green* be placed, as near as possible to the spot directly under the place where the ball lay in or on the *obstruction*, but not nearer the *hole*.

    The ball may be cleaned when lifted under this Rule.

    When a ball is in motion, an *obstruction* that might influence the movement of the ball, other than *equipment* of any player or the *flagstick* when attended, removed or held up, must not be moved.

(Exerting influence on ball – see Rule 1-2)

> **NOTE**
>
> If a ball to be dropped or placed under this Rule is not immediately recoverable, another ball may be *substituted*.

MOVABLE OBSTRUCTION

If the ball lies on an obstruction on the putting green, the obstruction may be removed and the ball is then placed on the green under the spot where it was on the obstruction.

BALL AGAINST RAKE MOVES WHEN RAKE REMOVED

If the ball lies against an obstruction, like a rake, it can be moved. If the ball moves, it must be replaced. If it does not move, the ball is played as it lies.

24-2. Immovable Obstruction
a. Interference

Interference by an immovable *obstruction* occurs when a ball lies in or on the *obstruction*, or when the *obstruction* interferes with the player's *stance* or the area of his intended swing. If the player's ball lies on the *putting green*, interference also occurs if an immovable *obstruction* on the *putting green* intervenes on his *line of putt*. Otherwise, intervention on the *line of play* is not, of itself, interference under this Rule.

b. Relief

Except when the ball is in a *water hazard* or a *lateral water hazard*, a player may take relief from interference by an immovable *obstruction* as follows:

(i) Through the Green: If the ball lies *through the green*, the player must lift the ball and drop it, without penalty, within one club-length of and not nearer the *hole* than the *nearest point of relief*. The *nearest point of relief* must not be in a *hazard* or on a *putting green*. When the ball is dropped within one club-length of the *nearest point of relief*, the ball must first strike a part of the *course* at a spot that avoids interference by the immovable *obstruction* and is not in a *hazard* and not on a *putting green*.

(ii) In a Bunker: If the ball is in a *bunker*, the player must lift the ball and drop it either:

    (a) Without penalty, in accordance with Clause (i) above, except that the *nearest point of relief* must be in the *bunker* and the ball must be dropped in the *bunker*; or

    (b) **Under penalty of one stroke**, outside the *bunker* keeping the point where the ball lay directly between the *hole* and the spot on which the ball is dropped, with no limit to how far behind the *bunker* the ball may be dropped.

(iii) On the Putting Green: If the ball lies on the *putting green*, the player must lift the ball and place it, without penalty, at the *nearest point of relief* that is not in a *hazard*. The *nearest point of relief* may be off the *putting green*.

(iv) On the Teeing Ground: If the ball lies on the *teeing ground*, the player must lift the ball and drop it, without penalty, in accordance with Clause (i) above.

    The ball may be cleaned when lifted under this Rule.

(Ball rolling to a position where there is interference by the condition from which relief was taken – see Rule 20-2c(v))

Exception:

A player may not take relief under this Rule if (a) interference by anything other than an immovable *obstruction* makes the *stroke* clearly impracticable or (b) interference by an immovable *obstruction* would occur only through the use of a clearly unreasonable *stroke* or an unnecessarily abnormal *stance*, swing or direction of play.

NOTE 1

If a ball is in a *water hazard* (including a *lateral water hazard*), the player may not take relief from interference by an immovable *obstruction*. The player must play the ball as it lies or proceed under Rule 26-1.

NOTE 2

If a ball to be dropped or placed under this Rule is not immediately recoverable, another ball may be *substituted*.

NOTE 3

The *Committee* may make a Local Rule stating that the player must determine the nearest point of *relief* without crossing over, through or under the *obstruction*.

24-3. Ball in Obstruction Not Found

It is a question of fact whether a ball that has not been found after having been struck toward an *obstruction* is in the *obstruction*. In order to apply this Rule, it must be known or virtually certain that the ball is in the *obstruction*. In the absence of such knowledge or certainty, the player must proceed under Rule 27-1.

FLAGSTICK REMOVED WHEN BALL IN MOTION

When a ball is in motion, it is permissible to move a flagstick that has been removed and that might influence the movement of the ball.

a. Ball in Movable Obstruction Not Found

If it is known or virtually certain that the original ball that has not been found is in a movable *obstruction*, the player may *substitute* another ball and take relief without penalty under this Rule. If he elects to do so, he must remove the *obstruction* and *through the green* or in a *hazard* drop a ball, or on the *putting green* place a ball, as near as possible to the spot directly under the place where the ball last crossed the outermost limits of the movable *obstruction*, but not nearer the hole.

b. Ball in Immovable Obstruction Not Found

If it is known or virtually certain that a ball that has not been found is in an immovable *obstruction*, the player may take relief under this Rule. If he elects to do so, the spot where the ball last crossed the outermost limits of the *obstruction* must be determined and, for the purpose of applying this Rule, the ball is deemed to lie at this spot and the player must proceed as follows:

(i)   Through the Green: If the ball last crossed the outermost limits of the immovable *obstruction* at a spot *through the green*, the player may *substitute* another ball, without penalty, and take relief as prescribed in Rule 24-2b(i).

(ii) In a Bunker: If the ball last crossed the outermost limits of the immovable *obstruction* at a spot in a *bunker*, the player may *substitute* another ball, without penalty, and take relief as prescribed in Rule 24-2b(ii).

(iii) In a Water Hazard (including a Lateral Water Hazard): If the ball last crossed the outermost limits of the immovable *obstruction* at a spot in a *water hazard*, the player is not entitled to relief without penalty. The player must proceed under Rule 26-1.

(iv) On the Putting Green: If the ball last crossed the outermost limits of the immovable *obstruction* at a spot on the *putting green*, the player may *substitute* another ball, without penalty, and take relief as prescribed in Rule 24-2b(iii).

PENALTY FOR BREACH OF RULE:

Match play – Loss of hole; **Stroke play** – Two strokes.

BALL BEHIND IMMOVABLE OBSTRUCTION

If an obstruction intervenes on the line of play, but does not interfere with the lie, area of intended stance or area of intended swing, there is no relief without penalty.

ROADS AND PATHS

Am I entitled to relief without penalty from this road?

Yes. The road is an immovable obstruction, but your nearest point of relief will be in the bushes. You can, of course, play it as it lies.

Direction of play

DETERMINING NEAREST POINT OF RELIEF FROM IMMOVABLE OBSTRUCTION

I have interference from these steps, which are an immovable obstruction, the nearest point of relief appears to be outside the bunker, is that correct?

No. You are entitled to relief but your nearest point of relief must be in the bunker and the ball must be dropped in the bunker. Alternatively, you may drop out of the bunker under penalty of one stroke, keeping the point where the ball lay directly between the hole and the spot on which the ball is dropped.

RELIEF FOR SIDEWAYS STROKE

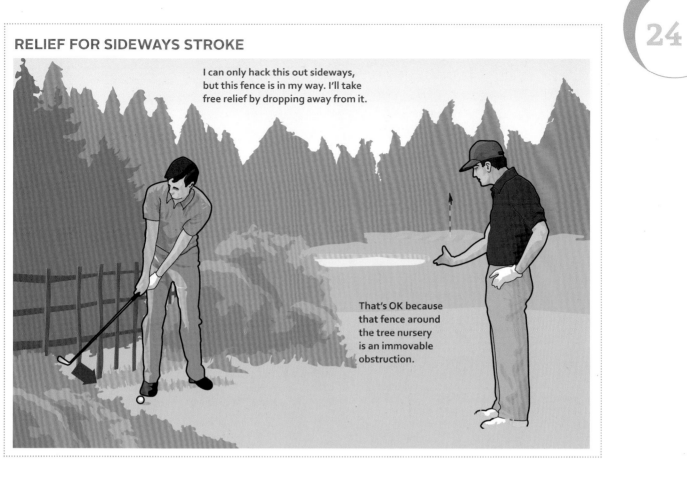

I can only hack this out sideways, but this fence is in my way. I'll take free relief by dropping away from it.

That's OK because that fence around the tree nursery is an immovable obstruction.

RELIEF FROM OBSTRUCTION GIVES RELIEF FOR LINE OF PLAY

Now I've dropped the ball I'm in a far better position. Can I go for the green?

Yes. After dropping the ball, the Rules permit you to play in any direction you wish. Also, the Rules don't distinguish between fairway and rough and it is your good fortune that you can now play past that bush to the green.

NO RELIEF WITHOUT PENALTY IN WATER HAZARD

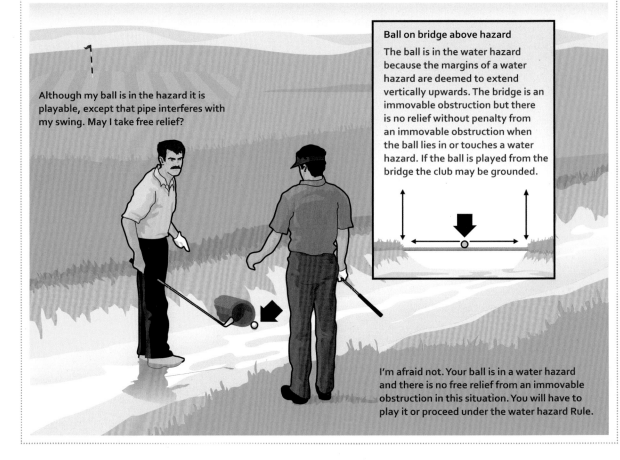

Although my ball is in the hazard it is playable, except that pipe interferes with my swing. May I take free relief?

Ball on bridge above hazard

The ball is in the water hazard because the margins of a water hazard are deemed to extend vertically upwards. The bridge is an immovable obstruction but there is no relief without penalty from an immovable obstruction when the ball lies in or touches a water hazard. If the ball is played from the bridge the club may be grounded.

I'm afraid not. Your ball is in a water hazard and there is no free relief from an immovable obstruction in this situation. You will have to play it or proceed under the water hazard Rule.

RELIEF FROM IMMOVABLE OBSTRUCTION ON PUTTING GREEN

When taking relief from an immovable obstruction on the putting green, the ball is placed at the nearest point of relief.

RULE 24 INCIDENTS

The size of an obstruction does not alter the fact that it is what it is under the Rules. A bottle cap and a building are both obstructions – it's just that one is movable and one is immovable.

The clubhouse behind the 18th green at Pinehurst No. 2 is in-bounds and, therefore, to be treated as an immovable obstruction should a ball find its way to a spot where the building interferes with a player's stance or the area of his intended swing.

During the second round of the 2005 U.S. Open, Nick Jones was playing the 18th hole as his 9th because his group started the round at the 10th tee. Jones's drive finished in the right rough near some pine trees that interfered on a direct line to the flagstick. He decided to play a full shot toward the green and then deal with whatever circumstances resulted – a greenside bunker, the rough or interference from the massive grandstand.

His approach shot went high into the clear morning sky on a direct line to the far right corner of the grandstand located at the left of the green. In the bright sunlight, both Jones and the walking Rules official lost sight of the ball as it approached the seated spectators. A clearly discernible metal noise was then reported followed by laughter and murmuring from the crowd.

Arriving at the grandstand, Jones was informed that his ball had struck a metal railing and rebounded 20 yards or so to a resting position on the flat roof of the clubhouse. Several television cameras were positioned on the roof. It being early in the day, only one cameraman was on duty, but he was able to confirm that Jones's ball was indeed near him and at rest on the roof.

In the heat of the moment, it seemed most logical to Jones to take the relief from the obstruction (the clubhouse) to which he was entitled, get the ball back down on the ground and finish play of the hole. However, another option available to him under the Rules was to play the ball as it lay from its flat, unobstructed position on the roof. In hindsight, this would probably have produced a better score.

However, Jones chose to take relief. The cameraman tossed the ball down from the roof. The relief point from the clubhouse resulted in interference from the grandstand, which was a temporary immovable obstruction. Relief was then determined from that temporary immovable obstruction and Jones put his ball

back in play at a point to the left of the green between the grandstand and a greenside bunker. He took five more strokes to complete the hole for a score of seven.

An obstruction can be declared by the Committee to be an integral part of the golf course. When that has been done, relief is not available under Rule 24. The ball must be played as it lies, and the player must simply deal with it.

The most famous hole in the world derives its name from the road that is an integral part of the golf course and runs beside the putting green. The Road Hole, the penultimate at St. Andrews' Old Course, has been the scene of much demise and success through the years, just as it was on the final afternoon of the 1995 British Open.

Costantino Rocca struggled tenaciously over the closing holes that afternoon in hope of overcoming John Daly. Tied with Daly, Rocca missed an opportunity for birdie at the 16th, and then missed the 17th green with his approach shot. According to the 1995 Open Annual, Rocca's ball "skirted the front of the (17th) green, shot across the road, slammed into the stone wall, then rebounded back onto the road and sat in a small depression."

The depression made it impossible for a lofted club to move under the ball, and Rocca was forced to putt. Putting from asphalt produces inexact results. After being struck with the putter, Rocca's ball popped into the air, "carried over the road, caught a piece of turf that shot it forward, climbed the bank, jumped onto the green and rolled within four feet of the cup (sic)." He holed his putt for par.

At the 18th, following a disastrous pitch, the Italian holed a 60-foot birdie putt from the Valley of Sin to force a play-off with Daly, which Daly ultimately won.

The location of the ball, rather than that of the obstruction, is of primary importance when determining relief from an obstruction. While that may sound perfectly obvious, it is not always, as Nick Dougherty realized at the 2005 Caltex Masters in Singapore.

Dougherty's drive from the 16th tee on the final day was pulled to the left and appeared to have

Because Nick Dougherty's ball was lying just in front of some wooden cross ties that bordered a hazard just outside the bunker, he was instructed to drop the ball within one club-length of his nearest point of relief, under Rule 24-2(i). Read a description of this incident below.

finished in a bunker next to some large, wooden cross ties that bordered the hazard. However, the ball had run through the bunker coming to rest on grass-covered ground just in front of the wooden obstructions.

By definition, such grass-covered ground is not part of a bunker. Therefore, because his ball was lying outside the bunker, Dougherty was entitled to take relief from the obstruction within one club-length of and not nearer the hole than the nearest point of relief – and that point must not be in a hazard or on a putting green.

Had his ball been in the bunker, his options would have been to take relief in the bunker without penalty or, at the cost of one penalty stroke, to drop outside the bunker keeping the point where the ball lay directly between the hole and the spot on which the ball is dropped, with no limit to how far behind the bunker the ball may be dropped.

As can be the case in free relief situations, Dougherty's drop put him in a much more favorable position from which he played to within three feet of the hole. With Colin Montgomerie just one shot back, Dougherty's good fortune allowed him to maintain a one-shot lead and go on to win the tournament.

Frequently asked questions

An immovable obstruction is close to my ball and mentally interferes, but does not otherwise interfere. Do I get relief?

No, relief is only available if the immovable obstruction interferes with your lie, stance or area of intended swing.

May a player move a movable obstruction that does not interfere with the lie of the ball, his area or intended swing or stance?

A movable obstruction (see Definition of "Obstructions") may be moved at any time and from any place without penalty, whether or not the player has interference from the obstruction – see Rule 24-1a.

Rule 25 ABNORMAL GROUND CONDITIONS, EMBEDDED BALL AND WRONG PUTTING GREEN

DEFINITIONS
All defined terms are in *italics* and are listed alphabetically in the Definitions section – see pages 10–23.

25-1. Abnormal Ground Conditions
a. Interference

Interference by an *abnormal ground condition* occurs when a ball lies in or touches the condition or when the condition interferes with the player's *stance* or the area of his intended swing. If the player's ball lies on the *putting green*, interference also occurs if an *abnormal ground condition* on the *putting green* intervenes on his *line of putt*. Otherwise, intervention on the *line of play* is not, of itself, interference under this Rule.

> **NOTE**
>
> The *Committee* may make a Local Rule stating that interference by an *abnormal ground condition* with a player's *stance* is deemed not to be, of itself, interference under this Rule.

b. Relief

Except when the ball is in a *water hazard* or a *lateral water hazard*, a player may take relief from interference by an *abnormal ground condition* as follows:

(i) Through the Green: If the ball lies *through the green*, the player must lift the ball and drop it, without penalty, within one club-length of and not nearer the *hole* than the *nearest point of relief*. The *nearest point of relief* must not be in a *hazard* or on a *putting green*. When the ball is dropped within one club-length of the *nearest point of relief*,

---

GROUND UNDER REPAIR DECLARED BY COMMITTEE

A rut made by a tractor is not ground under repair, but the Committee would be justified in declaring a deep rut to be ground under repair (far left).

A fallen tree still attached to its stump is not ground under repair, but it can be so declared by the Committee (left).

25

RELIEF FROM ABNORMAL GROUND CONDITIONS

The first step in taking relief from an abnormal ground condition (such as casual water) is to find the nearest point of relief. Then, the ball must be dropped within one club-length of that point, no closer to the hole.

the ball must first strike a part of the *course* at a spot that avoids interference by the condition and is not in a *hazard* and not on a *putting green*.

(ii) In a Bunker: If the ball is in a *bunker*, the player must lift the ball and drop it either:

(a) Without penalty, in accordance with Clause (i) above, except that the *nearest point of relief* must be in the *bunker* and the ball must be dropped in the *bunker*, or if complete relief is impossible, as near as possible to the spot where the ball lay, but not nearer the *hole*, on a part of the *course* in the *bunker* that affords maximum available relief from the condition; or

(b) **Under penalty of one stroke**, outside the *bunker*, keeping the point where the ball lay directly between the *hole* and the spot on which the ball is dropped, with no limit to how far behind the *bunker* the ball may be dropped.

(iii) On the Putting Green: If the ball lies on the *putting green*, the player must lift the ball and place it, without penalty, at the *nearest point of relief* that is not in a *hazard*, or if complete relief is impossible, at the nearest position to where it lay that affords maximum available relief from the condition, but not nearer the *hole* and not in a *hazard*. The *nearest point of relief* or maximum available relief may be off the *putting green*.

(iv) On the Teeing Ground: If the ball lies on the *teeing ground*, the player must lift the ball and drop it, without penalty, in accordance with Clause (i) above.

The ball may be cleaned when lifted under Rule 25-1b.

(Ball rolling to a position where there is interference by the condition from which relief was taken – see Rule 20-2c(v))

Exception:

A player may not take relief under this Rule if (a) interference by anything other than an *abnormal ground condition* makes the *stroke* clearly impracticable or (b) interference by an *abnormal ground condition* would occur only through the use of a clearly unreasonable *stroke* or an unnecessarily abnormal *stance*, swing or direction of play.

NOTE 1

If a ball is in a *water hazard* (including a *lateral water hazard*), the player is not entitled to relief without penalty from interference by an *abnormal ground condition*. The player must play the ball as it lies (unless prohibited by Local Rule) or proceed under Rule 26-1.

NOTE 2

If a ball to be dropped or placed under this Rule is not immediately recoverable, another ball may be *substituted*.

c. Ball in Abnormal Ground Condition Not Found

It is a question of fact whether a ball that has not been found after having been struck toward an *abnormal ground condition* is in such a condition. In order to apply this Rule, it must be known or virtually certain that the ball is in the *abnormal ground condition*. In the absence of such knowledge or certainty, the player must proceed under Rule 27-1.

If it is known or virtually certain that a ball that has not been found is in an *abnormal ground condition*, the player may take relief under this Rule. If he elects to do so, the spot where the ball last crossed the outermost limits of the *abnormal ground condition* must be determined and, for the purpose of applying this Rule, the ball is deemed to lie at this spot and the player must proceed as follows:

(i) Through the Green: If the ball last crossed the outermost limits of the *abnormal ground condition* at a spot *through the green*, the player may *substitute* another ball, without penalty, and take relief as prescribed in Rule 25-1b(i).

(ii) In a Bunker: If the ball last crossed the outermost limits of the *abnormal ground condition* at a spot in a *bunker*, the player may *substitute* another ball, without penalty, and take relief as prescribed in Rule 25-1b(ii).

CASUAL WATER ON PUTTING GREEN

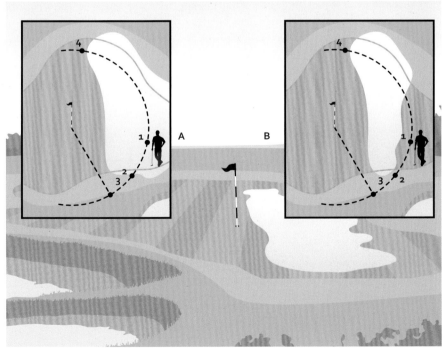

In both illustrations the player's ball lies on the putting green at Point 1. In illustration A his ball is in casual water, while in illustration B casual water intervenes on his line of putt. In either case, if relief is taken, the player must place the ball at Point 3, the "nearest point of relief," even though it is not on the putting green.

BALL CLOSE TO CASUAL WATER: LEFT-HANDED STROKE NOT REASONABLE

No. You always play right-handed and there's no reason for you not to do so here.

If I said I was going to play left-handed, would you give me free relief from the casual water?

BALL CLOSE TO CASUAL WATER: LEFT-HANDED STROKE REASONABLE

A player who can't play a normal right-handed stroke because of a tree may decide to play left-handed, in which case she would be standing in casual water.

Direction of play

She is entitled to relief from the casual water for a left-handed stroke and, having dropped the ball, she may then play right-handed or left-handed.

BALL IN CASUAL WATER IN BUNKER

If the player's ball is in a bunker and she wishes to take relief from casual water without penalty, relief must be taken in the bunker.

EMBEDDED BALL

A ball is considered embedded when it lies in its own pitch-mark and part of the ball is below the level of the ground.

WHEN BALL IS EMBEDDED

Ball embedded – Part of the ball (embedded in its own pitch-mark) is below the level of the ground.

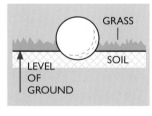

GRASS

LEVEL OF GROUND

SOIL

Ball embedded – Despite the fact that the ball is not touching the soil, part of the ball (embedded in its own pitch-mark) is below the level of the ground.

Ball not embedded – Even when the Local Rule extending relief for an embedded ball to anywhere through the green has been introduced, relief would not be available for the ball in this diagram because, while the ball is sitting down in grass, no part of the ball is below the level of the ground.

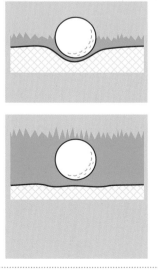

(iii) In a Water Hazard (including a Lateral Water Hazard): If the ball last crossed the outermost limits of the *abnormal ground condition* at a spot in a *water hazard*, the player is not entitled to relief without penalty. The player must proceed under Rule 26-1.

(iv) On the Putting Green: If the ball last crossed the outermost limits of the *abnormal ground condition* at a spot on the *putting green*, the player may *substitute* another ball, without penalty, and take relief as prescribed in Rule 25-1b(iii).

25-2. Embedded Ball

If a player's ball is embedded in any closely-mown area *through the green*, it may be lifted, cleaned and dropped, without penalty, as near as possible to the spot where it lay but not nearer the hole. The ball when dropped must first strike a part of the *course through the green*.

NOTE 1
A ball is "embedded" when it is in its own pitch-mark and part of the ball is below the level of the ground. A ball does not necessarily have to touch the soil to be embedded (e.g. grass, *loose impediments* and the like may intervene between the ball and the soil).

NOTE 2
"Closely-mown area" means any area of the course, including paths through the rough, cut to fairway height or less.

NOTE 3

The *Committee* may adopt the Local Rule as provided for in Appendix I allowing a player relief, without penalty, for a ball embedded anywhere *through the green*.

25-3. Wrong Putting Green
a. Interference

Interference by a *wrong putting green* occurs when a ball is on the *wrong putting green*.

Interference to a player's *stance* or the area of his intended swing is not, of itself, interference under this Rule.

b. Relief

If a player's ball lies on a *wrong putting green* he must not play the ball as it lies. He must take relief, without penalty, as follows:

The player must lift the ball and drop it within one club-length of and not nearer the *hole* than the *nearest point of relief*. The *nearest point of relief* must not be in a *hazard* or on a *putting green*. When dropping the ball within one club-length of the *nearest point of relief*, the ball must first strike a part of the *course* at a spot that avoids interference by the *wrong putting green* and is not in a *hazard* and not on a *putting green*. The ball may be cleaned when lifted under this Rule.

PENALTY FOR BREACH OF RULE:
Match play – Loss of hole; **Stroke play** – Two strokes.

RELIEF FROM A WRONG PUTTING GREEN

I am going to be standing on this wrong putting green to play my stroke. Must I take relief?

No. Relief must be taken if your ball lies on a wrong putting green, but relief is not available for interference to your stance.

STANCE INTERFERED WITH BY BURROWING ANIMAL HOLE: BALL UNPLAYABLE BECAUSE OF OTHER CONDITION

My ball is clearly unplayable in the roots of this tree. Can I take free relief because I would have to stand on the burrowing animal hole if I was able to play it?

No. I am afraid you are not entitled to take a free drop because it is clearly impracticable for you to play a stroke at your ball.

RULE 25 INCIDENTS

During the second round of the 2014 Barclays at Ridgewood C.C. in Paramus, New Jersey, Seung-Yul Noh was playing the 11th hole when he struck his tee shot and it came to rest on the 3rd putting green (a wrong putting green).

Rule 25-3 prohibits play from a wrong putting green to protect greens from being damaged in cases like this one. Unfortunately for Noh, he played his next stroke from the wrong putting green before being made aware of the infraction. As a result, he was penalized two strokes.

Asked later on about whether the violation was covered by a Local Rule, Brad Fabel, a PGA Tour rules official and former Tour player, confirmed that it was a Rule of golf.

Slugger White, PGA Tour Vice President of Rules and Competition, was equally astonished, saying "I've been out here 33 years. We have never seen this happen."

Frequently asked question

A player steps all around his ball to force up water on the surface. He then claims his ball lies in casual water. What is the ruling?

Casual water does not exist in this case. The Definition of "Casual Water" states that it is water that is visible before or after the player takes his stance.

Rule 26 WATER HAZARDS (INCLUDING LATERAL WATER HAZARDS)

DEFINITIONS
All defined terms are in *italics* and are listed alphabetically in the Definitions section – see pages 10–23.

26-1. Relief for Ball in Water Hazard

It is a question of fact whether a ball that has not been found after having been struck toward a *water hazard* is in the *hazard*. In the absence of knowledge or virtual certainty that a ball struck toward a *water hazard*, but not found, is in the *hazard*, the player must proceed under Rule 27-1.

If the ball is found in the *water hazard* or if it is known or virtually certain that a ball that has not been found is in the *water hazard* (whether the ball lies in water or not), the player may **under penalty of one stroke**:

a. Proceed under the stroke and distance provision of Rule 27-1 by playing a ball as nearly as possible at the spot from which the original ball was last played (see Rule 20-5); or

b. Drop a ball behind the *water hazard*, keeping the point at which the original ball last crossed the margin of the *water hazard* directly between the *hole* and the spot on which the ball is dropped, with no limit to how far behind the *water hazard* the ball may be dropped; or

c. As additional options available only if the ball last crossed the margin of a *lateral water hazard*, drop a ball outside the *water hazard* within two club-lengths of and not nearer the *hole* than (i) the point where the original ball last crossed the margin of the *water hazard* or (ii) a point on the opposite margin of the *water hazard* equidistant from the *hole*.

When proceeding under this Rule, the player may lift and clean his ball or *substitute* a ball.

(Prohibited actions when ball is in hazard — see Rule 13-4)

(Ball moving in water in a water hazard — see Rule 14-6)

RULE 26-1. RELIEF FOR BALL IN WATER HAZARD

Jean Van de Velde's difficulty with the Barry Burn at the 72nd hole of the 1999 British Open resulted in a three-way play-off for the championship. See the details of his unfortunate brush with Rule 26-1 in the incident on pages 137–138.

KNOWLEDGE OR VIRTUAL CERTAINTY BALL IN WATER HAZARD

It cannot be assumed that a ball is in a water hazard because there is a possibility that the ball is in the water hazard. Without knowledge or virtual certainty that a player's ball lies in a water hazard, he must proceed under stroke and distance (Rule 27-1).

26-2. Ball Played Within Water Hazard
a. Ball Comes to Rest in Same or Another Water Hazard

If a ball played from within a *water hazard* comes to rest in the same or another *water hazard* after the stroke, the player may:

(i) **under penalty of one stroke**, play a ball as nearly as possible at the spot from which the last stroke from outside a *water hazard* was made (see Rule 20-5); or

(ii) proceed under Rule 26-1a, 26-1b or, if applicable, 26-1c, incurring the **penalty of one stroke under that Rule**. For purposes of applying Rule 26-1b or 26-1c, the reference point is the point where the original ball last crossed the margin of the *hazard* in which it lies.

NOTE

If the player proceeds under Rule 26-1a by dropping a ball in the *hazard* as near as possible to the spot from which the original ball was last played, but elects not to play the dropped ball, he may then proceed under Clause (i) above, Rule 26-1b or, if applicable, Rule 26-1c. If he does so, **he incurs a total of two *penalty strokes*:** the penalty of one stroke for proceeding under Rule 26-1a, and an additional penalty of one stroke for then proceeding under Clause (i) above, Rule 26-1b or Rule 26-1c.

b. Ball Lost or Unplayable Outside Hazard or Out of Bounds

If a ball played from within a *water hazard* is lost or deemed unplayable outside the *hazard* or is *out of bounds*, the player may, after taking a **penalty of one stroke under Rule 27-1 or 28a**, play a ball as nearly as possible at the spot in the *hazard* from which the original ball was last played (see Rule 20-5).

If the player elects not to play a ball from that spot, he may:

(i) **add an additional penalty of one stroke** (making a total of two *penalty strokes*) and play a ball as nearly as possible at the spot from which the last stroke from outside a *water hazard* was made (see Rule 20-5); or

(ii) proceed under Rule 26-1b or, if applicable, Rule 26-1c, **adding the additional penalty of one stroke** prescribed by the Rule (making a total of two *penalty strokes*) and using as the reference point the point where the original ball last crossed the margin of the

hazard before it came to rest in the *hazard*.

NOTE 1

When proceeding under Rule 26-2b, the player is not required to drop a ball under Rule 27-1 or 28a. If he does drop a ball, he is not required to play it. He may alternatively proceed under Clause (i) or (ii) above. If he does so, **he incurs a total of two penalty strokes**: the penalty of one stroke under Rule 27-1 or 28a, and an additional penalty of one stroke for then proceeding under Clause (i) or (ii) above.

NOTE 2

If a ball played from within a *water hazard* is deemed unplayable outside the *hazard*, nothing in Rule 26-2b precludes the player from proceeding under Rule 28b or c.

PENALTY FOR BREACH OF RULE:

Match play – Loss of hole; **Stroke play** – Two strokes.

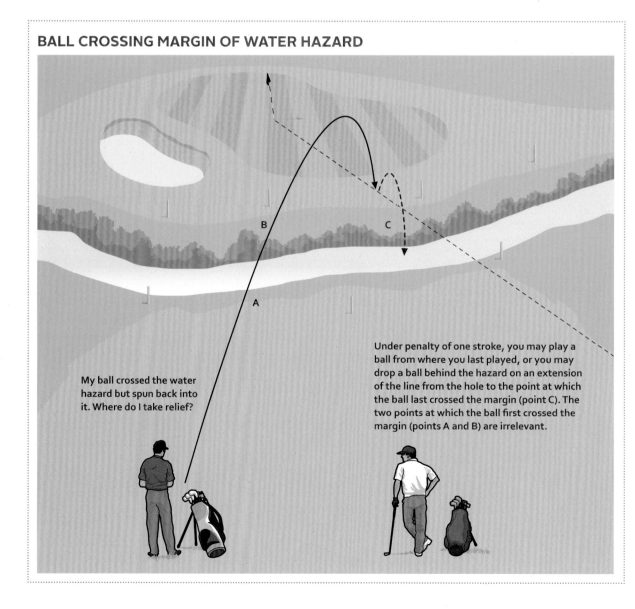

BALL CROSSING MARGIN OF WATER HAZARD

My ball crossed the water hazard but spun back into it. Where do I take relief?

Under penalty of one stroke, you may play a ball from where you last played, or you may drop a ball behind the hazard on an extension of the line from the hole to the point at which the ball last crossed the margin (point C). The two points at which the ball first crossed the margin (points A and B) are irrelevant.

RELIEF FROM LATERAL WATER HAZARD

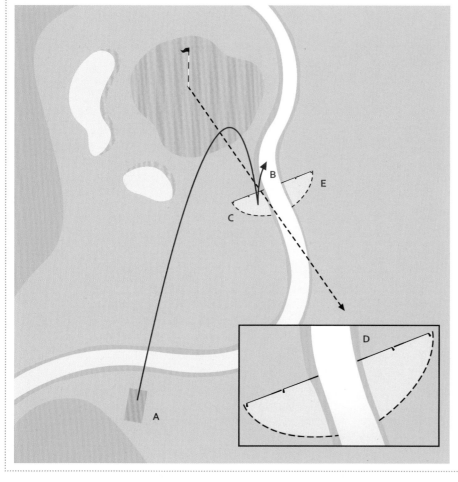

The player has played a ball from the teeing ground (Point A) into the lateral water hazard at Point B. It last crossed the margin of the hazard at Point C and the point on the opposite margin, equidistant from the hole is Point E. He may play the ball as it lies or, under penalty of one stroke; (i) play another ball from the tee – Rule 26-1a; (ii) drop a ball anywhere on the far side of the hazard on the dotted line from the hole through Point C, e.g., Line D – Rule 26-1b; (iii) drop a ball in the area on the near side of the hazard which is all ground within two club-lengths of Point C – Rule 26-1c(i); or (iv) drop a ball in the area on the far side of the hazard which is all ground within two club-lengths of Point E – Rule 26-1c(ii).

BALL PLAYED FROM WITHIN WATER HAZARD

If this player fails to get his ball out of the water hazard, he has several options (i) play the ball as it lies or, under penalty of one stroke: (ii) drop a ball at the spot where he last played; (iii) drop a ball behind the hazard, using the point where it last crossed the hazard margin as the reference point; or (iv) play again from the last place he played outside the hazard.

Rule 26 Incidents

During the first round of the 2005 Masters Tournament, Tiger Woods used his options under Rule 26 to their logical advantage after putting into Rae's Creek at Augusta National's 13th hole.

The lightning-fast speed of the green helped to propel Woods' ball past the hole and down the closely mown bank of the creek that runs immediately in front of the green. Woods was completely aware of his available options which were, firstly without penalty, to play his ball from where it lay in the hazard; or secondly for a one-stroke penalty, to drop his ball on the fairway side of the creek and pitch back to the green; or thirdly for a one-stroke penalty, to play again from where he last played.

Woods chose to play again from where he last played, i.e., to putt again. To comply with Rule 20-5, Woods was required to place his ball on the putting green, rather than drop it. He also used his option under Rule 26 to substitute a ball rather than retrieving the ball he had played into the hazard. Putting again was by far his best option. Woods went on to win three days later.

One of the most remorseful Rules incidents of the past decade involved Jean Van de Velde playing the 72nd hole of the 1999 British Open. The Frenchman needed only a double bogey at Carnoustie's home hole to become the first from his country to win the championship since 1907.

A short time after playing from the tee, he was standing in the Barry Burn, his navy blue trousers rolled to his knees, contemplating his fate and his options under Rule 26.

Having played a driver from the 18th tee, Van de Velde's ball finished well right but safely on a peninsula created by a bend in the burn. Instead of laying up with his second, the Frenchman attempted to play a 2-iron to the distant green. His shot was a bit wayward, and it ricocheted off a grandstand railing, a stone wall and finally settled behind the second crossing of the burn into some heavy rough.

Attempting to chop his ball out of the rough and over the burn, Van de Velde instead chunked it badly, and the ball finished in the shallow water of the burn. As the stream flows perpendicular to the line of play, it was marked with a yellow line indicating a water hazard – not the red line of a lateral water hazard.

He had three options: He could play the ball without penalty as it lay. For a one-stroke penalty, he could play again from where he last played, or he could drop behind the hazard keeping the point at which his ball last crossed the margin of the hazard directly between the hole and the spot on which the ball would be dropped, with no limit to how far behind the hazard he might want to go.

Three in the water, Van de Velde needed a six to win the British Open. He contemplated avoiding a penalty stroke by playing the ball from the water. To assess his chances, he decided to step into the water to see what the shot required. Having removed his shoes and socks, Van de Velde rolled up his trouser legs and lowered himself down the stone wall and into the water.

There he stood in the dark water, wedge in hand, assessing his ability to play the submerged ball out of the hazard. After several minutes, discretion became the better part of valor and the Frenchman chose option b under Rule 26-1. He dropped a ball behind the hazard on the stipulated line, suffered a penalty stroke and played his fifth shot to the right greenside bunker. His up-and-down from the bunker resulted in a score of seven, as well as a play-off between Paul Lawrie, Justin Leonard and Van de Velde, which Lawrie won.

During the 2010 U.S. Open at Pebble Beach, the meaning of the term "virtual certainty" came into play on the short dog-leg par-4 3rd hole, when Dustin Johnson tried to cut the corner of the dog-leg with his tee shot. His ball sailed far to the left and disappeared in the direction of a grove of trees, consisting of long grass, undergrowth and a small lateral water hazard. No one saw exactly where the ball had come to rest, either in the water hazard or any other area.

After a five-minute search, Johnson's ball was not found. At this point he did not have knowledge or virtual certainty that his ball was in the water hazard. It is a question of fact whether a ball that has not been found after having been struck toward a water hazard is in the hazard. In order to apply Rule 26-1, it must be known or virtually certain that the ball is in the hazard. Johnson's only option was to proceed under the lost ball Rule (Rule 27-1).

Shortly after Johnson began his return to the tee to play under a penalty of stroke and distance, his original ball was found. He could not play the original ball since after a five-minute search his ball was lost according to the definition of lost ball.

Given the nature of the 3rd hole, it was not possible for Dustin Johnson to establish virtual certainty that his tee shot was in the lateral water hazard. Therefore, following a five-minute search, Dustin Johnson had to proceed under penalty of stroke and distance and return to the tee for a lost ball.

Frequently asked questions

The ball landed on the putting green side of a pond (marked as a yellow water hazard) in front of the green, but rolled back in. Where does the player drop?

Under penalty of one stroke, the player may play a ball as nearly as possible to where the original ball was last played (Rule 26-1a, i.e., stroke and distance) or drop a ball behind the hazard keeping the point where the ball last crossed the margin of the hazard between him and the hole (Rule 26-1b). Under this option, the ball must be dropped behind the water hazard; not on the green side of the hazard. Decision 26-1/1.5 illustrates the options under Rule 26-1b. The player cannot drop a ball within two club lengths of where the ball last crossed the hazard margin. This option is only available for a lateral water hazard (red stakes or lines).

Can I drop on the "line of flight" when using option b of the water hazard Rule?

No. Under the Rules of Golf, dropping the ball on the "line of flight" is never an option, however, it is often confused with the concept provided in Rule 26-1b. The reference points when using Rule 26-1b are the flagstick and the point where the ball last crossed the margin of the water hazard. Point D in Decision 26-1/15 provides a nice illustration of this option.

Rule 27 BALL LOST OR OUT OF BOUNDS; PROVISIONAL BALL

DEFINITIONS
All defined terms are in *italics* and are listed alphabetically in the Definitions section – see pages 10–23.

27-1. Stroke and Distance; Ball Out of Bounds; Ball Not Found Within Five Minutes

a. Proceeding Under Stroke and Distance

At any time, a player may, **under penalty of one stroke**, play a ball as nearly as possible at the spot from which the original ball was last played (see Rule 20-5), i.e., proceed under penalty of stroke and distance.

Except as otherwise provided in the *Rules*, if a player makes a *stroke* at a ball from the spot at which the original ball was last played, he is deemed to have proceeded **under penalty of stroke and distance**.

b. Ball Out of Bounds

If a ball is *out of bounds*, the player must play a ball, **under penalty of one stroke**, as nearly as possible at the spot from which the original ball was last played (see Rule 20-5).

c. Ball Not found Within Five Minutes

If a ball is *lost* as a result of not being found or identified as his by the player within five minutes after the player's *side* or his or their *caddies* have begun to search for it, the player must play a ball, **under penalty of one stroke**, as nearly as possible at the spot from which the original ball was last played (see Rule 20-5).

PLAYERS UNABLE TO IDENTIFY THEIR BALLS

My ball is a number 3 with black writing.

So is mine. Unless we can identify which is which, both balls are "lost."

Exception:

If it is known or virtually certain that the original ball, that has not been found, has been *moved* by an *outside agency* (Rule 18-1), is in an *obstruction* (Rule 24-3), is in an *abnormal ground condition* (Rule 25-1), or is in a *water hazard* (Rule 26-1), the player may proceed under the applicable *Rule*.

PENALTY FOR BREACH OF RULE 27-1:
Match play – Loss of hole; **Stroke play** – Two strokes.

27-2. Provisional Ball
a. Procedure

If a ball may be lost outside a *water hazard* or may be *out of bounds*, to save time the player may play another ball provisionally in accordance with Rule 27-1. The player must:

(i)   announce to his *opponent* in match play or his *marker* or a *fellow-competitor* in stroke play that he intends to play a *provisional ball*; and

(ii) play the *provisional ball* before he or his *partner* goes forward to search for the original ball.

If a player fails to meet the above requirements prior to playing another ball, that ball is not a *provisional ball* and becomes the *ball in play* under penalty of stroke and distance (Rule 27-1); the original ball is *lost*.

(Order of play from teeing ground – see Rule 10-3)

BALL NOT FOUND WITHIN FIVE MINUTES

A player may receive help in searching for his ball, but if it is not found or identified within 5 minutes of his side or any caddie of the side starting to search, he must play under stroke and distance.

NOTE

If a provisional ball *played under Rule 27-2a might be* lost *outside a* water hazard *or* out of bounds, *the player may play another* provisional ball. *If another* provisional ball *is played, it bears the same relationship to the previous* provisional ball *as the first* provisional ball *bears to the original ball.*

b. When Provisional Ball Becomes Ball in Play

The player may play a *provisional ball* until he reaches the place where the original ball is likely to be. If he makes a *stroke* with the *provisional ball* from the place where the original ball is likely to be or from a point nearer the *hole* than that place, the original ball is *lost* and the *provisional ball* becomes the *ball in play* **under penalty of stroke and distance** (Rule 27-1).

If the original ball is *lost* outside a *water hazard* or is *out of bounds*, the *provisional ball* becomes the *ball in play*, u**nder penalty of stroke and distance** (Rule 27-1).

Exception:

If it is known or virtually certain that the original ball, that has not been found, has been *moved* by an *outside agency* (Rule 18-1), or is in an *obstruction* (Rule 24-3) or an *abnormal ground condition* (Rule 25-1c), the player may proceed under the applicable *Rule*.

c. When Provisional Ball to Be Abandoned

If the original ball is neither *lost* nor *out of bounds*, the player must abandon the *provisional ball* and continue playing the original ball. If it is known or virtually certain that the original ball is in a *water hazard*, the player may proceed in accordance with Rule 26-1. In either situation, if the player makes any further *strokes* at the *provisional ball*, he is playing a *wrong ball* and the provisions of Rule 15-3 apply.

NOTE

If a player plays a provisional ball *under Rule 27-2a, the* strokes *made after this Rule has been invoked with a* provisional ball *subsequently abandoned under Rule 27-2c and penalties incurred solely by playing that ball are disregarded.*

PROVISIONAL BALL PLAYED: ORIGINAL BALL FOUND UNPLAYABLE

A player plays a provisional ball as his ball may be lost. The original ball is found within five minutes and before the provisional ball has become the ball in play, but the ball is unplayable. The player must abandon the provisional ball and proceed with the original ball.

PROVISIONAL BALL BECOMES BALL IN PLAY

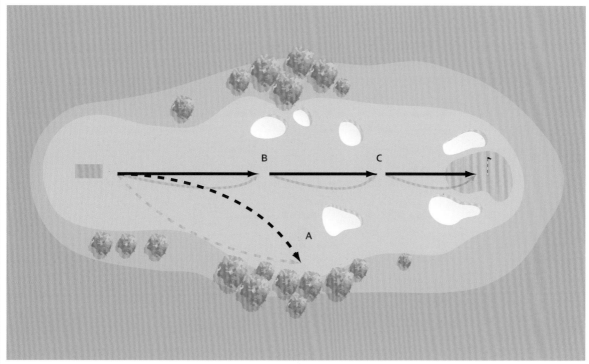

The player has played from the tee and his ball may be lost at A. He plays a provisional ball to B and then from B to C. The player decides not to look for his original ball at A and plays his provisional ball from C to the green. Consequently, the provisional ball becomes the ball in play, under penalty of stroke and distance and the original ball is by definition lost. This is because the player has played a stroke with the provisional ball from a point nearer the hole than the place where the original ball is likely to be.

RULE 27 INCIDENTS

While the Rules allot five minutes of time to search for a lost ball, sometimes it is to a player's advantage not to find his original ball. Phil Mickelson would have been at a distinct advantage had a diligent gallery marshal not found his ball during the third play-off hole of the 2001 Buick Invitational at Torrey Pines.

From the tee, first Mickelson and then Frank Lickliter played their drives into a rough canyon to the left of the 17th hole. Each then played a provisional ball in case his original ball turned out to be lost in the canyon.

Lickliter's first ball was soon found, requiring him to abandon his provisional ball in the fairway (Rule 27-2c). After inspecting his lie, he decided that his best course of action was to deem his ball unplayable and replay from the tee, as was his option under the unplayable ball Rule (Rule 28).

Watching the events unfold and preferring his chances lying three in the fairway with his provisional ball, Mickelson asked that the search stop for his original ball in the canyon. "Don't find it," directed Mickleson.

"I don't want to find it." He clearly understood that under the Rules a ball couldn't be declared lost.

A well-intended marshal in the canyon never heard Mickelson's request, continued his search, and was successful in finding Mickelson's original ball. Fuming at the turn of events, Mickelson could be heard to say, "Did I not ask him to get out of there?"

The marshal informed Mickelson that his ball was found, even though Mickelson preferred to continue play with this provisional ball. Mickelson was obligated to have a look at the found ball and, by Rule 27-2c, if the found ball was his original, abandon his provisional ball and continue play with the original.

Because Mickelson's provisional ball was nearer the hole than his original ball was likely to be, had Mickelson made a stroke with this provisional ball before his original ball was found, the provisional ball would have become the ball in play. It would not have mattered if his original were subsequently found.

However, with his original ball found, Mickelson was required to deal with its circumstances just as Lickliter had been required to deal with his. Both players' troublesome drives were found, both players' provisional balls had to be abandoned, both deemed their original balls unplayable and both returned to the tee to play their third stroke.

Mickelson, the defending champion, ultimately won with a double-bogey six.

During the third round of the 1998 British Open at Royal Birkdale, Mark O'Meara's second shot drifted too far to the right into knee-high grass and scrub trees at the 480-yard 6th hole.

By the time O'Meara and his caddie reached the area where they thought his ball had finished, a number of spectators were already engaged in searching for it. The Rules observer with the group was Reed Mackenzie, then vice-president of the USGA and chairman of the association's Rules of Golf Committee. When O'Meara arrived on the scene, Mackenzie started timing the five-minute search period allowed under the Rules.

To everyone in the immediate area of the search, O'Meara announced the type of ball he was playing and stated that it was embossed with his logo. Several balls were found, but none were his.

After searching for approximately four minutes, O'Meara suspected that his ball was lost, left the search area, took another ball from his caddie and started back down the fairway to play again from where his original ball had last been played.

About 30 seconds later, a spectator announced, "Here it is! I have it." Someone called to O'Meara, who did not hear and continued walking. An official went to where the spectator had found the ball and saw that it was the type O'Meara was using and did have his logo on it.

By this time, it was nearing the end of the five-minute search period, and it was clear that O'Meara

would not be able to get back to the ball in order to identify it within the five-minute period. The Definition of "Lost Ball" states that a ball is lost if it is not "found **or** identified" within the five-minute search. If the Definition stated, "found **and** identified," the procedure would have been clear. A radio call was made for a roving Rules official to make a decision.

Mike Shea, at that time the senior Rules director of the PGA Tour in the U.S., was working in the area and took the call. David Rickman, Rules secretary for The R&A, was also on hand. Shea arrived first and brought O'Meara in a cart to discuss the situation with Rickman. Rickman was advised that the ball had been found, but not identified by the player, within the five-minute time limit. Considering the facts, Rickman determined that the ball had been found within the five-minute search period, that O'Meara was entitled to identify it outside the stipulated five-minute period and, if it was his ball, be was entitled to play it without penalty. Everyone returned to the area where the ball had been found.

However, during search, the area had become trampled, and a misguided spectator, believing the ball had been abandoned, had lifted it.

O'Meara and Rickman went to the spot, the ball was not there, but the spectator was close by and returned the ball to O'Meara, who identified it as his. Although the spectator said he knew exactly where the ball had been before he lifted it, his pinpointing turned out to be only an approximation.

Under Rules 18-1 and 20-3c, O'Meara was therefore required to drop as near as possible to the spot where the ball had been before the spectator lifted it. When O'Meara dropped the ball, it then rolled more than two club-lengths from the spot where it struck a part of the course thus requiring a re-drop. Upon re-dropping, the ball rolled nearer the hole. Therefore, O'Meara placed it on the spot where it first struck a part of the course when re-dropped. He then played his shot and continued the round, winning the championship the following day.

If a ball is found within five minutes, the player is allowed enough time to reach the area and identify it even though the identification takes place after the five-minute search period has elapsed.

As fate would have it, a month before O'Meara's predicament, Lee Janzen was in a similar circumstance during the final round of the 1998 U.S. Open. From the 5th tee at Olympic in San Francisco, Janzen's drive came to rest in a tree. After discussing the situation with marshals

Mark O'Meara returns to identify a ball found within the five-minute search period during the 1998 Championship.

in the area, Janzen assumed his ball remained up in the tree and was, therefore, lost. He headed back to the tee to put another ball into play (Rule 27).

Before a second ball could be played, Janzen's first ball fell from the tree and was identified by his caddie. Janzen was called back, and he identified the ball as his. All this took place within the five-minute search period and, therefore, there was no question that Janzen's ball was in play and no penalty was incurred.

Janzen's ball falling from the tree was propitious, as he went on to record a 68 for the day, which resulted in a one-stroke win over Payne Stewart and his second U.S. Open victory in six starts.

Frequently asked questions

After going forward to search in the area where his ball is likely located, may a player return to where he last played in order to play a provisional ball?

No. If the player played another ball at this point, it would become his ball in play and the original ball would be lost (See Rule 27-2a and Definition of "Lost Ball"). A provisional ball must be played "before going forward to search" as the principle of the provisional ball Rule is saving time.

A player hit his tee shot into deep woods. He correctly played a provisional ball to the fairway. Before reaching the provisional ball the player finds the original ball lying against the base of a tree. Can the player still continue with the provisional ball?

No. Once the original ball is found the provisional ball must be abandoned (Rule 27-2c) and the player must continue play with the original ball or declare it unplayable (Rule 28). If the ball is declared unplayable and the player chooses to play under stroke and distance (Rule 28a) he must return to the tee and play again from there.

Rule 28 BALL UNPLAYABLE

DEFINITIONS

All defined terms are in *italics* and are listed alphabetically in the Definitions section – see pages 10–23.

The player may deem his ball unplayable at any place on the *course*, except when the ball is in a *water hazard*. The player is the sole judge as to whether his ball is unplayable.

If the player deems his ball to be unplayable, he must, **under penalty of one stroke**:

a. Proceed under the stroke and distance provision of Rule 27-1 by playing a ball as nearly as possible at the spot from which the original ball was last played (see Rule 20-5); or

b. Drop a ball behind the point where the ball lay, keeping that point directly between the *hole* and the spot on which the ball is dropped, with no limit to how far behind that point the ball may be dropped; or

c. Drop a ball within two club-lengths of the spot where the ball lay, but not nearer the *hole*.

If the unplayable ball is in a *bunker*, the player may proceed under Clause a, b or c. If he elects to proceed under Clause b or c, a ball must be dropped in the *bunker*.

When proceeding under this Rule, the player may lift and clean his ball or *substitute* a ball.

PENALTY FOR BREACH OF RULE:

Match play – Loss of hole; **Stroke play** – Two strokes.

OTHER FORMS OF PLAY

BALL UNPLAYABLE IN BUSH: PLACE FOR DROPPING

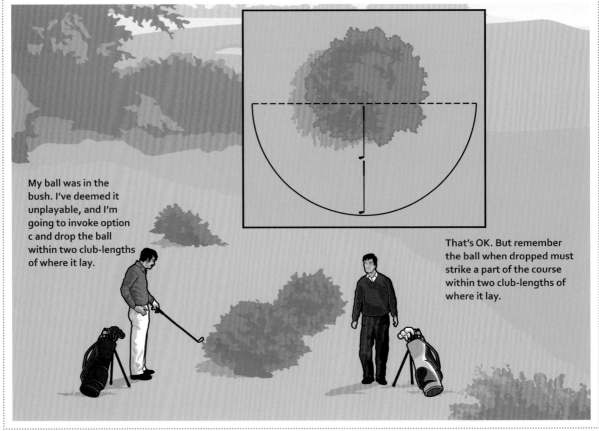

My ball was in the bush. I've deemed it unplayable, and I'm going to invoke option c and drop the ball within two club-lengths of where it lay.

That's OK. But remember the ball when dropped must strike a part of the course within two club-lengths of where it lay.

BALL UNPLAYABLE IN BUNKER: PLAYER'S OPTIONS

The player's tee shot comes to rest in a bunker, in an unplayable position. Under penalty of one stroke, she may: (a) play again from where she last played (i.e., the tee); or (b) drop a ball in the bunker behind the point where the ball lay (point 1), keeping that point directly between the hole and the spot on which the ball is dropped (i.e., line 1–2); or (c) drop a ball in the bunker within two club-lengths of where her ball lay (point 1), but not nearer the hole (i.e., the indicated area).

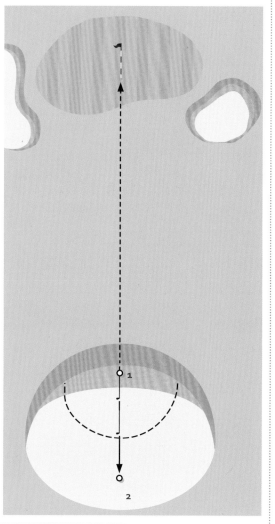

RULE 28 INCIDENTS

It is the responsibility of every player to know the Rules, and it is incumbent upon the Committee to enforce them. In stroke play, the Committee's primary responsibility is the protection of the entire field. This responsibility lasts throughout all rounds of the competition. If there is an infraction in the first round that does not come to light until play of the fourth round, the Committee is authorized to respond retroactively. This ensures the correctness of the entire competition.

An unplayable ball (Rule 28) also requires proper adherence to dropping procedures (Rule 20). While the penalty for an unplayable ball is one stroke, the violation

for an improper drop that results in playing from a wrong place results in a penalty of two strokes.

During the third round of the 2005 Samsung World Championship, Michelle Wie's ball came to rest in a bush during play of the 7th hole. She deemed her ball unplayable and selected the option that required her to drop within two club-lengths of the spot on the ground immediately below the position of the ball in the bush, no nearer the hole. Wie dropped the ball, made a stroke, finished the round and returned her score card.

The following day, the Committee became aware

Michelle Wie plays from a wrong place after dropping improperly from an unplayable lie. Unaware of the two-stroke penalty for her infraction, she failed to include it in her third round score and was ultimately disqualified for returning a score lower than she actually made.

that Wie might have dropped improperly and, therefore, played from a wrong place. The Committee prudently sought all sources of information in making its determination. Videotape of the incident was reviewed. Following play of the fourth round and before the close of competition, Wie and her caddie were asked to recreate the drop.

The Committee concluded that Wie had indeed dropped in and played from a wrong place. The penalty for both breaches was three strokes – one for an unplayable ball, and two for playing from a wrong place.

Because she was unaware that she had played from the wrong place, Wie unintentionally and regrettably failed to include the two penalty strokes on her score card for the third round. This was an additional breach (Rule 6-6d) for returning a score for a hole lower than the score actually made. Because the competition was not yet closed, Wie was disqualified but her marker was absolved, as she was unaware that an infraction had taken place.

The Committee is obligated to use all sources and methods in protecting the field for the entire competition. In this way, the propriety of the competition is preserved. Once the competition is closed, unintentional infractions that come to light are not penalized. There is, however, no time limit for penalizing an infraction that a competitor knowingly commits but fails to include in his score.

Because Wie was unaware of her improper drop and the resulting penalty, had the infraction come to light after the close of the competition, the lower score would have stood without penalty (Rule 34-1b).

Because of the addition of the exception to Rule 6-6d in 2016, had this incident occurred in 2016, Wie would not have been disqualified but rather would have been penalized two strokes for a violation of Rule 28 and an additional two strokes for a breach of Rule 6-6d. (See Rule 6 incidents for other situations where Rule 6-6d might apply.)

When is a player permitted to drop a ball within one club-length of a designated spot and when is a player permitted to drop a ball within two club-lengths of a designated spot?

The answer is that there are several Rules addressing these conditions, among which are the obstruction Rule (Rule 24) and the unplayable ball Rule (Rule 28).

Rule 24 calls for dropping a ball within one club-length of and not nearer the hole than the nearest point of relief.

Rule 28 calls for dropping a ball within two club-lengths of the spot where the ball lay, but not nearer the hole.

When proceeding under Rule 24, it would be a violation if the ball were to be dropped and played from a spot two club-lengths from the nearest point of relief. However, it would not be a violation when proceeding under Rule 28, if the player were to drop and play a ball only one club-length from where the original ball lay. Not knowing the difference in the requirements of these two Rules may have consequences. Ian Poulter once unexplainably proceeded in sequence: (i) correctly according to Rule 28 then (ii) incorrectly according to Rule 24 because he measured two club-lengths for the application of each Rule. In the latter case, he played from a wrong place thus incurring a two-stroke penalty.

During the second round of the 2014 Volvo China Open, Poulter sprayed his tee shot on the 13th hole way to the right into a group of heavy trees and bushes beyond a paved cart path. Deeming his ball unplayable, he dropped it to the left and properly two club-lengths from where it lay, the ball coming to rest on the cart path. He then took relief from the obstruction but unfortunately dropped the ball two club-lengths from the nearest point of relief, playing it from there with the resultant two-stroke penalty.

Poulter was quoted as saying, "It was a schoolboy error. I have just made a mistake. We make them and I guess that was a fun one. I took two club-lengths as opposed to one and it's a two shot penalty, which turned a bad six into a really bad eight, so not the best of holes. Sometimes we are a bit thick and that was one of those times. Guess I need to get the Rules book back out. It's the most simple Rule and I had been given it the day before."

Frequently asked questions

May a player declare a ball in a hazard unplayable?

The answer depends on the type of hazard the ball is in. If the ball is in a water hazard, the player may not declare the ball unplayable. He may play the ball as it lies, or proceed under the water hazard Rule (Rule 26-1). If the unplayable ball lies in a bunker, the player may proceed under any of the options listed in Rule 28. However, if he elects option b or c, the ball must be dropped in the bunker.

What is the ruling if I deem my ball unplayable, drop it and it rolls back into the original position or another unplayable position?

As long as the ball did not roll into a position where it must be re-dropped (see Rule 20-2c), you must play the ball as it lies or declare the ball unplayable again, incurring an additional one-stroke penalty.

Rule 29

OTHER FORMS OF PLAY

THREESOMES AND FOURSOMES

DEFINITIONS
All defined terms are in *italics* and are listed alphabetically in the Definitions section – see pages 10–23.

29-1. General

In a *threesome* or a *foursome*, during any *stipulated round* the *partners* must play alternately from the *teeing grounds* and alternately during the play of each hole. *Penalty strokes* do not affect the order of play.

FOURSOMES: ORDER OF PLAY WHEN PARTNER DRIVES OUT OF BOUNDS

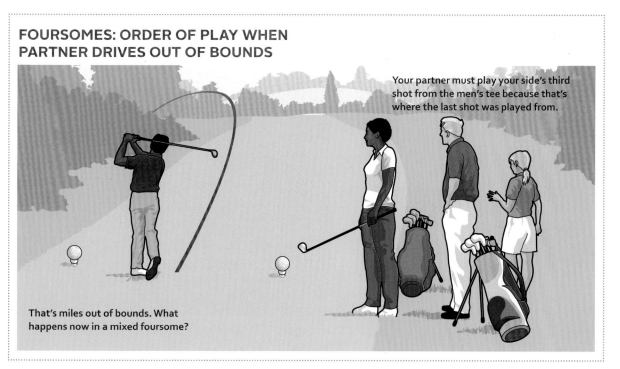

Your partner must play your side's third shot from the men's tee because that's where the last shot was played from.

That's miles out of bounds. What happens now in a mixed foursome?

FOURSOMES: WHICH PARTNER DROPS BALL

We are entitled to free relief from the casual water. Do I drop the ball or do you?

It's my turn to play the next shot so I drop the ball.

See Rule 20-2a which requires a ball to be dropped by the player himself.

ORDER OF PLAY IN FOURSOMES

In foursomes, if player A hits the tee shot out of bounds, player B must play next from the tee.

29-2. Match Play

If a player plays when his *partner* should have played, **his *side* loses the hole**.

29-3. Stroke Play

If the *partners* make a *stroke* or *strokes* in incorrect order, such *stroke* or *strokes* are canceled and **the *side* incurs a penalty of two strokes**. The *side* must correct the error by playing a ball in correct order as nearly as possible at the spot from which it first played in incorrect order (see Rule 20-5). If the *side* makes a *stroke* on the next *teeing ground* without first correcting the error or, in the case of the last hole of the round, leaves the *putting green* without declaring its intention to correct the error, **the *side* is disqualified**.

RULE 29 INCIDENTS

During the 2010 Ryder Cup matches at the Celtic Manor Resort in Newport, Wales, the American foursome of Jim Furyk and Rickie Fowler eventually salvaged a half in their match with Lee Westwood and Martin Kaymer, but an unusual ruling on the 4th hole left the Americans two down at the time.

Furyk had driven left of the fairway into an area of mud and water caused by the heavy rains that plagued the competition from the start. The referee with the match, Simon Higginbottom, declared the area where Furyk's ball lay to be an abnormal ground condition, which entitled the Americans to relief

During foursome play at the 2010 Ryder Cup, Rickie Fowler wrongly substituted a ball when taking relief under Rule 25-1. The error resulted in a loss of hole penalty for the American team in a match that eventually ended in a tie.

without penalty under Rule 25-1. In the alternate shot format of foursome play prescribed by Rule 29-1, it was Fowler's turn to make the next stroke. Additionally, according to Rule 20-2a, it is "the player himself" who must drop the ball, thus, the member of the side whose turn it is to play must drop the ball in foursome competitions.

At this point, Fowler made a costly mistake by not recovering Furyk's ball from the abnormal ground condition, which he easily could have done. Rather, he abandoned Furyk's ball, reached into his pocket, dropped one of his own balls and played it. Rule 25-1 only allows substitution of another ball if the ball to be dropped is not immediately recoverable. Had the error been discovered before the substituted ball had been played, he could have corrected the mistake under Rule 20-6 by recovering Furyk's ball and dropping it. However, having played the substituted ball, the side incurred a loss of hole penalty and the Americans were now two down.

The practice putting green at the Old Course in St. Andrews lies just off the course and a short distance from the 1st tee. Paired together on the second day for the morning foursomes of the 1975 Walker Cup Match, the U.S. side of veteran William C. Campbell and newcomer John Grace reported to the tee a little ahead of their starting time. They had already decided that Grace would drive at the odd-numbered holes, so Campbell decided to use the extra time before the match began to hit a few putts on the practice green – some 50 yards from the 1st tee.

As the visiting team, Campbell and Grace had the honor. The wind was gusting from the west, which carried the announcement of the match's beginning beyond Campbell's earshot.

As the breeze momentarily died, Campbell heard "the click" of Grace's drive just before striking a practice putt, and he was unable to interrupt his practice stroke. Therefore, Campbell had practiced during play of the hole. Instantly and instinctively recognizing his infraction of the Rules, Campbell walked onto the fairway and reported to the referee. The U.S. had just lost the first hole (Rule 7-2).

The referee for the match, John Pasquill, from the Royal and Ancient Golf Club, accepted Campbell's report but made no immediate announcement to the other players. Because play of the hole had ended with the Rules violation and the loss of hole, Campbell was free to play his side's second toward the 1st green. Strokes made in continuing the play of a hole, the result of which has been decided, are not practice strokes.

Walking across the Swilken Burn, Campbell told Grace what had taken place. "He was incredulous, to say the least," Campbell recalls.

The fact that the practice green was off the course, beyond the out-of-bounds markers, gave Grace reason to believe they might have a chance on appeal, though there is no such distinction within the Rules.

Campbell reported to Pasquill that his partner wished to protest the ruling and appeal to the Committee. In a neutral voice, Pasquill appropriately replied, "On the golf course, I am the Committee." Thus, the Americans lost the first hole and eventually the match to Mark James and Richard Eyles.

Frequently asked question

Who plays a provisional ball in foursomes?

If the player makes a stroke and the ball might be out of bounds or lost outside a water hazard, the provisional ball must be played by the partner. For example, if Jack and Jill are playing in a mixed foursome competition, and Jill hits her tee shot towards an area which is out of bounds, Jack must play the provisional ball from the teeing ground where Jill played the original ball..

Rule 30

THREE-BALL, BEST-BALL AND FOUR-BALL MATCH PLAY

DEFINITIONS
All defined terms are in *italics* and are listed alphabetically in the Definitions section – see pages 10–23.

30-1. General

The Rules of Golf, so far as they are not at variance with the following specific Rules, apply to *three-ball*, *best-ball* and *four-ball matches*.

30-2. Three-Ball Match Play
a. Ball at Rest Moved or Purposely Touched by an Opponent

If an *opponent* incurs a *penalty stroke* under Rule 18-3b, that penalty is incurred only in the match with the player whose ball was touched or *moved*. No penalty is incurred in his match with the other player.

b. Ball Deflected or Stopped by an Opponent Accidentally

If a player's ball is accidentally deflected or stopped by an *opponent*, his *caddie* or *equipment*, there is no penalty. In his match with that *opponent* the player may, before another *stroke* is made by either *side*, cancel the *stroke* and play a ball, without penalty, as nearly as possible at the spot from which the original ball was last played (see Rule 20-5) or he may play the ball as it lies. In his match with the other *opponent*, the ball must be played as it lies.

Exception:

Ball striking person attending or holding up *flagstick* or anything carried by him – see Rule 17-3b.
(Ball purposely deflected or stopped by *opponent* – see Rule 1-2)

BREACH OF RULE BY ONE PARTNER IN MATCH PLAY

I'll just remove this twig before playing my ball.

I'm afraid you're disqualified from the hole for removing a loose impediment from the bunker. Fortunately, although I'm in the same bunker, I'm not penalized because your breach of Rule 13-4 did not assist my play.

THREE-BALL MATCH PLAY

John, my ball has struck your bag. What do I do now?

In your match with me, you may either play the ball as it lies or cancel that stroke and replay it. In your match with Jim, you must play your original ball as it lies.

That means I'm going to have two balls in play at the same time.

That's right. Rule 30-2b.

FOUR-BALL MATCH PLAY: ONE PLAYER MAY REPRESENT SIDE

Your partner's late. Are you disqualified or just your partner?

Fortunately, neither of us. Because this is a four-ball match, I am entitled to represent the side. Let's start. My partner is allowed to join us later, between holes.

30-3. Best-Ball and Four-Ball Match Play
a. Representation of Side

A *side* may be represented by one *partner* for all or any part of a match; all *partners* need not be present. An absent *partner* may join a match between holes, but not during play of a hole.

b. Order of Play

Balls belonging to the same *side* may be played in the order the *side* considers best.

c. Wrong Ball

If a player incurs the loss of hole penalty under Rule 15-3a for making a *stroke* at a *wrong ball*, **he is disqualified for that hole**, but his *partner* incurs no penalty even if the *wrong ball* belongs to him. If the *wrong ball* belongs to another player, its owner must place a ball on the spot from which the *wrong ball* was first played.
(Placing and Replacing – see Rule 20-3)

d. Penalty to Side

A *side* is penalized for a breach of any of the following by any *partner*:

- o   Rule 4 – Clubs
- o   Rule 6-4 – Caddie
- o   Any Local Rule or Condition of Competition for which the penalty is an adjustment to the state of the match.

e. Disqualification of Side

(i) **A side is disqualified** if any *partner* incurs a penalty of disqualification under any of the following:

- ○ Rule 1-3 – Agreement to Waive Rules
- ○ Rule 4 – Clubs
- ○ Rule 5-1 or 5-2 – The Ball
- ○ Rule 6-2a – Handicap
- ○ Rule 6-4 – Caddie
- ○ Rule 6-7 – Undue Delay; Slow Play
- ○ Rule 11-1 – Teeing
- ○ Rule 14-3 – Artificial Devices and Unusual Equipment; Abnormal Use of Equipment
- ○ Rule 33-7 – Disqualification Penalty Imposed by Committee

(ii) **A side is disqualified** if all *partners* incur a penalty of disqualification under any of the following:

- ○ Rule 6-3 – Time of Starting and Groups
- ○ Rule 6-8 – Discontinuance of Play

(iii) In all other cases where a breach of a *Rule* would result in disqualification, **the player is disqualified for that hole only**.

f. Effect of Other Penalties

If a player's breach of a *Rule* assists his *partner's* play or adversely affects an *opponent's* play, **the *partner* incurs the applicable penalty in addition to any penalty incurred by the player**.

In all other cases where a player incurs a penalty for breach of a *Rule*, the penalty does not apply to his *partner*. Where the penalty is stated to be loss of hole, **the effect is to disqualify the player for that hole**.

RULE 30 INCIDENTS

The specific Rules governing four-ball match play are practical modifications to the Rules designed to accommodate the form of play. The most commonly applied Rules are: (1) the side may be represented by one partner for all or any part of a match; (2) balls belonging to the same side may be played in the order the side considers best; (3) a side is penalized for a breach of Rule 4, Rule 6-4 and any Local Rule for which the penalty is an adjustment to the state of the match; and (4) if a player's breach of a Rule assists his partner's play or adversely affects an opponent's play, the partner incurs the applicable penalty in addition to any penalty incurred by the player. Where the penalty is stated to be loss of hole in the Rules other than for four-ball match play, the effect is to disqualify the player for that hole.

One of the difficulties in applying the Rules to four-ball match play is sorting out penalties as to who incurs

the penalty and if there is a correction required.

Here are two examples:

Two players (A and B), members of the same side, after striking their shots from the tee of the 1st hole of the match, arrived where their balls had come to rest in the fairway. At this point, player A discovered that he had begun the match with 15 clubs in his bag. The referee who was accompanying the match was asked for a ruling. The referee ruled that player A was in breach of Rule 4-4 for starting with more than 14 clubs and that Rule 30-3d requires that the side is to be penalized for a breach of Rule 4-4, not just player A. The penalty statement for Rule 4-4 requires that at the conclusion of the 1st hole, the state of the match be adjusted by deducting one hole from side A-B. Thus, the match should continue to a conclusion of the 1st hole and then the adjustment will be made. If side A-B should win the hole, then the match will be all square after the adjustment.

Two players (A and B), members of the same side, are searching for the ball of player A. Player B finds a ball in deep rough that is believed to be that of player A, who then chips the ball onto the fairway. It is then discovered that player A has played the ball of player B. The referee who was accompanying the match was asked for a ruling. The referee ruled that Rule 30-3c applies: therefore player A is disqualified for the hole but player B incurs no penalty. Player B must now represent the side alone until the hole is completed.

At the 1st U.S. Amateur Four-Ball Championship conducted in 2015 at The Olympic Club, San Francisco, CA, during the first round of match play, Sam Burns and his partner Austin Connelly ran afoul of the third most commonly applied Rule mentioned above – a side is penalized for a breach of any Local Rule (or Condition of Competition) for which the penalty is an adjustment to the state of the match (Rule 30-3d).

After completion of the 4th hole, Burns and his partner were 3up. Following his tee shot from the 5th tee and while waiting on the group ahead to finish the 5th hole, Burns requested a ride to a nearby restroom from a local club representative who was driving a golf cart. Shortly, they were in route to the restroom. Unfortunately, neither the match's referee nor observer could prevent this violation of the Transportation Condition in effect for the Championship, which stated that, "Players must not ride on any form of transportation during a stipulated round unless authorized by the Committee."

Although the referee knew that the Transportation Condition had been breached, he

Austin Connelly and Sam Burns

asked for confirmation as to whether the penalty applied to the player only or to the side. The Director of the Championship, Bill McCarthy, responded that Rule 30-3d indeed would apply to this situation.

The player was immediately told of his violation and the associated penalty, which in match play is, "At the conclusion of the hole at which the breach is discovered, the state of the match is adjusted by deducting one hole for each hole at which a breach occurred."

After the ruling, play of the 5th hole continued with each side eventually scoring four on the hole. At this point, since Burns and Connelly had begun the 5th hole 3up and the hole had been halved, the side was 3up before the adjustment. However, the adjustment required by the Rules was a deduction of one hole with the result that the side was now 2up beginning play of the 6th hole.

Ultimately, Burns and Connelly won the match by a margin of 3 and 2, and moved on to the second round of match play.

Frequently asked question

In a four ball match, if my partner's next stroke is conceded by our opponents, but he putts the ball anyway, what is the ruling?

There is no penalty for holing out in this circumstance. However, if hitting the putt assists you (e.g., it is on your line of putt and allows you to see the break), you are disqualified from the hole.

Rule 31 FOUR-BALL STROKE PLAY

DEFINITIONS
All defined terms are in *italics* and are listed alphabetically in the Definitions section – see pages 10–23.

31-1. General

The Rules of Golf, so far as they are not at variance with the following specific Rules, apply to *four-ball* stroke play.

31-2. Representation of Side

A *side* may be represented by either *partner* for all or any part of a *stipulated round*; both *partners* need not be present. An absent *competitor* may join his *partner* between holes, but not during play of a hole.

31-3. Scoring

The *marker* is required to record for each hole only the gross score of whichever *partner's* score is to count. The gross scores to count must be individually identifiable; otherwise, **the *side* is disqualified**. Only one of the *partners* need be responsible for complying with Rule 6-6b.

(Wrong score – see Rule 31-7a)

31-4. Order of Play

Balls belonging to the same *side* may be played in the order the *side* considers best.

31-5. Wrong Ball

If a *competitor* is in breach of Rule 15-3b for making a *stroke* at a *wrong ball*, **he incurs a penalty of two strokes** and must correct his mistake by playing the correct ball or by proceeding under the *Rules*. His *partner* incurs no penalty even if the *wrong ball* belongs to him.

If the *wrong ball* belongs to another *competitor*, its owner must place a ball on the spot from which the *wrong ball* was first played.

(Placing and Replacing – see Rule 20-3)

31-6. Penalty to Side

A *side* is penalized for a breach of any of the following by either *partner*:

o   Rule 4 – Clubs

FOUR-BALL STROKE PLAY: REPRESENTATION OF SIDE

In four ball, the side can be represented by one partner for all or any part of a round.

FOUR-BALL STROKE PLAY

Date __3RD APRIL 2015__

Competition __SPRING OPEN FOUR-BALL__

PLAYER A __J. SUTHERLAND__   Handicap __16__   Strokes __12__

PLAYER B __W. B. TAYLOR__   Handicap __12__   Strokes __9__

Hole	Length Yards	Par	Stroke Index	Gross Score A	Gross Score B	Net Score A	Net Score B	Won X Lost – Half O	Mar. Score	Hole	Length Yards	Par	Stroke Index	Gross Score A	Gross Score B	Net Score A	Net Score B	Won X Lost – Half O	Mar. Score
1	437	4	4		4		3			10	425	4	3		5		4		
2	320	4	14		4		4			11	141	3	17	3		3			
3	162	3	18		4		4			12	476	5	9	6		5			
4	504	5	7	6		5				13	211	3	11		4		4		
5	181	3	16	4		4				14	437	4	5		5		4		
6	443	4	2		5		4			15	460	4	1		5		4		
7	390	4	8		5		4			16	176	3	15	4		4			
8	346	4	12	5		4				17	340	4	13		4		4		
9	340	4	10	4		3				18	435	4	6	6		5			
Out	3123	35				35				In	3101	34				37			
										Out	3123	35				35			
										T'tl	6224	69				72			

Player's Signature _____

Marker's Signature __R. J. Parker__

Handicap

Net Score

Partner's scores to be individually identified

1 The lower score of the partners is the score for the hole (Rule 31).

2 Only one of the partners need be responsible for complying with Rule 6-6b, i.e., recording scores, checking scores, countersigning and returning the card (Rule 31-3).

3 The competitor is solely responsible for the correctness of the gross score recorded. Although there is no objection to the competitor (or his marker) entering the net score, it is the Committee's responsibility to record the better ball score for each hole, to add up the scores and to apply the handicaps recorded on the card (Rule 33-5). Thus, there is no penalty for an error by the competitor (or his marker) for recording an incorrect net score.

4 Scores of the two partners must be individually identifiable, otherwise it is impossible for the Committee to apply the correct handicap. If the scores of both partners, having different handicaps, are not individually identifiable, the Committee has no alternative but to disqualify both partners (Rule 31-7 and Rule 6-6 apply).

5 The Committee is responsible for laying down the conditions under which a competition is to be played (Rule 33-1), including the method of handicapping. In the above illustration the Committee laid down that 3/4 handicaps would apply.

o Rule 6-4 – Caddie

o Any Local Rule or Condition of Competition for which there is a maximum penalty per round.

31-7. Disqualification Penalties
a. Breach by One Partner

A side is disqualified from the competition if either *partner* incurs a penalty of disqualification under any of the following:

- Rule 1-3 – Agreement to Waive Rules
- Rule 3-4 – Refusal to Comply with a Rule
- Rule 4 – Clubs
- Rule 5-1 or 5-2 – The Ball
- Rule 6-2b – Handicap
- Rule 6-4 – Caddie
- Rule 6-6b – Signing and Returning Score Card
- Rule 6-6d – Wrong Score for Hole
- Rule 6-7 – Undue Delay; Slow Play
- Rule 7-1 – Practice Before or Between Rounds
- Rule 10-2c – Sides Agree to Play Out of Turn
- Rule 11-1 – Teeing
- Rule 14-3 – Artificial Devices and Unusual Equipment; Abnormal Use of Equipment
- Rule 22-1 – Ball Assisting Play
- Rule 31-3 – Gross Scores to Count Not Individually Identifiable
- Rule 33-7 – Disqualification Penalty Imposed by Committee

b. Breach by Both Partners

A *side* is disqualified from the competition:

(i) if each *partner* incurs a penalty of disqualification for a breach of Rule 6-3 (Time of Starting and Groups) or Rule 6-8 (Discontinuance of Play), or

(ii) if, at the same hole, each *partner* is in breach of a *Rule* the penalty for which is disqualification from the competition or for a hole.

c. For the Hole Only

In all other cases where a breach of a *Rule* would result in disqualification, **the *competitor* is disqualified only for the hole at which the breach occurred.**

31-8. Effect of Other Penalties

If a *competitor's* breach of a *Rule* assists his *partner's* play, **the *partner* incurs the applicable penalty in addition to any penalty incurred by the *competitor*.**

In all other cases where a *competitor* incurs a penalty for breach of a *Rule*, the penalty does not apply to his *partner*.

RULE 31 INCIDENTS

The Rules governing four-ball stroke play start with the innocent-sounding phrase, "The Rules of Golf, so far as they are not at variance with the following specific Rules, apply to four-ball stroke play." Examining these specific Rules, it is clear that each member of a side must play his best and hope that his partner will play well enough on any hole where he is not at his best. In the event of a violation of the Rules, the first question will be: Does this Rule assess a penalty to both players when it is only one who is in violation but not the other? The answer must come from a careful reading of the specific Rules.

The Rules governing four-ball stroke play are not complex and the most commonly applied Rules are: (1) the side may be represented by one partner for all or any part of a match; (2) balls belonging to the same side may be played in the order the side considers best; (3) a side is penalized for a breach of Rule 4, Rule 6-4 and any Local Rule for which there is a maximum penalty per round; and (4) if a competitor's breach of a Rule assists his partner's play, the partner incurs the applicable penalty in addition to any penalty incurred by the competitor.

An interesting situation arose in the four-ball part of the 2001 WGC-EMC2 World Cup in Gotemba, Japan, for the American side of Tiger Woods and David Duval. On the 16th green after the side had holed out, Duval made a practice stroke with his putter. The pair had not understood the Local Rule sheet that stated,

"A player shall not play any practice stroke on or near the putting green of the hole last played," with a penalty of two strokes applied to the following hole.

After Duval's infraction was reported to John Paramor, a Chief Referee for the European Tour, he raced to inform the side, where he found them on the 17th green. The question would arise regarding Rule 31-6 that assigns a penalty to the side for a violation of any Local Rule for which there is a maximum penalty per round. Fortunately for the Americans, this would not include the Local Rule that Duval had violated, since there was no maximum penalty statement associated with this Rule.

When Paramor informed them of Duval's violation, this significantly changed the American's strategy for playing the hole. Duval had previously struck his tee shot on the par-3 hole close enough that he thought he had a tap-in putt for a birdie, which now would become a 4 if made. In view of the potential birdie by Duval, Woods was about to pick up his ball since the best he could score was a par or 3. In view of the message from Paramour, the side needed Woods's putt for the lower score. Woods made the short putt and the lower score for the side was 3.

The important element of this four-ball situation is that the Local Rule penalty applies only to the player in violation, not to the side.

Frequently asked questions

In four-ball stroke play, what score must be recorded on the score card?
Only the gross score of whichever partner's score is to count for the hole must be recorded on the card. The score of the other player does not need to be recorded. Additionally, the scores must be individually identifiable so the Committee can determine which partner's score is recorded.

Do both partners have to sign the score card in a four-ball stroke play competition?
No. Only one of the partners needs to sign the score card.

Rule 32 BOGEY, PAR AND STABLEFORD COMPETITIONS

DEFINITIONS
All defined terms are in *italics* and are listed alphabetically in the Definitions section – see pages 10–23.

32-1. Conditions

Bogey, par and Stableford competitions are forms of stroke play in which play is against a fixed score at each hole. The *Rules* for stroke play, so far as they are not at variance with the following specific Rules, apply.

In handicap bogey, par and Stableford Competitions, the *competitor* with the lowest net score at a hole takes the *honor* at the next *teeing ground*.

a. Bogey and Par Competitions

The scoring for bogey and par competitions is made as in match play.

Any hole for which a *competitor* makes no return is regarded as a loss. The winner is the *competitor* who is most successful in the aggregate of holes.

The *marker* is responsible for marking only the gross number of *strokes* for each hole where the *competitor* makes a net score equal to or less than the fixed score.

NOTE 1

The *competitor's* score is adjusted by **deducting a hole or holes under the applicable Rule** when a penalty other than disqualification is incurred under any of the following:

o   Rule 4 – Clubs
o   Rule 6-4 – Caddie
o   Any Local Rule or Condition of Competition for which there is a maximum penalty per round.

The *competitor* is responsible for reporting the facts regarding such a breach to the *Committee* before he returns his score card so that the *Committee* may apply the penalty. If the *competitor* fails to report his breach to the *Committee*, **he is disqualified.**

NOTE 2

If the *competitor* is in breach of Rule 6-3a (Time of Starting) but arrives at his starting point, ready to play, within five minutes after his starting time, or is in breach of Rule 6-7 (Undue Delay; Slow Play), the *Committee* will **deduct one hole from the aggregate of holes.** For a repeated offense under Rule 6-7, see Rule 32-2a.

NOTE 3

If the *competitor* incurs the additional two-stroke penalty provided in the Exception to Rule 6-6d, that additional penalty is applied by **deducting one hole from the aggregate of holes scored for the round. The penalty the competitor failed to include in his score is applied to the hole where the breach occurred.** However, neither penalty applies when a breach of Rule 6-6d does not affect the result of the hole.

b. Stableford Competitions

The scoring in Stableford competitions is made by points awarded in relation to a fixed score at each hole as follows:

Hole Played In	Points	Hole Played In	Points
More than one over fixed score or no score returned	0	One under fixed score	3
		Two under fixed score	4
One over fixed score	1	Three under fixed score	5
Fixed score	2	Four under fixed score	6

The winner is the *competitor* who scores the highest number of points.

The *marker* is responsible for marking only the gross number of *strokes* at each hole where the *competitor's* net score earns one or more points.

NOTE 1

If a competitor is in breach of a Rule for which there is a maximum penalty per round, he must report the facts to the Committee before returning his score card; if he fails to do so, **he is disqualified.** The Committee will, from the total points scored for the round, **deduct two points for each hole at which any breach occurred, with a maximum deduction per round of four points for each Rule breached.**

NOTE 2

If the *competitor* is in breach of Rule 6-3a (Time of Starting) but arrives at his starting point, ready to play, within five minutes after his starting time, or is in breach of Rule 6-7 (Undue Delay; Slow Play), the *Committee* will **deduct two points from the total points scored for the round**. For a repeated offense under Rule 6-7, see Rule 32-2a.

NOTE 3

If the *competitor* incurs the additional two-stroke penalty provided in the Exception to Rule 6-6d, that additional penalty is applied by **deducting two points from the total points scored for the round. The penalty the competitor failed to include in his score is applied to the hole where the breach occurred.** However, neither penalty applies when a breach of Rule 6-6d does not affect the points scored on the hole.

NOTE 4

For the purposes of preventing slow play, the *Committee* may, in the conditions of a competition (Rule 33-1), establish pace of play guidelines, including maximum periods of time allowed to complete a *stipulated round*, a hole or a *stroke*.

The *Committee* may, in such a condition, modify the penalty for a breach of this Rule as follows:

First offense – Deduction of one point from the total points scored for the round;

Second offense – Deduction of a further two points from the total points scored for the round;

For subsequent offense – Disqualification.

32-2. Disqualification Penalties
a. From the Competition

A *competitor* is **disqualified** from the competition if he incurs a penalty of disqualification under any of the following:

o   Rule 1-3 – Agreement to Waive Rules
o   Rule 3-4 – Refusal to Comply with Rule
o   Rule 4 – Clubs
o   Rule 5-1 or 5-2 – The Ball
o   Rule 6-2b – Handicap
o   Rule 6-3 – Time of Starting and Groups
o   Rule 6-4 – Caddie
o   Rule 6-6b – Signing and Returning Score Card

- Rule 6-6d – Wrong Score for Hole, i.e., when the recorded score is lower than actually taken, except that no penalty is incurred when a breach of this Rule does not affect the result of the hole
- Rule 6-7 – Undue Delay; Slow Play
- Rule 6-8 – Discontinuance of Play
- Rule 7-1 – Practice Before or Between Rounds
- Rule 10-2c – Playing Out of Turn
- Rule 11-1 – Teeing
- Rule 14-3 – Artificial Devices and Unusual Equipment; Abnormal Use of Equipment
- Rule 22-1 – Ball Assisting Play
- Rule 33-7 – Disqualification Penalty Imposed by Committee

b. For a Hole

In all other cases where a breach of a *Rule* would result in disqualification, **the *competitor* is disqualified only for the hole at which the breach occurred.**

Rule 33

DEFINITIONS
All defined terms are in *italics* and are listed alphabetically in the Definitions section – see pages 10–23.

ADMINISTRATION
THE COMMITTEE

33-1. Conditions; Waiving Rule

The *Committee* must establish the conditions under which a competition is to be played.

The *Committee* has no power to waive a Rule of Golf.

The number of holes of a stipulated round must not be reduced once play has commenced for that round.

Certain specific *Rules* governing stroke play are so substantially different from those governing match play that combining the two forms of play is not practicable and is not permitted. The result of a match played in these circumstances is null and void and, in the stroke-play competition, **the *competitors* are disqualified.**

In stroke play the *Committee* may limit a *referee's* duties.

33-2. The Course
a. Defining Bounds and Margins

The *Committee* must define accurately:

(i) the *course* and *out of bounds*,

(ii) the margins of *water hazards* and *lateral water hazards*,

(iii) *ground under repair*, and

(iv) *obstructions* and integral parts of the *course*.

b. New Holes

New *holes* should be made on the day on which a stroke-play competition begins and at such other times as the *Committee* considers necessary, provided all *competitors* in a single round play with each *hole* cut in the same position.

Exception:

When it is impossible for a damaged *hole* to be repaired so that it conforms with the Definition, the *Committee* may make a new *hole* in a nearby similar position.

RULE 33-2d. COURSE UNPLAYABLE

If the course is not in a playable condition, the Committee may have to temporarily suspend play. In stroke play only, if further play becomes impossible, the Committee may have to declare play null and void.

NOTE

Where a single round is to be played on more than one day, the *Committee* may provide, in the conditions of a competition (Rule 33-1), that the *holes* and *teeing grounds* may be differently situated on each day of the competition, provided that, on any one day, all *competitors* play with each *hole* and each *teeing ground* in the same position.

c. Practice Ground

Where there is no practice ground available outside the area of a competition *course*, the *Committee* should establish the area on which players may practice on any day of a competition, if it is practicable to do so. On any day of a stroke-play competition, the *Committee* should not normally permit practice on or to a *putting green* or from a *hazard* of the competition *course*.

d. Course Unplayable

If the *Committee* or its authorized representative considers that for any reason the *course* is not in a playable condition or that there are circumstances that render the proper playing of the game impossible, it may, in match play or stroke play, order a temporary suspension of play or, in stroke play, declare play null and void and cancel all scores for the round in question. When a round is canceled, all penalties incurred in that round are canceled. (Procedure in discontinuing and resuming play – see Rule 6-8)

33-3. Times of Starting and Groups

The *Committee* must establish the times of starting and, in stroke play, arrange the groups in which *competitors* must play.

When a match-play competition is played over an extended period, the *Committee* establishes the limit of time within which each round must be completed. When players are allowed to arrange the date of their match within these limits, the *Committee* should announce that the match must be played at a stated time on the last day of the period, unless the players agree to a prior date.

33-4. Handicap Stroke Table

The *Committee* must publish a table indicating the order of holes at which handicap strokes are to be given or received.

33-5. Score Card

In stroke play, the *Committee* must provide each *competitor* with a score card containing the date and the *competitor's* name or, in *foursome* or *four-ball* stroke play, the *competitors'* names.

In stroke play, the *Committee* is responsible for the addition of scores and the application of the handicap recorded on the score card.

In *four-ball* stroke play, the *Committee* is responsible for recording the better-ball score for each hole and in the process applying the handicaps recorded on the score card and adding the better-ball scores.

In bogey, par and Stableford competitions, the *Committee* is responsible for applying the handicap recorded on the score card and determining the result of each hole and the overall result or points total.

NOTE

The *Committee* may request that each *competitor* record the date and his name on his score card.

33-6. Decision of Ties

The *Committee* must announce the manner, day and time for the decision of a halved match or of a tie, whether played on level terms or under handicap.

A halved match must not be decided by stroke play. A tie in stroke play must not be decided by a match.

33-7. Disqualification Penalty; Committee Discretion

A penalty of disqualification may in exceptional individual cases be waived, modified or imposed if the *Committee* considers such action warranted.

Any penalty less than disqualification must not be waived or modified.

If a *Committee* considers that a player is guilty of a serious breach of etiquette, it may impose a penalty of disqualification under this Rule.

33-8. Local Rules
a. Policy

The *Committee* may establish Local Rules for local abnormal conditions if they are consistent with the policy set forth in Appendix I.

b. Waiving or Modifying a Rule

A Rule of Golf must not be waived by a Local Rule. However, if a *Committee* considers that local abnormal conditions interfere with the proper playing of the game to the extent that it is necessary to make a Local Rule that modifies the Rules of Golf, the Local Rule must be authorized by the USGA.

RULE 33 INCIDENTS

Rule 33 states that the Committee must establish the conditions under which a competition is to be played and lists very specific areas that require attention, such as starting times, score cards, definition of the bounds and margins of the course and what to do in case of a tie.

Each of the four major championships uses a different method for settling a tie. Each is also very specific in outlining exactly what will take place:

Masters Tournament – If there is a tie after 72 holes of play, a hole-by-hole play-off will commence at hole no. 18. Hole numbers 18 and 10 will be played alternatively until a champion is decided.

U.S. Open – In the case of a tie after 72 holes, an 18-hole play-off will be held on the Monday following. If this play-off results in a tie, play will immediately continue hole-by-hole until a winner is determined.

British Open – In the event of a tie after four rounds [at St. Andrew's in 2015], the winner will be decided by a four-hole aggregate play-off. The play-off will start as soon as practicable after the last players have finished their round.

The player with the lowest aggregate over the four extra holes will be declared the winner. If the players are still tied having played these four holes, a hole-by-hole play-off will be played.

PGA Championship – In the event of a tie for first place after 72 holes [at Oak Hill in 2011], there will be a three-hole aggregate play-off. If a tie still remains, there will be a sudden-death play-off.

Prior to the opening round of the second U.S. Open, the USGA's first president, Theodore Havemeyer, made what is arguably the most important ruling in the championship's long history.

The championship was to be held during July 1896 at Shinnecock Hills Golf Club on Long Island and was precluded by a situation that led Havemeyer to establish the Committee's unequivocal authority, as stated in Rule 33, to lay down the conditions under which a competition is to be played.

Gathering before the opening round, a group of competitors, comprised of proficient or professional players mostly from Scotland, England and private clubs in New York, New England and Chicago, objected to John Shippen being accepted into the competitive field. Shippen's mother was a Shinnecock Indian and

his father was a black Presbyterian minister on the nearby Shinnecock Indian Reservation.

The objectors threatened that if forced to play with Shippen, they would withdraw from the competition, thereby leaving a weaker field and a dubious U.S. Open Champion. At this early point in the game's American history, those less knowledgeable of the game generally deferred to those proficient in its playing to help mold competitive policies and procedures. Such a dilemma extended to golf in the 1890s. Fortunately, Havemeyer provided insight and direction on his side of the equation.

He met with the objectors and made the USGA's argument succinctly: An open competition was to be held; in order to be an open competition, applications had been accepted from all qualified individuals; to limit the field on any basis other than proficiency would invalidate the open nature of the competition and, in turn, the identification of the national open champion.

Havemeyer emphasized that it was the objectors' unquestioned right to withdraw. However, as far as the national championship was concerned, if Shippen chose to play and he were the only competitor in the field, he would be the national champion.

Feeling the intransigence of Havemeyer's argument and his irrefutable logic, those objecting reversed themselves and chose to compete. James Foulis, a Scottish professional playing out of the Chicago Golf Club, was the champion with a score of 152. Shippen tied for fifth place.

Frequently asked questions

If my ball comes to rest in a creek that is unmarked (i.e., there are no stakes or lines) how should I proceed?
Even though the Committee has not properly marked the golf course, the creek does not lose its status as a water hazard and you may proceed under the water hazard Rule (Rule 26-1). If it is impossible to drop behind the water hazard under Rule 26-1b, the creek meets the Definition of a "Lateral Water Hazard," and you may proceed under Rule 26-1c.

Can our Club establish a dropping zone on the green side of a yellow water hazard which is difficult to carry?
No. A Committee cannot make a Local Rule which alters or waives the Rules of Golf. This Local Rule would allow players to drop a ball on a part of the course where the Rules do not allow.

Rule 34 DISPUTES AND DECISIONS

DEFINITIONS
All defined terms are in *italics* and are listed alphabetically in the Definitions section – see pages 10–23.

34-1. Claims and Penalties
a. Match Play

If a claim is lodged with the *Committee* under Rule 2-5, a decision should be given as soon as possible so that the state of the match may, if necessary, be adjusted. If a claim is not made in accordance with Rule 2-5, it must not be considered by the *Committee*.

There is no time limit on applying the disqualification penalty for a breach of Rule 1-3.

b. Stroke Play

In stroke play, a penalty must not be rescinded, modified or imposed after the competition has closed. A competition is closed when the result has been officially announced or, in stroke-play qualifying followed by match play, when the player has teed off in his first match.

Exception:

A penalty of disqualification must be imposed after the competition has closed if a *competitor*:

(i) was in breach of Rule 1-3 (Agreement to Waive Rules); or

(ii) returned a score card on which he had recorded a handicap that, before the competition closed, he knew was higher than that to which he was entitled, and this affected the number of strokes received (Rule 6-2b); or

(iii) returned a score for any hole lower than actually taken (Rule 6-6d) for any reason other than failure to include one or more *penalty strokes* that, before the competition closed, he did not know he had incurred; or

(iv) knew, before the competition closed, that he had been in breach of any other *Rule* for which the penalty is disqualification.

34-2. Referee's Decision

If a *referee* has been appointed by the *Committee*, his decision is final.

34-3. Committee's Decision

In the absence of a *referee*, any dispute or doubtful point on the *Rules* must be referred to the *Committee*, whose decision is final.

If the *Committee* cannot come to a decision, it may refer the dispute or doubtful point to the Rules of Golf Committee of the USGA, whose decision is final.

If the dispute or doubtful point has not been referred to the Rules of Golf Committee, the player or players may request that an agreed statement be referred through a duly authorized representative of the *Committee* to the Rules of Golf Committee for an opinion as to the correctness of the decision given. The reply will be sent to this authorized representative.

If play is conducted other than in accordance with the Rules of Golf, the Rules of Golf Committee will not give a decision on any question.

RULE 34 INCIDENTS

Rule 34 is one that governs disputes and decisions, thus is of great interest to the Committee but seldom referred to by a player. One of the key provisions of this Rule is that if the Committee appoints a referee, his decision is final (Rule 34-2). This provision has several implications. If a referee authorizes a player to infringe a Rule then the player is absolved from penalty in such a case. If a referee makes a decision that a player disagrees with, the player may make an appeal to the Committee but only if the referee consents. In this last situation, a good referee almost always allows the player a chance to obtain a second opinion.

The good news for a player is that if a referee makes a mistake, there are sometimes avenues for a correction to be made by the referee or the Committee.

At a U.S. Open sectional qualifier at Woodmont Country Club, MD, in 2000, an official erred with the result that a player who proceeded correctly was told that he had proceeded incorrectly. The result of the official's error was that the player left the putting green under the impression that he had scored six on the 17th hole of the North course. Upon playing from the tee of the 18th hole, the error was discovered and the player's score was correctly adjusted to 4.

In play of the 17th hole, the player was playing the course for the first time and had struck his tee shot in the direction of some trees to the left side of the fairway. Because he reasonably thought that his ball might be lost outside a water hazard, he announced and properly played a provisional ball (Rule 27-2) that came to rest in the center of the fairway. Upon reaching the place where he hoped to find his original ball, he was fortunate to find it in a playable position but just inside a lateral water hazard that was not visible from the tee and unknown to him at the time of playing the provisional ball.

An official incorrectly told the player that he was not entitled to play a provisional ball when his ball was struck in the direction of a water hazard and that he must consider his second ball from the tee as his ball in play with a one-stroke penalty, thus he would lie three with that ball. The player continued with the ball in the fairway, taking three additional strokes to complete the hole for an apparent score of 6.

After reviewing the situation, the Committee reached the following decision. Since the player had proceeded correctly with the second ball from the tee, it was a provisional ball and the Rules required that he abandon that ball when the original ball was found (Rule 27-2c) and continue play with the original ball. At that point, further play of the provisional ball would be play of a wrong ball. However, since this was at the direction of the official, the player would not be penalized for doing so. Moreover, since he was required to abandon the provisional ball, there would be no penalty under Rule 27-1 that was associated with the second ball as a provisional ball. The Committee determined that his score for the hole was 4, which included the stroke from the tee with the original ball plus the three strokes made with the wrong ball after the incorrect ruling and with no penalty strokes. This is an unusual case where the player must count the strokes with a wrong ball as otherwise he would have no score for the hole.

If the player had doubt about the official's original decision, he could have asked for a second opinion, but he did not do so.

Frequently asked questions

My friends and I were playing a 4-man scramble event. On one hole, I hit a chip and my ball struck and moved my friend's ball on the putting green. What is the ruling?
A scramble is not a format covered by the Rules of Golf. Therefore, the Committee in charge of the competition must decide the outcome of any situations which arise and its decision is final (Rule 34-3).

During the final round of a stroke-play competition, a competitor accidentally moved his ball in the fairway. He knew it was a penalty, but forgot to include the one stroke penalty in his score. After the competition closed, he informed the Committee and was disqualified. Is that correct?
Yes. Exception (iii) to Rule 34-1b says that a player must be disqualified if he knew, before the competition closed, that he had incurred a penalty but intentionally or unintentionally failed to include the penalty in his score. If he did not know he had incurred the penalty, the result of the competition must stand.

APPENDICES

APPENDIX I
LOCAL RULES; CONDITIONS OF THE COMPETITION

Definitions

All defined terms are in *italics* and are listed alphabetically in the Definitions section – see pages 10-23.

APPENDIX I INCIDENTS

At the rear of the Rules of Golf, Appendix I is where you will find very specific instructions about Local Rules and Conditions of Competition. Many of the nuances reflected here are useful when employing the Rules for situations that arise at all levels of competition. Environmentally sensitive areas, protection of young trees, mud, stones in bunkers, deciding ties, etc. are all addressed.

In many national competitions, including the U.S. Women's Amateur, motorized transportation is prohibited under a Condition of Competition. Unless provided or sanctioned by a Rules official, a player is never allowed to ride.

In match play, a violation of the transportation condition does not trigger an immediate loss of hole penalty, but rather a "state of the match" adjustment penalty. In other words, the hole where the infraction took place or is discovered is played out and, following that, the state of the match is altered accordingly. In the event of a breach between the play of two holes, the penalty applies at the conclusion of the next hole.

At the 2003 U.S. Women's Amateur at Philadelphia C.C., Maru Martinez was 2-up in her match with Michelle Wie after the first nine holes of the first round. At the turn, Martinez made a quick stop in the clubhouse. Emerging from the building, she was offered and accepted a ride to the 10th tee by a well-meaning volunteer. Neither player was aware of the breach by Martinez until both players had played their tee shots at the 10th hole.

Discovering the breach during play of the 10th hole, the referee initially ruled Martinez lost the hole, which led to both players lifting their balls from the fairway and heading to the 11th tee. Before either player had played from the 11th tee, the referee realized the error, directed the players to replace the lifted balls and play out the hole.

Play of the 10th hole was completed with the result that Wie won with a conceded birdie. The state of the match was then adjusted with 1-up being taken from Martinez. The match was now all square. Martinez went on to win 1-up.

"I was very mad," she said later, "but I just said I've got to start all over again. It was my responsibility."

Temporary Immovable Obstruction (TIO) is the term used to describe the various obstructions that are specific to national championships. Grandstands, concession stands, score boards, television booths, camera stands, cables and cranes can all fall into this category. They are unusual to the normal playing of the course and for that reason relief is granted. Although the logic is consistent, many times the relief appears to favor a wayward shot that would otherwise have the player playing from a more penal place.

During the second round of the 2006 WGC-Bridgestone Invitational, Tiger Woods's 167-yard second shot to the 9th green bounced off a concrete walkway near the clubhouse, onto and over the roof and into a cart of a kitchen employee. Unaware of where the ball had come from, the employee put it into one of the cup holders and drove off. Once it became known where the ball had finished before the kitchen-hand drove off with it, it was decided that the grandstands near the clubhouse had interfered with Woods's line to the hole. This entitled him to free relief under the Local Rule for TIOs. The resulting drop gave Woods an unobstructed line to the hole. He was able to make a bogey five when superficially it appeared his score would be much greater.

One of the more common Local Rules implemented across both regular club play and high level competitions, including the U.S. Open, is the one that provides relief for an embedded ball anywhere through the green.

Rule 25-2 provides relief, without penalty, for a ball embedded in its own pitch-mark in any closely mown area through the green. "Closely mown area" means any area of the course, including paths through the rough, cut to fairway height or less. The Local Rule extends relief to all areas through the green including those that are not closely mown. However, there is an important exception to the Local Rule in that there is no relief for a ball embedded in sand in an area that is not closely mown.

An unusual incident occurred in the first round of the 2007 U.S. Open at Oakmont C. C. involving this Local Rule as well as several other Rules, illustrating the importance of understanding the interrelationship among various Rules when proceeding under one or more Rules.

Playing the 3rd hole, Steve Stricker struck his tee shot to the left of the fairway in the direction of the famous "church pew" bunkers, which are surrounded by tall grass. Arriving at the bunkers where he believed his ball to lie, search began with Steve and his fellow-competitors, Joey Sindelar and Joe Durant, plus their caddies actively probing and raking sand and loose impediments in the bunkers as authorized by Rule 12-1.

Near the four-minute mark of search, Sindelar found a ball embedded close to but outside a bunker, but Stricker could not immediately tell if the found ball was his. Acting under Rule 12-2, he announced to Sindelar that he had reason to believe this ball was his and that it was necessary to lift it in order to identify it. He marked the position of the ball, lifted it and determined that it was the ball he struck from the tee. While the ball was lifted, he realized that he might be entitled to relief under the Local Rule for an embedded ball. A Rules official cautioned that it must first be determined that the ball was in fact embedded, that is, it must have been in its own pitch-mark with part of the ball below the level of the ground. Furthermore, since he would be operating under the Local Rule not Rule 25-2, it must be determined that the ball was not embedded in sand, which was possible because of its proximity to the bunkers.

Fortunately for Stricker, it was determined that the ball was embedded, not in sand, and that he was entitled to relief under the Local Rule. His next question was, "May I clean the ball before dropping it?" The answer was, "Yes and the ball must be dropped as near as possible to the spot where it lay, not nearer the hole."

When the ball was dropped, it first struck a part of the course outside the bunker near where it was embedded but rolled and came to rest in the bunker. According to Rule 20-2c(i), a dropped ball must be re-dropped, without penalty, if it rolls into and comes to rest in a hazard. Stricker again dropped the ball with the same result. At this point, Rule 20-2c tells the player that the ball must be placed as near as possible to the spot where it first struck a part of the course when re-dropped.

Stricker attempted to place the ball as required by the Rule but it failed to come to rest on the spot on which it was placed. He then followed Rule 20-3d and attempted to place the ball on the nearest spot where it would remain at rest, not nearer the hole and not in the bunker.

He found such a spot several inches away from where it first struck a part of the course when re-dropped and played his second shot on the hole toward the green.

This situation is remarkable because of the number of Rules that governed the player's procedures. Simply knowing Rule 25-2 would not have been sufficient as it was the Local Rule that applied to his situation together with all the referenced parts of Rule 20 that came into play.

PART A
Local Rules

Definitions

All defined terms are in *italics* and are listed alphabetically in the Definitions section – see pages 10-23.

General

As provided in Rule 33-8a, the *Committee* may make and publish Local Rules for local abnormal conditions if they are consistent with the policies established in this Appendix. In addition, detailed information regarding acceptable and prohibited Local Rules is provided in *Decisions on the Rules of Golf* under Rule 33-8 and in *How to Conduct a Competition*.

If local abnormal conditions interfere with the proper playing of the game and the *Committee* considers it necessary to modify a Rule of Golf, authorization from the USGA must be obtained.

Within the policies established in Appendix I, the *Committee* may adopt Specimen Local Rules by referring, on a score card or notice board, to the examples given below. However, Specimen Local Rules of a temporary nature should not be printed on a score card.

1. Course – Defining Boundaries, Margins and Status of Objects

The *Committee* may adopt Local Rules:

o Specifying means used to define *out of bounds*, *water hazards*, *lateral water hazards*, *ground under repair*, *obstructions* and integral parts of the *course* (Rule 33-2a).

o Clarifying the status of *water hazards* that may be *lateral water hazards* (Rule 26).

o Clarifying the status of objects that may be *obstructions* (Rule 24).

o Declaring any construction to be an integral part of the *course* and, accordingly, not an *obstruction*, e.g., built-up sides of *teeing grounds*, *putting greens* and *bunkers* (Rules 24 and 33-2a).

o Declaring artificial surfaces and sides of roads to be integral parts of the *course*.

o Providing relief of the type afforded under Rule 24-2b from roads and paths not having artificial surfaces and sides, if they could unfairly affect play.

o Defining temporary obstructions installed on or adjoining the *course* as movable, immovable or temporary immovable obstructions.

2. Course Protection

a. Ground Under Repair; Play Prohibited

If the *Committee* wishes to protect any area of the *course*, including turf nurseries, young plantations and other parts of the *course* under cultivation, it should declare it to be *ground under repair* and prohibit play from within that area.

The following Local Rule is recommended:

"The _____(defined by ____) is *ground under repair* from which play is prohibited. If a player's ball lies in the area, or if it interferes with the player's stance or the area of his intended swing, the player must take relief under Rule 25-1.

PENALTY FOR BREACH OF LOCAL RULE:
Match play – Loss of hole; **Stroke Play** – Two strokes."

b. Protection of Young Trees

When it is desired to prevent damage to young trees, the following Local Rule is recommended:

"Protection of young trees identified by _____. If such a tree interferes with a player's *stance* or area of his intended swing, the ball must be lifted, without penalty, and dropped in accordance with the procedure prescribed in Rule 24-2b (Immovable Obstruction). If the ball lies in a *water hazard*, the player must lift and drop the ball in accordance with Rule 24-2b(i), except that the *nearest point of relief* must be in the *water hazard* and the ball must be dropped in the *water hazard*, or the player may proceed under Rule 26. The ball may be cleaned when lifted under this Local Rule.

Exception

A player may not obtain relief under this Local Rule if (a) interference by anything other than such a tree makes the *stroke* clearly impracticable or (b) interference by such a tree would occur only through the use of a clearly unreasonable *stroke* or an unnecessarily abnormal *stance*, swing or direction of play.

PENALTY FOR BREACH OF LOCAL RULE:
Match play – Loss of hole; **Stroke Play** – Two strokes."

c. Environmentally-Sensitive Areas

If an appropriate authority (i.e. a Government Agency or the like) prohibits entry into and/or play from an area on or adjoining the *course* for environmental reasons, the *Committee* should make a Local Rule clarifying the relief procedure. The *Committee* may not declare an area to be environmentally-sensitive.

The *Committee* has some discretion in terms of whether the area is defined as *ground under repair*, a *water hazard* or *out of bounds*. However, it may not simply define an area to be a *water hazard* if it does not meet the Definition of a "*Water Hazard*" and it should attempt to preserve the character of the *hole*.

The following Local Rule is recommended:

"1. Definition

An environmentally-sensitive area (ESA) is an area so declared by an appropriate authority, entry into and/or play from which is prohibited for environmental reasons.

The_____(defined by_____) are 'environmentally-sensitive areas' (ESAs). These areas are to be played as (*ground under repair* – *water hazards* – *out of bounds*).

2. Ball in Environmentally-Sensitive Area

Ground Under Repair:

If a ball is in an ESA defined as *ground under repair*, a ball must be dropped in accordance with Rule 25-1b.

If it is known or virtually certain that a ball that has not been found is in an ESA defined as *ground under repair*, the player may take relief, without penalty, as prescribed in Rule 25-1c.

Water Hazards and Lateral Water Hazards:

If the ball is found in or if it is known or virtually certain that a ball that has not bzen found is in an ESA defined as a *water hazard* or *lateral water hazard*, the player must, under penalty of one stroke, proceed under Rule 26-1.

If a ball dropped in accordance with Rule 26 rolls into a position where the ESA interferes with the player's *stance* or the area of his intended swing, the player must take relief as provided in Clause 3 of this Local Rule.

Out of Bounds:

If a ball is in an ESA defined as *out of bounds*, the player must play a ball, under penalty of one stroke, as nearly as possible at the spot from which the original ball was last played (see Rule 20-5).

3. Interference with Stance or Area of Intended Swing

Interference by an ESA occurs when the ESA interferes with the player's *stance* or the area of his intended swing. If interference exists, the player must take relief as follows:

(a) **Through the Green:** If the ball lies *through the green*, the point on the *course* nearest to where the ball lies must be determined that (a) is not nearer the *hole*, (b) avoids interference by the ESA and (c) is not in a *hazard* or on a *putting green*. The player must lift the ball and drop it, without penalty, within one club-length of the point so determined on

a part of the *course* that fulfills (a), (b) and (c) above.

(b) **In a Hazard:** If the ball is in a *hazard*, the player must lift the ball and drop it either:

(i) Without penalty, in the *hazard*, as near as possible to the spot where the ball lay, but not nearer the *hole*, on a part of the *course* that provides complete relief from the ESA; or

(ii) Under penalty of one *stroke*, outside the *hazard*, keeping the point where the ball lay directly between the *hole* and the spot on which the ball is dropped, with no limit to how far behind the *hazard* the ball may be dropped. Additionally, the player may proceed under Rule 26 or 28 if applicable.

(c) **On the Putting Green:** If the ball lies on the *putting green*, the player must lift the ball and place it, without penalty, in the nearest position to where it lay that affords complete relief from the ESA, but not nearer the *hole* or in a *hazard*.

The ball may be cleaned when lifted under Clause 3 of this Local Rule.

Exception

A player must not take relief under Clause 3 of this Local Rule if (a) interference by anything other than an ESA makes the *stroke* clearly impracticable or (b) interference by an ESA

ENVIRONMENTALLY SENSITIVE AREAS

The Links course at Spanish Bay in California has areas of sand dunes which have been declared environmentally sensitive. A player may not play from or enter these areas.

would occur only through the use of a clearly unreasonable *stroke* or an unnecessarily abnormal stance, swing or direction of play.

PENALTY FOR BREACH OF LOCAL RULE:
Match play – Loss of hole; **Stroke Play** – Two strokes.

NOTE

In the case of a serious breach of this Local Rule, the Committee may impose a penalty of disqualification."

3. Course Conditions
a. Embedded Ball

Course conditions, including mud and extreme wetness, may interfere with proper playing of the game and warrant relief for an embedded ball anywhere *through the green*.

Rule 25-2 provides relief, without penalty, for a ball embedded in its own pitch-mark in any closely-mown area *through the green*. On the *putting green*, a ball may be lifted and damage caused by the impact of a ball may be repaired (Rules 16-1b and c). When permission to take relief for an embedded ball anywhere *through the green* would be warranted, the following Local Rule is recommended:

"*Through the green*, a ball that is embedded may be lifted, cleaned and dropped, without penalty, as near as possible to the spot where it lay but not nearer the *hole*. The ball when dropped must first strike a part of the *course through the green*.

NOTE

A ball is "embedded" when it is in its own pitch-mark and part of the ball is below the level of the ground. A ball does not necessarily have to touch the soil to be embedded (e.g., grass, *loose impediments* and the like may intervene between the ball and the soil).

Exceptions

1. A player may not take relief under this Local Rule if the ball is wembedded in sand in an area that is not closely-mown.
2. A player may not take relief under this Local Rule if interference by anything other than the condition covered by this Local Rule makes the *stroke* clearly impracticable.

PENALTY FOR BREACH OF LOCAL RULE:
Match play – Loss of hole; **Stroke Play** – Two strokes."

b. "Preferred Lies" and "Winter Rules"

Ground under repair is provided for in Rule 25, and occasional local abnormal conditions that might interfere with fair play and are not widespread should be defined as *ground under repair*.

However, adverse conditions, such as heavy snows, spring thaws, prolonged rains or extreme heat can make fairways unsatisfactory and sometimes prevent use of heavy mowing equipment. When these conditions are so general throughout a *course* that the *Committee* believes "preferred lies" or "winter rules" would promote fair play or help protect the *course*, the following Local Rule (which should be withdrawn as soon as conditions warrant) is recommended:

"A ball lying on a closely-mown area *through the green* (or specify a more restricted area, e.g., at the 6th hole) may be lifted without penalty and cleaned. Before lifting the ball, the player must mark its position. Having lifted the ball, he must place it on a spot within (specify area, e.g., six inches, one club-length, etc.) of and not nearer the *hole* than where it originally lay, that is not in a *hazard* and not on a *putting green*.

A player may place his ball only once, and it is in *play* when it has been placed (Rule 20-4). If the ball fails to come to rest on the spot on which it was placed, Rule 20-3d applies. If the ball when placed comes to rest on the spot on which it is placed and it subsequently *moves*, there is no penalty and the ball must be played as it lies, unless the provisions of any other *Rule* apply.

If the player fails to mark the position of the ball before lifting it, moves the ball-marker prior to putting the ball back into play or moves the ball in any other manner, such as rolling it with a club, he incurs a penalty of one stroke.

NOTE

"Closely-mown area" means any area of the course, including paths through the rough, cut to fairway height or less.

---

*PENALTY FOR BREACH OF LOCAL RULE:
Match play – Loss of hole; **Stroke play** – Two strokes.
*If a player incurs the general penalty for a breach of this Local Rule, no additional penalty under the Local Rule is applied."

c. Cleaning Ball

Conditions, such as extreme wetness causing significant amounts of mud to adhere to the ball, may be such that permission to lift, clean and replace the ball would be appropriate. In these circumstances, the following Local Rule is recommended:

"(Specify area, e.g., at the 6th hole, on a closely-mown area, anywhere *through the green*, etc.) a ball may be lifted and cleaned without penalty. The ball must be replaced.

NOTE

The position of the ball must be marked before it is lifted under this Local Rule – see Rule 20-1.

PENALTY FOR BREACH OF LOCAL RULE:

Match play – Loss of hole; **Stroke Play** – Two strokes."

d. Aeration Holes

When a *course* has been aerated, a Local Rule permitting relief, without penalty, from an aeration hole may be warranted. The following Local Rule is recommended:

"*Through the green*, a ball that comes to rest in or on an aeration hole may be lifted without penalty, cleaned and dropped as near as possible to the spot where it lay but not nearer the *hole*. The ball when dropped must first strike a part of the *course through the green*.

On the *putting green*, a ball that comes to rest in or on an aeration hole may be placed at the nearest spot not nearer the *hole* that avoids the situation.

PENALTY FOR BREACH OF LOCAL RULE:

Match play – Loss of hole; **Stroke Play** – Two strokes."

e. Seams of Cut Turf

If a *Committee* wishes to allow relief from seams of cut turf, but not from the turf itself, the following Local Rule is recommended:

"*Through the green*, seams of cut turf (not the turf itself) are deemed to be *ground under repair*. However, interference by a seam with the player's *stance* is deemed not to be, of itself, interference under Rule 25-1. If the ball lies in or touches the seam or the seam interferes with the area of intended swing, relief is available under Rule 25-1. All seams within the cut turf area are considered the same seam.

PENALTY FOR BREACH OF LOCAL RULE:

Match play – Loss of hole; **Stroke Play** – Two strokes."

f. Stones in Bunkers

Stones are, by definition, *loose impediments* and, when a player's ball is in a *hazard*, a stone lying in or touching the *hazard* may not be touched or moved (Rule 13-4). However, stones in *bunkers* may represent a danger to players (a player could be injured by a stone struck by the player's club in an attempt to play the ball) and they may interfere with the proper playing of the game.

When permission to lift a stone in a *bunker* is warranted, the following Local Rule is recommended:

"Stones in *bunkers* are movable *obstructions* (Rule 24-1 applies)."

RELIEF FROM STONES IN BUNKERS

While normally loose impediments, a Committee may choose to declare stones in bunkers to be movable obstructions.

4. Obstructions

a. Immovable Obstructions Close to Putting Green (e.g., Sprinkler Heads)

Rule 24-2 provides relief, without penalty, from interference by an immovable *obstruction*, but it also provides that, except on the *putting green*, intervention on the *line of play* is not, of itself, interference under this Rule.

However, on some courses, the aprons of the *putting green* are so closely-mown that players may wish to putt from just off the green. In such conditions, immovable *obstructions* on the apron may interfere with the proper playing of the game and the introduction of the following Local Rule providing additional relief, without penalty, from intervention by an immovable *obstruction* would be warranted:

"Relief from interference by an immovable *obstruction* may be taken under Rule 24-2.

In addition, if a ball lies *through the green* and an immovable *obstruction* on or within two club-lengths of the *putting green* and within two club-lengths of the ball intervenes on the *line of play* between the ball and the *hole*, the player may take relief as follows:

The ball must be lifted and dropped at the nearest point to where the ball lay that (a) is not nearer the *hole*, (b) avoids intervention and (c) is not in a *hazard* or on a *putting green*.

If the player's ball lies on the *putting green* and an immovable *obstruction* within two club-lengths of the *putting green* intervenes on his *line of putt*, the player may take relief as follows:

The ball must be lifted and placed at the nearest point to where the ball lay that (a) is not nearer the *hole*, (b) avoids intervention and (c) is not in a *hazard*.

The ball may be cleaned when lifted.

Exception

A player may not take relief under this Local Rule if interference by anything other than the immovable *obstruction* makes the *stroke* clearly impracticable.

PENALTY FOR BREACH OF LOCAL RULE:
Match play – Loss of hole; **Stroke Play** – Two strokes."

NOTE

The Committee may restrict this Local Rule to specific holes, to balls lying only in closely-mown areas, to specific obstructions, or, in the case of obstructions that are not on the putting green, to obstructions in closely-mown areas if so desired. "Closely-mown area" means any area of the course, including paths through the rough, cut to fairway height or less.

b. Temporary Immovable Obstructions

When temporary obstructions are installed on or adjoining the *course*, the *Committee* should define the status of such obstructions as movable, immovable or temporary immovable obstructions.

If the *Committee* defines such obstructions as temporary immovable obstructions, the following Local Rule is recommended:

"1. Definition

A temporary immovable obstruction (TIO) is a non-permanent artificial object that is often erected in conjunction with a competition and is fixed or not readily movable. Examples of TIOs include, but are not limited to, tents, scoreboards, grandstands, television towers and lavatories.

Supporting guy wires are part of the TIO, unless the *Committee* declares that they are to be treated as elevated power lines or cables.

2. Interference

Interference by a TIO occurs when (a) the ball lies in front of and so close to the TIO that the TIO interferes with the player's *stance* or the area of his intended swing, or (b) the ball lies in, on, under or behind the TIO so that any part of the TIO intervenes directly between the player's ball and the *hole* and is on his *line of play*; interference also exists if the ball lies within one club-length of a spot equidistant from the *hole* where such intervention would exist.

NOTE

A ball is under a TIO when it is below the outermost edges of the TIO, even if these edges do not extend downwards to the ground.

RULE 24-2. IMMOVABLE OBSTRUCTION

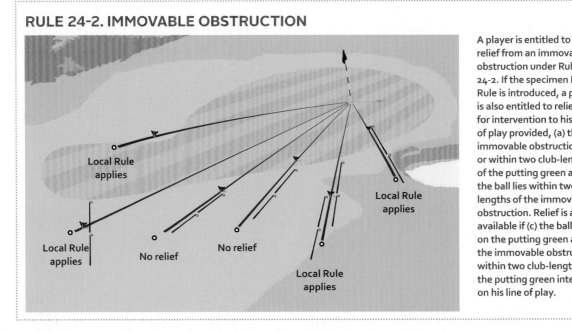

Local Rule applies

Local Rule applies

No relief

No relief

Local Rule applies

Local Rule applies

Local Rule applies

A player is entitled to relief from an immovable obstruction under Rule 24-2. If the specimen Local Rule is introduced, a player is also entitled to relief for intervention to his line of play provided, (a) the immovable obstruction is on or within two club-lengths of the putting green and (b) the ball lies within two club-lengths of the immovable obstruction. Relief is also available if (c) the ball lies on the putting green and the immovable obstruction within two club-lengths of the putting green intervenes on his line of play.

TEMPORARY IMMOVABLE OBSTRUCTIONS

If there are temporary immovable obstructions, such as grandstands, on the course, the Committee should introduce a Local Rule providing for relief from such temporary immovable obstructions.

3. Relief

A player may obtain relief from interference by a TIO, including a TIO that is *out of bounds*, as follows:

(a) **Through the Green:** If the ball lies *through the green*, the point on the *course* nearest to where the ball lies must be determined that (a) is not nearer the *hole*, (b) avoids interference as defined in Clause 2 and (c) is not in a *hazard* or on a *putting green*. The player must lift the ball and drop it, without penalty, within one club-length of the point so determined on a part of the *course* that fulfills (a), (b) and (c) above.

(b) **In a Hazard:** If the ball is in a *hazard*, the player must lift and drop the ball either:

(i) Without penalty, in accordance with Clause 3(a) above, except that the nearest part of the *course* affording complete relief must be in the *hazard* and the ball must be dropped in the *hazard*, or, if complete relief is impossible, on a part of the course within the *hazard* that affords maximum available relief; or

(ii) Under penalty of one *stroke*, outside the *hazard* as follows: the point on the *course* nearest to where the ball lies must be determined that (a) is not nearer the *hole*, (b) avoids

interference as defined in Clause 2 and (c) is not in a *hazard*. The player must drop the ball within one club-length of the point so determined on a part of the *course* that fulfils (a), (b) and (c) above.

The ball may be cleaned when lifted under Clause 3.

NOTE 1
If the ball lies in a *hazard*, nothing in this Local Rule precludes the player from proceeding under Rule 26 or Rule 28, if applicable.

NOTE 2
If a ball to be dropped under this Local Rule is not immediately recoverable, another ball may be *substituted*.

NOTE 3
A *Committee* may make a Local Rule (a) permitting or requiring a player to use a dropping zone when taking relief from a TIO or (b) permitting a player, as an additional relief option, to drop the ball on the opposite side of the TIO from the point established under Clause 3, but otherwise in accordance with Clause 3.

Exceptions

If a player's ball lies in front of or behind the TIO (not in, on or under the TIO), he may not obtain relief under Clause 3 if:

1.   Interference by anything other than the TIO makes it clearly impracticable for him to make a *stroke* or, in the case of intervention, to make a *stroke* such that the ball could finish on a direct line to the *hole*;

2.   Interference by the TIO would occur only through use of a clearly unreasonable *stroke* or an unnecessarily abnormal *stance*, swing or direction of play; or

3.   In the case of intervention, it would be clearly impracticable to expect the player to be able to strike the ball far enough towards the *hole* to reach the TIO.

A player who is not entitled to relief due to these exceptions may, if the ball lies *through the green* or in a *bunker*, obtain relief as provided in Rule 24-2b, if applicable. If the ball lies in a *water hazard*, the player may lift and drop the ball in accordance with Rule 24-2b(i), except that the *nearest point of relief* must be in the *water hazard* and the ball must be dropped in the *water hazard*, or the player may proceed under Rule 26-1.

4.   Ball in TIO Not Found

If it is known or virtually certain that a ball that has not been found is in, on or under a TIO, a ball may be dropped under the provisions of Clause 3 or Clause 5, if applicable. For the purpose of applying Clauses 3 and 5, the ball is deemed to lie at the spot where it last crossed the outermost limits of the TIO (Rule 24-3).

5.   Dropping Zones

If the player has interference from a TIO, the *Committee* may permit or require the use of a dropping zone. If the player uses a dropping zone in taking relief, he must drop the ball in the dropping zone nearest to where his ball originally lay or is deemed to lie under Clause 4 (even though the nearest dropping zone may be nearer the *hole*).

NOTE
A *Committee* may make a Local Rule prohibiting the use of a dropping zone that is nearer the hole.

PENALTY FOR BREACH OF LOCAL RULE:
Match play – Loss of hole; **Stroke Play** – Two strokes."

c.   Temporary Power Lines and Cables

When temporary power lines, cables or telephone lines are installed on the *course*, the following Local Rule is recommended:

"Temporary power lines, cables, telephone lines and mats covering or stanchions supporting them are *obstructions*:

1.   If they are readily movable, Rule 24-1 applies.

2.   If they are fixed or not readily movable, the player may, if the ball lies *through the green* or in a *bunker*, obtain relief as provided in Rule 24-2b. If the ball lies in a *water hazard*, the player may lift and drop the ball in accordance with Rule 24-2b(i), except that the *nearest point of relief* must be in the *water hazard* and the ball must be dropped in the *water hazard* or the player may proceed under Rule 26.

3.   If a ball strikes an elevated power line or cable, the *stroke* is canceled and the player must play a ball as nearly as possible at the spot from which the original ball was played in accordance with Rule 20-5 (Making Next Stroke from Where Previous Stroke Made).

NOTE
Guy wires supporting a temporary immovable obstruction are part of the temporary immovable obstruction, unless the *Committee*, by Local Rule, declares that they are to be treated as elevated power lines or cables.

Exception
A *stroke* that results in a ball striking an elevated junction section of cable rising from the ground must not be replayed.

4.   Grass-covered cable trenches are *ground under repair*, even if not marked, and Rule 25-1b applies.

PENALTY FOR BREACH OF LOCAL RULE:
Match play – Loss of hole; **Stroke Play** – Two strokes."

5.   Water Hazards - Playing Ball Provisionally Under Rule 26-1

If a *water hazard* (including a *lateral water hazard*) is of such size and shape and/or located in such a position that:

(i)   it would be impracticable to determine whether the ball is in the *hazard* or to do so would unduly delay play, and

(ii)   if the original ball is not found, it is known or virtually certain that it is in the *water hazard*,

the *Committee* may introduce a Local Rule permitting the play of a ball provisionally under Rule 26-1. The ball is played provisionally under any of the applicable options under Rule 26-1 or any applicable Local Rule. In such a case, if a ball is played provisionally and the original ball is in a *water hazard*, the player may play the original ball as it lies or continue with the ball played provisionally, but he may not proceed under Rule 26-1 with regard to the original ball.

DROPPING ZONE

The most common example of a dropping zone is one used for a water hazard.

In these circumstances, the following Local Rule is recommended:

"If there is doubt whether a ball is in or is *lost* in the *water hazard* (specify location), the player may play another ball provisionally under any of the applicable options in Rule 26-1.

If the original ball is found outside the *water hazard*, the player must continue play with it.

If the original ball is found in the *water hazard*, the player may either play the original ball as it lies or continue with the ball played provisionally under Rule 26-1.

If the original ball is not found or identified within the five-minute search period, the player must continue with the ball played provisionally.

PENALTY FOR BREACH OF LOCAL RULE:
Match play – Loss of hole; **Stroke Play** – Two strokes."

6. Dropping Zones

The *Committee* may establish dropping zones on which balls may or must be dropped when the *Committee* considers that it is not feasible or practicable to proceed exactly in conformity with Rule 24-2b or Rule 24-3 (Immovable Obstruction), Rule 25-1b or 25-1c (Abnormal Ground Conditions), 25-3 (Wrong Putting Green), Rule 26-1 (Water Hazards and Lateral Water Hazards) or Rule 28 (Ball Unplayable).

Generally, such dropping zones should be provided as an additional relief option to those available under the Rule itself, rather than being mandatory.

Using the example of a dropping zone for a *water hazard*, when such a dropping zone is established, the following Local Rule is recommended:

"If a ball is in or it is known or virtually certain that a ball that has not been found is in the *water hazard* (specify location), the player may:

(i) proceed under Rule 26-1; or

(ii) as an additional option, drop a ball, under penalty of one stroke, in the dropping zone.

PENALTY FOR BREACH OF LOCAL RULE:
Match play – Loss of hole; **Stroke Play** – Two strokes."

NOTE

When using a dropping zone the following provisions apply regarding the dropping and re-dropping of the ball:

(a) The player does not have to stand within the dropping zone when dropping the ball.

(b) The dropped ball must first strike a part of the course within the dropping zone.

(c) If the dropping zone is defined by a line, the line is within the dropping zone.

(d) The dropped ball does not have to come to rest within the dropping zone.

(e) The dropped ball must be re-dropped if it rolls and comes to rest in a position covered by Rule 20-2c(i-vi).

(f) The dropped ball may roll nearer the *hole* than the spot where it first struck a part of the *course*, provided it comes to rest within two club-lengths of that spot and not into any of the positions covered by (e).

(g) Subject to the provisions of (e) and (f), the dropped ball may roll and come to rest nearer the *hole* than:

o its original position or estimated position (see Rule 20-2b);

o the *nearest point of relief* or maximum available relief (Rule 24-2, 25-1 or 25-3); or

o the point where the original ball last crossed the margin of the *water hazard* or *lateral water hazard* (Rule 26-1).

7. Distance-Measuring Devices

If the *Committee* wishes to act in accordance with the Note under Rule 14-3, the following Local Rule is recommended:

"(Specify as appropriate, e.g., In this competition, or For all play at this *course*, etc.), a player may obtain distance information by use of a distance-measuring device. If, during a *stipulated round*, a player uses a distance-measuring device to gauge or measure other conditions that might affect his play (e.g., elevation changes, wind speed, etc.), the player is in breach of Rule 14-3."

PART B
Conditions of the Competition

Definitions

All defined terms are in *italics* and are listed alphabetically in the Definitions section – see pages 10-23.

General

Rule 33-1 provides, "The *Committee* must establish the conditions under which a competition is to be played." The conditions should include many matters such as method of entry, eligibility, number of rounds to be played, etc. which it is not appropriate to deal with in the Rules of Golf or this Appendix. Detailed information regarding these conditions is provided in "Decisions on the Rules of Golf" under Rule 33-1 and in "How to Conduct a Competition".

However, there are a number of matters that might be covered in the Conditions of the Competition to which the Committee's attention is specifically drawn. These are:

1. Specification of Clubs and the Ball

The following conditions are recommended only for competitions involving expert players:

a. List of Conforming Driver Heads

On its website (www.usga.org) the USGA periodically issues a List of Conforming Driver Heads that lists driving clubheads that have been evaluated and found to conform with the Rules of Golf. If the *Committee* wishes to limit players to drivers that have a clubhead, identified by model and loft, that is on the List, the List should be made available and the following condition of competition used:

"Any driver the player carries must have a clubhead, identified by model and loft, that is named on the current List of Conforming Driver Heads issued by the USGA.

Exception

A driver with a clubhead that was manufactured prior to 1999 is exempt from this condition.

---

*PENALTY FOR CARRYING, BUT NOT MAKING STROKE WITH, CLUB OR CLUBS IN BREACH OF CONDITION:

Match play – At the conclusion of the hole at which the breach is discovered, the state of the match is adjusted by deducting one hole for each hole at which a breach occurred; maximum deduction per round – Two holes.

Stroke play – Two strokes for each hole at which any breach occurred; maximum penalty per round – Four strokes (two strokes at each of the first two holes at which any breach occurred).

Match play or stroke play – If a breach is discovered between the play of two holes, it is deemed to have been discovered during play of the next hole, and the penalty must be applied accordingly.

Bogey and par competitions – See Note 1 to Rule 32-1a.
Stableford competitions – See Note 1 to Rule 32-1b.
*Any club or clubs carried in breach of this condition must be declared out of play by the player to his *opponent* in match play or his marker or a fellow-competitor in stroke

play immediately upon discovery that a breach has occurred. If the player fails to do so, he is disqualified.

PENALTY FOR MAKING STROKE WITH CLUB IN BREACH OF CONDITION:

Disqualification."

b. List of Conforming Golf Balls

On its website (www.usga.org) the USGA eriodically issues a List of Conforming Golf Balls that lists balls that have been tested and found to conform with the Rules of Golf. If the *Committee* wishes to require players to play a model of golf ball on the List, the List should be made available and the following condition of competition used:

"The ball the player plays must be named on the current List of Conforming Golf Balls issued by the USGA.

PENALTY FOR BREACH OF CONDITION:

Disqualification."

c. One Ball Condition

If it is desired to prohibit changing brands and models of golf balls during a *stipulated round*, the following condition is recommended:

"Limitation on Balls Used During Round: (Note to Rule 5-1)

(i) "One Ball" Condition

During a *stipulated round*, the balls a player plays must be of the same brand and model as detailed by a single entry on the current List of Conforming Golf Balls.

Note

If a ball of a different brand and/or model is dropped or placed it may be lifted, without penalty, and the player must then proceed by dropping or placing a proper ball (Rule 20-6).

PENALTY FOR BREACH OF CONDITION:

Match play – At the conclusion of the hole at which the breach is discovered, the state of the match is adjusted by deducting one hole for each hole at which a breach occurred; maximum deduction per round – Two holes.

Stroke play – Two strokes for each hole at which any breach occurred; maximum penalty per round – Four strokes (two strokes at each of the first two holes at which any breach occurred).

Bogey and Par competitions – See Note 1 to Rule 32-1a.
Stableford competitions – See Note 1 to Rule 32-1b.

(ii) Procedure When Breach Discovered

When a player discovers that he has played a ball in breach of this condition, he must abandon that ball before playing from the next *teeing ground* and complete the round with a proper ball; otherwise, the player is disqualified. If discovery is made during play of a hole and the player elects to substitute a proper ball before completing that hole, the player must place a proper ball on the spot where the ball played in breach of the condition lay."

2. Caddie (Note to Rule 6-4)

Rule 6-4 permits a player to use a *caddie*, provided he has only one *caddie* at any one time. However, there may be circumstances where a Committee may wish to prohibit *caddies* or restrict a player in his choice of *caddie*, e.g., professional golfer, sibling, parent, another player in the competition, etc. In such cases, the following wording is recommended:

"Use of Caddie Prohibited

A player is prohibited from using a *caddie* during the *stipulated round*."

"Restriction on Who May Serve as Caddie

A player is prohibited from having _____ serve as his *caddie* during the *stipulated round*.

---

*PENALTY FOR BREACH OF CONDITION:

Match play – At the conclusion of the hole at which the breach is discovered, the state of the match is adjusted by deducting one hole for each hole at which a breach occurred; maximum deduction per round – Two holes.

Stroke play – Two strokes for each hole at which any breach occurred; maximum penalty per round – Four strokes (two strokes at each of the first two holes at which any breach occurred).

Match play or stroke play – If a breach is discovered between the play of two holes, it is deemed to have been discovered during play of the next hole, and the penalty must be applied accordingly.

Bogey and par competitions – See Note 1 to Rule 32-1a.
Stableford competitions – See Note 1 to Rule 32-1b.

*A player having a *caddie* in breach of this condition must immediately upon discovery that a breach has occurred ensure that he conforms with this condition for the remainder of the *stipulated round*. Otherwise, the player is disqualified."

3. Pace of Play (Note 2 to Rule 6-7)

The *Committee* may establish pace of play guidelines to help prevent slow play, in accordance with Note 2 to Rule 6-7

SUSPENSION OF PLAY DUE TO A DANGEROUS SITUATION

If the Note to Rule 6-8b is in effect and play is suspended for a dangerous situation, play must be immediately discontinued.

4. Suspension of Play Due to a Dangerous Situation (Note to Rule 6-8b)

As there have been many deaths and injuries from lightning on golf courses, all clubs and sponsors of golf competitions are urged to take precautions for the protection of persons against lightning. Attention is called to Rules 6-8 and 33-2d. If the *Committee* desires to adopt the condition in the Note under Rule 6-8b, the following wording is recommended:

"When play is suspended by the *Committee* for a dangerous situation, if the players in a match or group are between the play of two holes, they must not resume play until the *Committee* has ordered a resumption of play. If they are in the process of playing a hole, they must discontinue play immediately and not resume play until the *Committee* has ordered a resumption of play. If a player fails to discontinue play immediately, he is disqualified, unless circumstances warrant waiving the penalty as provided in Rule 33-7.

The signal for suspending play due to a dangerous situation will be a prolonged note of the siren."

The following signals are generally used and it is recommended that all *Committees* do similarly:

Discontinue Play Immediately: One prolonged note of siren.

Discontinue Play: Three consecutive notes of siren, repeated.

Resume Play: Two short notes of siren, repeated.

5. Practice

a. General

The *Committee* may make regulations governing practice in accordance with the Note to Rule 7-1, Exception (c) to Rule 7-2, Note 2 to Rule 7-2 and Rule 33-2c.

b. Practice Between Holes (Note 2 to Rule 7)

If the *Committee* wishes to act in accordance with Note 2 to Rule 7-2, the following wording is recommended:

"Between the play of two holes, a player must not make any practice stroke on or near the *putting green* of the hole last played and must not test the surface of the *putting green* of the hole last played by rolling a ball.

PENALTY FOR BREACH OF CONDITION:

Match play – Loss of next hole.

Stroke play – Two strokes at the next hole.

Match play or stroke play – In the case of a breach at the last hole of the stipulated round, the player incurs the penalty at that hole."

6. Advice in Team Competitions (Note to Rule 8)

If the *Committee* wishes to act in accordance with the Note under Rule 8, the following wording is recommended:
"In accordance with the Note to Rule 8 of the Rules of Golf, each team may appoint one person (in addition to the persons from whom *advice* may be asked under that Rule) who may give *advice* to members of that team. Such person (if it is desired to insert any restriction on who may be nominated insert such restriction here) must be identified to the *Committee* before giving *advice*."

7. New Holes (Note to Rule 33-2b)

The *Committee* may provide, in accordance with the Note to Rule 33-2b, that the *holes* and *teeing grounds* for a single round of a competition being held on more than one day may be differently situated on each day.

8. Transportation

If it is desired to require players to walk in a competition, the following condition is recommended:
"Players must not ride on any form of transportation during a *stipulated round* unless authorized by the *Committee*.

---

*PENALTY FOR BREACH OF CONDITION:

Match play – At the conclusion of the hole at which the breach is discovered, the state of the match is adjusted by deducting one hole for each hole at which a breach occurred; maximum deduction per round – Two holes.

Stroke play – Two strokes for each hole at which any breach occurred; maximum penalty per round – Four strokes (two strokes at each of the first two holes at which any breach occurred).

Match play or stroke play – If a breach is discovered between the play of two holes, it is deemed to have been discovered during play of the next hole, and the penalty must be applied accordingly.

Bogey and par competitions – See Note 1 to Rule 32-1a.

Stableford competitions – See Note 1 to Rule 32-1b.

*Use of any unauthorized form of transportation must be discontinued immediately upon discovery that a breach has occurred. Otherwise, the player is disqualified."

9. Anti-Doping

The *Committee* may require, in the conditions of competition, that players comply with an anti-doping policy.

10. How to Decide Ties

In both match play and stroke play, a tie can be an acceptable result. However, when it is desired to have a sole winner, the *Committee* has the authority, under Rule 33-6, to determine how and when a tie is decided. The decision should be published in advance.

The USGA recommends:

"Match Play

A match that ends all square should be played off hole by hole until one side wins a hole. The play-off should start on the hole where the match began. In a handicap match, handicap strokes should be allowed as in the *stipulated round*.

Stroke Play

(a) In the event of a tie in a scratch stroke-play competition, a play-off is recommended. The play-off may be over 18 holes or a smaller number of holes as specified by the *Committee*. If that is not feasible or there is still a tie, a hole-by-hole play-off is recommended.

(b) In the event of a tie in a handicap stroke play competition, a play-off with handicaps is recommended. The play-off may be over 18 holes or a smaller number of holes as specified by the *Committee*. It is recommended that any such play-off consist of at least three holes.

In competitions where the handicap stroke allocation table is not relevant, if the play-off is less than 18 holes, the percentage of 18 holes played should be applied to the players' handicaps to determine their play-off handicaps. Handicap stroke fractions of one half stroke or more should count as a full stroke and any lesser fraction should be disregarded.

In competitions where the handicap stroke table is relevant, such as four-ball stroke play and bogey, par and Stableford competitions, handicap strokes should be taken as they were assigned for the competition using the players' respective stroke allocation table(s).

(c) If a play-off of any type is not feasible, matching score cards is recommended. The method of matching cards should be announced in advance and should also provide what will happen if this procedure does not produce a winner. An acceptable method of matching cards is to determine the winner on the basis of the best score for the last nine holes. If the tying players have the same score for the last nine, determine the winner on the basis of the last six holes, last three holes and finally the 18th hole. If this method is used in a competition with a multiple tee start, it is recommended that the "last nine holes, last six holes, etc." wis considered to be holes 10–18, 13–18, etc.

For competitions where the handicap stroke table is not relevant, such as individual stroke play, if the last nine, last six, last three holes scenario is used, one-half, one-third, one-sixth, etc. of the handicaps should be deducted from the score for those holes. In terms of the use of fractions in such deductions, the *Committee* should act in accordance with the recommendations of the relevant handicapping authority.

In competitions where the handicap stroke table is relevant, such as *four-ball* stroke play and bogey, par and Stableford competitions, handicap strokes should be taken as they were assigned for the competition, using the players' respective stroke allocation table(s)."

11. Draw for Match Play

Although the draw for match play may be completely blind or certain players may be distributed through different quarters

or eighths, the General Numerical Draw is recommended if matches are determined by a qualifying round.

General Numerical Draw

For purposes of determining places in the draw, ties in qualifying rounds other than those for the last qualifying place are decided by the order in which scores are returned, with the first score to be returned receiving the lowest available number, etc. If it is impossible to determine the order in which scores are returned, ties are determined by a blind draw.

UPPER HALF	LOWER HALF	UPPER HALF	LOWER HALF
64 QUALIFIERS		**32 QUALIFIERS**	
1 vs. 64	2 vs. 63	1 vs. 32	2 vs. 31
32 vs. 33	31 vs. 34	16 vs. 17	15 vs. 18
16 vs. 49	15 vs. 50	8 vs. 25	7 vs. 26
17 vs. 48	18 vs. 47	9 vs. 24	10 vs. 23
8 vs. 57	7 vs. 58	4 vs. 29	3 vs. 30
25 vs. 40	26 vs. 39	13 vs. 20	14 vs. 19
9 vs. 56	10 vs. 55	5 vs. 28	6 vs. 27
24 vs. 41	23 vs. 42	12 vs. 21	11 vs. 22
4 vs. 61	3 vs. 62	**16 QUALIFIERS**	
29 vs. 36	30 vs. 35	1 vs. 16	2 vs. 15
13 vs. 52	14 vs. 51	8 vs. 9	7 vs. 10
20 vs. 45	19 vs. 46	4 vs. 13	3 vs. 14
5 vs. 60	6 vs. 59	5 vs. 12	6 vs. 11
28 vs. 37	27 vs. 38	**8 QUALIFIERS**	
12 vs. 53	11 vs. 54	1 vs. 8	2 vs. 7
21 vs. 44	22 vs. 43	4 vs. 5	3 vs. 6

Frequently asked questions

What does the "One Ball Condition" mean?

The Rules of Golf do not require a player to use the same brand and type of golf ball throughout the stipulated round. A player may use a different ball to start each hole. However, the Committee may adopt as a Condition of a Competition, the "One Ball Condition." When this condition is adopted, players are required to use the same brand and type of golf ball throughout the stipulated round.
Please refer to Appendix 1; Part B; Item 1c (Specification of the Ball).

Is there a penalty if, when playing "Preferred Lies," the player simply rolls the ball with his club instead of lifting and placing?

The Committee in charge of a competition or golf course may adopt a Local Rule allowing players to lift, clean and place their ball when conditions warrant such a Local Rule – see Appendix I; Part A; Item 3b. Before lifting the ball, the position of the ball must be marked. If the player fails to mark the position of the ball before lifting it, he incurs a penalty of one stroke.

APPENDIX II

Design of Clubs

A player in doubt as to the conformity of a club should consult the USGA.

A manufacturer should submit to the USGA sample of a club to be manufactured for a ruling as to whether the club conforms with the *Rules*. The sample becomes the property of the USGA or reference purposes. If a manufacturer fails to submit a sample or, having submitted a sample, fails to await a ruling before manufacturing and/or marketing the club, the manufacturer assumes the risk of a ruling that the club does not conform with the *Rules*.

The following paragraphs prescribe general regulations for the design of clubs, together with specifications and interpretations. Further information relating to these regulations and their proper interpretation is provided in "A Guide to the Rules on Clubs and Balls."

Where a club, or part of a club, is required to meet a specification within the *Rules*, it must be designed and manufactured with the intention of meeting that specification.

1. Clubs

a. General

A club is an implement designed to be used for striking the ball and generally comes in three forms: woods, irons and putters distinguished by shape and intended use. A putter is a club with a loft not exceeding ten degrees designed primarily for use on the *putting green*.

The club must not be substantially different from the traditional and customary form and make. The club must be composed of a shaft and a head and it may also have material added to the shaft to enable the player to obtain a firm hold (see 3 below). All parts of the club must be fixed so that the club is one unit, and it must have no external attachments. Exceptions may be made for attachments that do not affect the performance of the club.

b. Adjustability

All clubs may incorporate features for weight adjustment. Other forms of adjustability may also be permitted upon evaluation by the USGA. The following requirements apply to all permissible methods of adjustment:

(i) the adjustment cannot be readily made;

(ii) all adjustable parts are firmly fixed and there is no reasonable likelihood of them working loose during a round; and

(iii) all configurations of adjustment conform with the *Rules*. During a *stipulated round*, the playing characteristics of a club must not be purposely changed by adjustment or by any other means (see Rule 4-2a).

c. Length

The overall length of the club must be at least 18 inches (0.457 m) and, except for putters, must not exceed 48 inches (1.219 m).

For woods and irons, the measurement of length is taken when the club is lying on a horizontal plane and the sole is set against a 60 degree plane as shown in Fig. I. The length is defined as the distance from the point of the intersection between the two planes to the top of the grip. For putters, the measurement of length is taken from the top of the grip along the axis of the shaft or a straight line extension of it to the sole of the club.

d. Alignment

When the club is in its normal address position the shaft must be so aligned that:

(i) the projection of the straight part of the shaft on to the

CLUB LENGTH AND ALIGNMENT; SHAFT STRAIGHTNESS

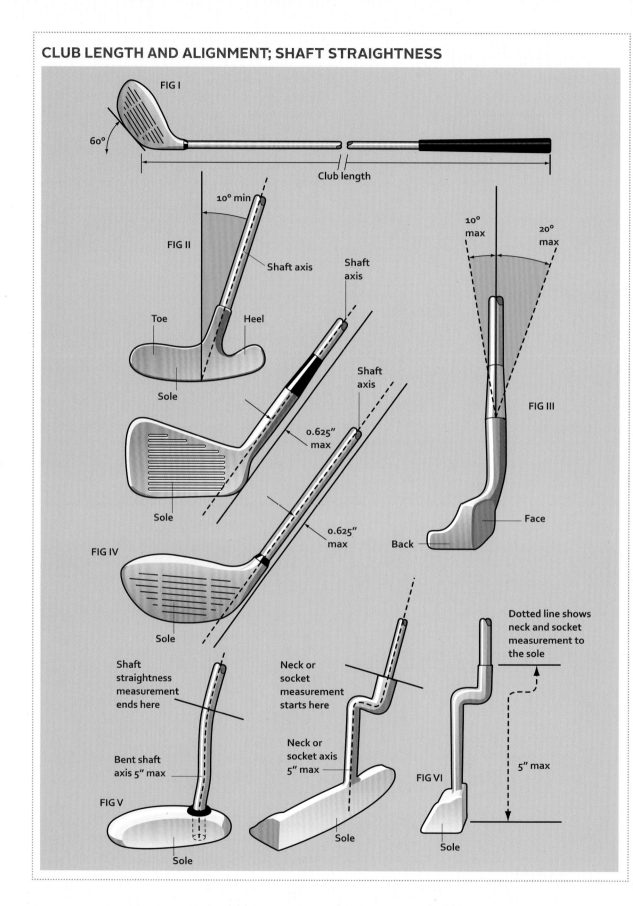

FIG I

60°

Club length

FIG II

10° min

Shaft axis

Toe

Heel

Sole

Shaft axis

Shaft axis

0.625" max

Sole

Shaft axis

0.625" max

10° max

20° max

FIG III

Face

Back

FIG IV

Sole

Shaft straightness measurement ends here

Bent shaft axis 5" max

FIG V

Sole

Neck or socket measurement starts here

Neck or socket axis 5" max

Sole

Dotted line shows neck and socket measurement to the sole

5" max

FIG VI

Sole

vertical plane through the toe and heel must diverge from the vertical by at least 10 degrees (see Fig. II). If the overall design of the club is such that the player can effectively use the club in a vertical or close-to-vertical position, the shaft may be required to diverge from the vertical in this plane by as much as 25 degrees;

(ii) the projection of the straight part of the shaft on to the vertical plane along the intended *line of play* must not diverge from the vertical by more than 20 degrees forwards or 10 degrees backwards (see Fig. III). Except for putters, all of the heel portion of the club must lie within 0.625 inches (15.88 mm) of the plane containing the axis of the straight part of the shaft and the intended (horizontal) *line of play* (see Fig. IV).

2. Shaft

a. Straightness

The shaft must be straight from the top of the grip to a point not more than 5 inches (127 mm) above the sole, measured from the point where the shaft ceases to be straight along the axis of the bent part of the shaft and the neck and/or socket (see Fig. V).

b. Bending and Twisting Properties

At any point along its length, the shaft must:

(i) bend in such a way that the deflection is the same regardless of how the shaft is rotated about its longitudinal axis; and

(ii) twist the same amount in both directions.

c Attachment to Clubhead

The shaft must be attached to the clubhead at the heel either directly or through a single plain neck and/or socket. The length from the top of the neck and/or socket to the sole of the club must not exceed 5 inches (127 mm), measured along the axis of, and following any bend in, the neck and/or socket (see Fig. VI). **Exception for Putters:** The shaft or neck or socket of a putter may be fixed at any point in the head.

3. Grip (see Fig. VII)

The grip consists of material added to the shaft to enable the player to obtain a firm hold. The grip must be fixed to the shaft, must be straight and plain in form, must extend to the end of the shaft and must not be molded for any part of the hands. If no material is added, that portion of the shaft designed to be held by the player must be considered the grip.

(i) For clubs other than putters the grip must be circular in cross-section, except that a continuous, straight, slightly raised rib may be incorporated along the full length of the grip, and a slightly indented spiral is permitted on a wrapped grip or a replica of one.

(ii) A putter grip may have a non-circular cross-section, provided the cross-section has no concavity, is symmetrical and remains generally similar throughout the length of the grip. (See Clause (v) below).

(iii) The grip may be tapered but must not have any bulge or waist. Its cross-sectional dimensions measured in any direction must not exceed 1.75 inches (44.45 mm).

(iv) For clubs other than putters the axis of the grip must coincide with the axis of the shaft.

(v) A putter may have two grips provided each is circular in cross-section, the axis of each coincides with the axis of the shaft, and they are separated by at least 1.5 inches (38.1 mm).

4. Clubhead

a. Plain in Shape

The clubhead must be generally plain in shape. All parts must be rigid, structural in nature and functional. The clubhead or its parts must not be designed to resemble any other object. It is not practicable to define plain in shape precisely and comprehensively. However, features that are deemed to be in breach of this requirement and are therefore not permitted include, but are not limited to:

(i) All Clubs

o holes through the face;

o holes through the head (some exceptions may be made for putters and cavity back irons);

o features that are for the purpose of meeting dimensional specifications;

o features that extend into or ahead of the face;

o features that extend significantly above the top line of the head;

o furrows in or runners on the head that extend into the face (some exceptions may be made for putters); and

o optical or electronic devices.

(ii) Woods and Irons

o all features listed in (i) above;

o cavities in the outline of the heel and/or the toe of the head that can be viewed from above;

o severe or multiple cavities in the outline of the back of the head that can be viewed from above;

o transparent material added to the head with the intention of rendering conforming a feature that is not otherwise permitted; and

o features that extend beyond the outline of the head when viewed from above.

GRIP AND CLUB FACE

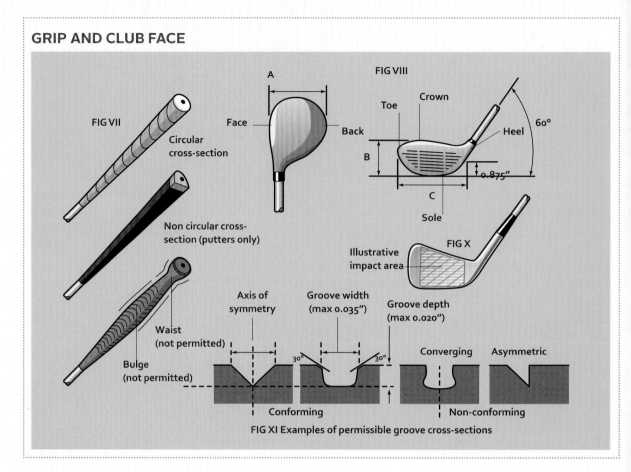

FIG VII — Circular cross-section

Non circular cross-section (putters only)

Waist (not permitted)

Bulge (not permitted)

A — Face — Back

FIG VIII — Toe, Crown, Heel, 60°, 0.875", B, C, Sole

Illustrative impact area — FIG X

Axis of symmetry — Groove width (max 0.035") — Groove depth (max 0.020")

30° 30° Converging Asymmetric

Conforming Non-conforming

FIG XI Examples of permissible groove cross-sections

b. Dimensions, Volume and Moment of Inertia

(i) Woods

When the club is in a 60 degree lie angle, the dimensions of the clubhead must be such that:

o the distance from the heel to the toe of the clubhead is greater than the distance from the face to the back;

o the distance from the heel to the toe of the clubhead is not greater than 5 inches (127 mm); and

o the distance from the sole to the crown of the clubhead, including any permitted features, is not greater than 2.8 inches (71.12 mm).

These dimensions are measured on horizontal lines between vertical projections of the outermost points of:

o the heel and the toe; and

o the face and the back (see Fig. VIII, dimension A); and on vertical lines between the horizontal projections of the outermost points of the sole and the crown (see Fig. VIII, dimension B). If the outermost point of the heel is not clearly defined, it is deemed to be 0.875 inches (22.23 mm) above the horizontal plane on which the club is lying (see Fig. VIII, dimension C).

The volume of the clubhead must not exceed 460 cubic centimeters (28.06 cubic inches), plus a tolerance of 10

cubic centimeters (0.61 cubic inches).

When the club is in a 60 degree lie angle, the moment of inertia component around the vertical axis through the clubhead's center of gravity must not exceed 5900 g cm² (32.259 oz in²), plus a test tolerance of 100 g cm² (0.547 oz in²).

(ii) Irons

When the clubhead is in its normal address position, the dimensions of the head must be such that the distance from the heel to the toe is greater than the distance from the face to the back.

(iii) Putters (see Fig. IX)

When the clubhead is in its normal address position, the dimensions of the head must be such that:

o the distance from the heel to the toe is greater than the distance from the face to the back;

o the distance from the heel to the toe of the head is less than or equal to 7 inches (177.8 mm);

o the distance from the heel to the toe of the face is greater than or equal to two thirds of the distance from the face to the back of the head;

o the distance from the heel to the toe of the face is greater than or equal to half of the distance from the heel to the toe of the head; and

o the distance from the sole to the top of the head, including any permitted features, is less than or equal to 2.5 inches (63.5 mm).

For traditionally shaped heads, these dimensions will be measured on horizontal lines between vertical projections of the outermost points of:

o the heel and the toe of the head;

o the heel and the toe of the face; and

o the face and the back; and on vertical lines between the horizontal projections of the outermost points of the sole and the top of the head. For unusually shaped heads, the toe to heel dimension may be made at the face.

c. Spring Effect and Dynamic Properties

The design, material and/or construction of, or any treatment to, the clubhead (which includes the club face) must not:

(i) have the effect of a spring which exceeds the limit set forth in the Pendulum Test Protocol on file with the USGA; or

(ii) incorporate features or technology including, but not limited to, separate springs or spring features, that have the intent of, or the effect of, unduly influencing the clubhead's spring effect; or

(iii) unduly influence the movement of the ball.

NOTE

(i) above does not apply to putters.

d. Striking Faces

The clubhead must have only one striking face, except that a putter may have two such faces if their characteristics are the same, and they are opposite each other.

5. Club Face

a. General

The face of the club must be hard and rigid and must not impart significantly more or less spin to the ball than a standard steel face (some exceptions may be made for putters). Except for such markings listed below, the club face must be smooth and must not have any degree of concavity.

b. Impact Area Roughness and Material

Except for markings specified in the following paragraphs, the surface roughness within the area where impact is intended (the "impact area") must not exceed that of decorative sandblasting, or of fine milling (see Fig. X).

The whole of the impact area must be of the same material (exceptions may be made for clubheads made of wood).

c. Impact Area Markings

If a club has grooves and/or punch marks in the impact area they must meet the following specifications:

(i) Grooves

o Grooves must be straight and parallel.

o Grooves must have a symmetrical cross-section and have sides which do not converge (see Fig. XI).

o *For clubs that have a loft angle greater than or equal to 25 degrees, grooves must have a plain cross-section.

o The width, spacing and cross-section of the grooves must be consistent throughout the impact area (some exceptions may be made for woods).

o The width (W) of each groove must not exceed 0.035 inches (0.9 mm), using the 30 degree method of measurement on file with the USGA.

o The distance between edges of adjacent grooves (S) must not be less than three times the width of the grooves, and

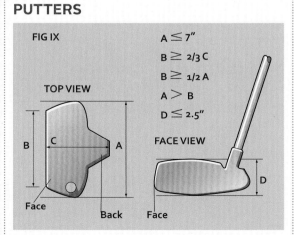

PUTTERS

FIG IX

TOP VIEW

$A \leq 7''$
$B \geq 2/3\,C$
$B \geq 1/2\,A$
$A > B$
$D \leq 2.5''$

FACE VIEW

B   C   A

Face   Back   Face

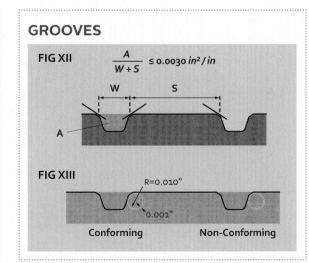

GROOVES

FIG XII

$$\frac{A}{W+S} \leq 0.0030\ in^2/in$$

W   S

A

FIG XIII

R=0.010"

0.001"

Conforming   Non-Conforming

not less than 0.075 inches (1.905 mm).

o The depth of each groove must not exceed 0.020 inches (0.508 mm).

o *For clubs other than driving clubs, the cross-sectional area (A) of a groove divided by the groove pitch (W+S) must not exceed 0.0030 square inches per inch (0.0762 mm²/mm) (see Fig. XII).

o Grooves must not have sharp edges or raised lips.

o *For clubs that have a loft angle greater than or equal to 25 degrees, groove edges must be substantially in the form of a round having an effective radius which is not less than 0.010 inches (0.254 mm) when measured as shown in Fig. XIII, and not greater than 0.020 inches (0.508 mm). Deviations in effective radius within 0.001 inches (0.0254 mm) are permissible.

(ii) Punch Marks

o The maximum dimension of any punch mark must not exceed 0.075 inches (1.905 mm).

o The distance between adjacent punch marks (or between punch marks and grooves) must not be less than 0.168 inches (4.27 mm), measured from center to center.

o The depth of any punch mark must not exceed 0.040 inches (1.02 mm).

o Punch marks must not have sharp edges or raised lips.

o *For clubs that have a loft angle greater than or equal to 25 degrees, punch mark edges must be substantially in the form of a round having an effective radius which is not less than 0.010 inches (0.254 mm) when measured as shown in Figure XIII, and not greater than 0.020 inches (0.508 mm). Deviations in effective radius within 0.001 inches (0.0254 mm) are permissible.

NOTE 1

The groove and punch mark specifications above indicated by an asterisk (*) apply only to new models of clubs manufactured on or after January 1, 2010 and any club where the face markings have been purposely altered, for example, by re-grooving. For further information on the status of clubs available before January 1, 2010 , refer to the Informational Club Database at www.usga.org.

NOTE 2

The Committee may require, in the conditions of competition, that the clubs the player carries must conform to the groove and punch mark specifications above indicated by an asterisk (*).

This condition is recommended only for competitions involving expert players. For further information, refer to Decision 4-1/1 in "Decisions on the Rules of Golf."

d. Decorative Markings

The center of the impact area may be indicated by a design within the boundary of a square whose sides are 0.375 inches (9.53 mm) in length. Such a design must not unduly influence the movement of the ball. Decorative markings are permitted outside the impact area.

e. Non-Metallic Club Face Markings

The above specifications do not apply to clubheads made of wood on which the impact area of the face is of a material of hardness less than the hardness of metal and whose loft angle is 24 degrees or less, but markings which could unduly influence the movement of the ball are prohibited.

f Putter Face Markings

Any markings on the face of a putter must not have sharp edges or raised lips. The specifications with regard to roughness, material and markings in the impact area do not apply.

APPENDIX III
The Ball

A player in doubt as to the conformity of a ball should consult the USGA.

A manufacturer should submit to the USGA samples of a ball to be manufactured for a ruling as to whether the ball conforms with the *Rules*. The samples become the property of the USGA for reference purposes. If a manufacturer fails to submit samples or, having submitted samples, fails to await a ruling before manufacturing and/or marketing the ball, the manufacturer assumes the risk of a ruling that the ball does not conform with the *Rules*.

The following paragraphs prescribe general regulations for the design of the ball, together with specifications and interpretations. Further information relating to these regulations and their proper interpretation is provided in "A Guide to the Rules on Clubs and Balls."

Where a ball is required to meet a specification within the Rules, it must be designed and manufactured with the intention of meeting that specificiation.

1. General

The ball must not be substantially different from the

traditional and customary form and make. The material and construction of the ball must not be contrary to the purpose and intent of the *Rules*.

2. Weight

The weight of the ball must not be greater than 1.620 ounces avoirdupois (45.93 g).

3. Size

The diameter of the ball must not be less than 1.680 inches (42.67mm).

4. Spherical Symmetry

The ball must not be designed, manufactured or intentionally modified to have properties which differ from those of a spherically symmetrical ball.

5. Initial Velocity

The initial velocity of the ball must not exceed the limit specified under the conditions set forth in the Initial Velocity Standard for golf balls on file with the USGA.

6. Overall Distance Standard

The combined carry and roll of the ball, when tested on apparatus approved by the USGA, must not exceed the distance specified under the conditions set forth in the Overall Distance Standard for golf balls on file with the USGA.

APPENDIX IV

Devices and Other Equipment

A player in doubt as to whether use of a device or other equipment would constitute a breach of the *Rules* should consult the USGA.

A manufacturer should submit to the USGA a sample of a device or other equipment to be manufactured for a ruling as to whether its use during a *stipulated round* would cause a player to be in breach of Rule 14-3. The sample becomes the property of the USGA for reference purposes. If a manufacturer fails to submit a sample or, having submitted a sample, fails to await a ruling before manufacturing and/or marketing the device or other equipment, the manufacturer assumes the risk of a ruling that use of the device or other equipment would be contrary to the *Rules*.

The following paragraphs prescribe general regulations for the design of devices and other equipment, together with specifications and interpretations. They should be read in conjunction with Rule 11-1 (Teeing) and Rule 14-3 (Artificial Devices, Unusual Equipment and Abnormal Use of Equipment).

1. Tees (Rule 11)

A tee is a device designed to raise the ball off the ground. A tee must not:

o   be longer than 4 inches (101.6 mm);
o   be designed or manufactured in such a way that it could indicate *line of play*;
o   unduly influence the movement of the ball; or
o   otherwise assist the player in making a *stroke* or in his play.

2. Gloves (Rule 14-3)

Gloves may be worn to assist the player in gripping the club, provided they are plain.

A "plain" glove must:

o   consist of a fitted covering of the hand with a separate sheath or opening for each digit (fingers and thumb); and
o   be made of smooth materials on the full palm and gripping surface of the digits.

A "plain" glove must not incorporate:

o   material on the gripping surface or inside of the glove, the primary purpose of which is to provide padding or which has the effect of providing padding. Padding is defined as an area of glove material which is more than 0.025 inches (0.635 mm) thicker than the adjacent areas of the glove without the added material;

NOTE

Material may be added for wear resistance, moisture absorption or other functional purposes, provided it does not exceed the definition of padding (see above).

o   straps to assist in preventing the club from slipping or to attach the hand to the club;
o   any means of binding digits together;
o   material on the glove that adheres to material on the grip;
o   features, other than visual aids, designed to assist the player in placing his hands in a consistent and/or specific position on the grip;
o   weight to assist the player in making a *stroke*;
o   any feature that might restrict the movement of a joint; or
o   any other feature that might assist the player in making a *stroke* or in his play.

3. Shoes (Rule 14-3)

Shoes that assist the player in obtaining a firm *stance* may be worn. Subject to the conditions of competition, features such as spikes on the sole are permitted, but shoes must not incorporate features:

○ designed to assist the player in taking his *stance* and/or building a *stance*;

○ designed to assist the player with his alignment; or

○ that might otherwise assist the player in making a *stroke* or in his play.

4. Clothing (Rule 14-3)

Articles of clothing must not incorporate features:

○ designed to assist the player with his alignment; or

○ that might otherwise assist the player in making a *stroke* or in his play.

5. Distance-Measuring Devices (Rule 14-3)

During a *stipulated round*, the use of any distance-measuring device is not permitted unless the *Committee* has introduced a Local Rule to that effect (see Note to Rule 14-3 and Appendix I; Part A; Section 7).

Even when the Local Rule is in effect, the device must not be used for any purposes that are prohibited by Rule 14-3, including but not limited to:

○ the gauging or measuring of slope;

○ the gauging or measuring of other conditions that might affect play (e.g., wind speed or direction);

○ recommendations that might assist the player in making a *stroke* or in his play (e.g., club selection, type of shot to be played, green reading or any other advice related matter); or

○ calculating the effective distance between two points based on elevation changes or other conditions affecting shot distance.

A multi-functional device, such as a smartphone or PDA, may be used as a distance-measuring device, but it must not be used to gauge or measure other conditions where doing so would be a breach of Rule 14-3.

ACKNOWLEDGMENTS

Photographic acknowledgments

Getty Images 101, 127 left; David Cannon 145; Adrian Dennis/AFP 151; Craig Jones 116; Donald Miralle 37, Hulton Archive 30; Richard Heathcote 126; Robert Laberge 148

Octopus Publishing Group Kevin Murray 77

PA Photos David James 50; Simon Barber/Jam Media 110

Peter Dazeley 127 right

Phil Sheldon Golf Picture Library 69, 80, 134, 173

Royal & Ancient 10 right

USGA 11 right, 34, 91, 102, 124, 175; Darren Carroll 11 left, 103, 156; Michael Cohen 38; JD Cuban 16 right, 19, 70, 87 bottom, 118, 121; Jonathan Ernst 135; Steve Gibbons 13, 41 right, 128, 139, 141, 147, 150, 157, 164; 179; Chris Keane 16 left, 21, 67, 68 left, 90, 119; Russell Kirk 9, 10 left, 15, 78 left, 120, 87 top; Joel Kowsky 57, 62; John Mummert 12, 22, 41 left, 63, 68 right, 78 right, 88, 93, 112,115, 131, 137, 177, 182; Fred Vuich 84; Robert Walker 44

An Hachette UK Company
www.hachette.co.uk

First published in Great Britain in 2003

This revised and updated edition published in 2015 by Hamlyn, a division of Octopus Publishing Group Ltd, Carmelite House, 50 Victoria Embankment, London, EC4Y 0DZ
www.octopusbooks.co.uk

Text copyright © United States Golf Association 2004, 2007, 2008, 2012, 2015

Design copyright © Octopus Publishing Group Ltd. 2004, 2007, 2008, 2012, 2015

Distributed in the US by Hachette Book Group USA, 1290 Avenue of the Americas, 4th and 5th Floors, New York, NY 10020, USA

ISBN: 978-0-600-63207-8

Printed and bound in China

10 9 8 7 6 5 4 3 2 1